$TOCK
INVESTING
for
EVERYONE

VOLUME II

Tools for Investing Like the Pros

Arshad Khan
Vaqar Zuberi

— S.A.G. —
Stocks Advisory Group
San Jose, California

Published by:
S.A.G. (Stocks Advisory Group)
P.O. Box 700003
San Jose, CA 95170
e-mail: StocksAG@aol.com

Volume One ISBN: 0-9660863-0-9
Volume Two ISBN: 0-9660863-1-7

Printed in the United States of America
Cover design: Lightbourne Images
Book production: Phelps and Associates

Library of Congress Catalog Card Number: 97-62349

Publisher's Cataloging-in-Publication
(Provided by Quality Books, Inc.)

Khan, Arshad Hassan, 1950-
        Stock investing for everyone. Vol. II, Tools for
investing like the pros / by Arshad Khan, Vaqar Zuberi.
        p. cm.
        Includes index.
        ISBN: 0-9660863-1-7

        1. Stocks--United States. 2. Investments. 3.
Finance, Personal. I. Zuberi, Vaqar. II. Title. III.
Title: Stock investing for everyone IV. Title: Tools for
investing like the pros

HG4661.K43 1998   332.63'22
                                    QBI98-988

INTRODUCTION

Stock Investing for Everyone: Tools for Investing Like the Pros, the second volume in the series, builds on the foundation developed in *Volume I*. While *Volume I* armed stock market investors with the basic stock market investing tools, *Volume II* provides more powerful tools to those who take their investing more seriously. *Volume II* is an appropriate resource for:

- investors who have used *Volume I* to develop the basic skills, have invested for sometime, and now desire to master the techniques that stock market professionals and savvy individual investors use
- professionals entering the securities industry
- experienced investors and professionals who want to refresh or upgrade their knowledge of various aspects of stock market investing

Volume II provides wide-ranging and in-depth knowledge to stock market investors. It introduces readers to the basics of fundamental and technical analysis. It contains a comprehensive description and practical interpretation of stock market variables (or indicators) such as earnings/share, moving averages, market breadth, etc. Also covered are sentiment and economic indicators.

In this volume, the behavior of individual stocks and the overall market is comprehensively described. Topics include bull and bear markets, corrections, recognizing a market top (and bottom), bullish and bearish signs, seasonal factors, and more. Detailed coverage is also given to related topics such as recognizing the behavior patterns of weakening stocks, the art of handling hot stocks, and group/sector monitoring.

The reader is given a thorough introduction to investment principles and strategies. Step-by-step instructions are provided on how to screen, rank and select stocks using different investment strategies. The book shows how to conduct comprehensive fundamental analysis on a company in order to determine if it has the potential to be a good investment. It also covers other important aspects of stock market investing, which often do not get the attention they deserve, such as selling strategies, risk management and portfolio management.

"Stock investing for everyone" is primarily based on the growth investing philosophy. However, a fair amount of coverage has been given to momentum investing. The reason is that the behavior of momentum players can considerably affect a stock, or even the overall market, in the short-term. Therefore, by understanding how momentum investors act and react, a knowledgeable investor will be in a better position to understand what at times appears to be the inexplicable behavior of stocks.

ACKNOWLEDGMENT

The writing and production of this two-volume book has been a long and challenging project, which could not have been completed without active help from many quarters. To our surprise, help and encouragement were available at every stage of this project and are gratefully acknowledged. Also acknowledged is the sacrifice and neglect that an author's wife and children have to endure during such a demanding project.

We would like to take this opportunity to thank Diana Singer and Jill Dawes for reviewing the manuscript and providing valuable comments. We also appreciate the dedication and professional attitude of Greg Sammons, who did the typesetting job for both volumes. Finally, we would like to thank Janice Phelps, of Phelps & Associates, for her invaluable and pivotal role in managing the book production process.

CONTENTS

INTRODUCTION

CHAPTER 1: Fundamental and Technical Analysis

CHAPTER 2: Stock Market Indicators

CHAPTER 3: More Stock Market Indicators

CHAPTER 4: Sentiment Indicators

CHAPTER 5: Economic Indicators

CHAPTER 6: Understanding Stock Market Behavior

CHAPTER 7: Understanding Stock Behavior

CHAPTER 8: Investment Principles and Strategies

CHAPTER 9: Screening and Selecting Stocks: An Overview

CHAPTER 10: Screening and Ranking Stocks: The Details

CHAPTER 11: Analyzing Stocks: The Details

CHAPTER 12: Selling Strategies

CHAPTER 13: Risk and Portfolio Management

APPENDIXES

GLOSSARY

INDEX

FIGURES AND TABLES

Figures

Tables

CHAPTER 1

Fundamental and Technical Analysis

SCHOOLS OF INVESTING

There are two basic methods, or philosophies, for analyzing the stock market. These are:

- fundamental analysis
- technical analysis

Fundamental analysis involves the study of various factors that affect a company's earnings and dividends which, in turn, influence its stock price. About 90% of investors use fundamental analysis. This approach emphasizes the analysis of company fundamentals, financial statements, business and industry conditions, as well as general economic data. This research leads to estimates for important valuation criteria such as future earnings, book value/share, and other related measures.

Technical analysis attempts to analyze various forces affecting the prices of individual stocks and the overall stock market. It is primarily based on the study of stock market price movements and fluctuations, and is highly focused on a stock's price behavior, volume behavior and pattern. Technical analysis is basically a short-term planning tool, which should not be used for long-term planning.

FUNDAMENTAL ANALYSIS

In fundamental analysis a company is researched in-depth within its business environment. Included in this analysis are its competitors and the industry group, or sector, to which it belongs. It should be noted that no specific benchmarks are used for comparison purposes.

Variables and ratios are analyzed in relation to industry norms, historical ranges, and the rest of the market.

Sources for analyzing a company

A number of sources can be tapped for conducting in-depth research on a company. The most commonly used sources are:

- company literature and press releases
- company research and earnings estimate reports (authored by stock analysts following the company)
- annual and quarterly reports (current and historical)
- 10K and 10Q reports (which contain more information than the annual and quarterly reports)
- financial statements
- industry and trade journals
- newspapers
- shareholders' meetings

Factors to be analyzed in fundamental analysis

The basic objective of an investor is to pick companies with the best price appreciation potential in the long run. Such companies usually have a superior record of earnings and dividends. To identify such companies the fundamentals of analyzing a company need to be learned. Factors that need to be identified and analyzed as part of this exercise are:

- company's business
- corporate purpose and mission
- profitability (current and projected)
- demand for products (current and future)
- competition and pricing pressures
- performance track record and accomplishments
- relative performance compared to similar companies and the market (current and historical)
- leadership status (whether the company is a leader or a follower)
- management quality (strengths and weaknesses)

Basic variables to be analyzed in-depth

There are many variables that affect a company's business, profitability, and stock price. Because an investor cannot analyze all these variables even in a cursory way, the practical approach is to pick a few important variables and analyze them in-depth. These can be supplemented by a few additional variables, if needed. The most important and widely used variables are:

- earnings per share
- earnings growth rate
- revenue (sales) growth
- return on equity
- cash flow
- debt level and ratios
- dividends

Analyzing financial statements

One of the basic requirements in fundamental analysis is the study of financial statements. Analysis of these statements allows an investor to determine a company's financial viability and profitability. The three financial statements most commonly analyzed are:

- balance sheet
- income statement
- statement of cash flows

Basic approach

Analysis of any financial statement generally involves three types of comparisons:

- relative size of items within a set of statements
- changes in each item and in the relative size of individual items
- comparison of financial measures of the company to similar companies (or to industry averages); this can include single line item comparison or ratio analysis

A potential stock market investor need not panic at the thought of having to become a financial wizard. Keep in mind that only a few key items in these statements need to be analyzed. These items are usually provided in an easy-to-read format, after they have been extracted from financial statements, in company research reports that are readily available to all investors. These reports often provide additional valuable data, not available in the original statements, such as comparison of various line items to the industry or group to which the company belongs (Appendixes A-C).

Balance sheet

This is a snapshot of a company's financial status that lists its assets and liabilities on a given date. It indicates a company's financial condition: what it owns, owes and the stockholder's equity (net worth). Balance sheets list values for the company's assets, its liabilities (debt, long-term/short-term), and the stockholders equity (assets/ liabilities), with the basic equation being:

equity = assets - liabilities

(Appendix B includes a summarized balance sheet and other financial data for Oracle Corporation, which can be the basis for analysis as shown in Chapter 11.)

Income statement

An income statement compares a company's total income to total expenses. The difference between the two is the profits earned or net earnings. An income statement reconciles revenues (sales), expenses, and profits and losses for a specific accounting period. It shows the annual business results, which include numbers for sales, costs and earnings. It also includes a comparison of results against the previous year. (Appendix B contains an analysis of Oracle Corporation's income statement.)

Statement of cash flows

Cash flow is the net cash generated during the reporting period (Appendix B) and is generally defined as the net income before the deduction of charges such as depreciation and amortization. A statement of cash flow indicates how a company's financial position changed during the fiscal year. It shows where the funds came from, where they were spent and is useful in the analysis of profit trends.

This type of analysis can be revealing. For example, while a company may have positive earnings, it does not necessarily mean that it is generating cash. Inventory and accounts receivable could be increasing which, in turn, can cause cash to be consumed. (Appendix B contains an analysis of Oracle's cash flow over a multi-year period.)

What to look for in financial statements

An investor should determine whether this year's results were better or worse than the previous year. The cause(s) of positive and negative items and trends should be determined. Any management changes should be noted, which in some cases can materially affect the company. Where possible, performance should be compared to industry benchmarks and averages, because that is an important aspect of any analysis. When reviewing these statements, ensure that:

- the balance sheet is strong and allows company flexibility to finance its growth
- revenues are growing at a healthy pace, indicating that ample demand exists for the company's products and/or services
- net income and earnings/share (net income divided by the number of outstanding shares) is rising
- margins are rising:
  - if margins are not rising, they should remain steady; ideally, a company should have 15%+ pretax margins
  - gross margin (revenues minus the direct cost of producing the product/service) is an excellent indicator of the efficiency with which the company produces goods; it is stated as a percentage of revenue
- research and development (R&D) expenditures are not decreasing as a percentage of annual revenues because:
  - R&D is an investment in the company's future that indicates whether new products will continue to be introduced
  - adequate R&D is a requirement for survival in a competitive environment
- number of outstanding shares are not increasing significantly
- cash reserves are ample: this can help a company to fund its growth, weather a downturn, pay dividends, buy back stock or make an acquisition
- company has managed to generate cash rather than consume it
- any account receivable and inventory growth approximates growth in sales: too high receivable or inventory levels are warning signals
- profitability is not impacted by excessive debt levels

A very important aspect of financial analysis is the study of a company's debt level and ratios, which can be obtained from company research reports (Appendixes A-C). These should be steady or improving. Small, successful, companies usually have low debt. A company with low debt has flexibility. High debt ratios are highly undesirable, especially during poor business conditions. When analyzing the debt ratio of any company, compare it to the industry average and similar companies.

The debt ratio is often reported as a percentage of long-term debt to capitalization (capitalization ratio), which is equal to:

long-term debt/(long-term debt + stockholders' equity)

Financial statements include many footnotes that may contain significant information. These notes should be checked to ensure that there are no hidden surprises.

Analyzing the industry

It is not sufficient to research a company without observing the environment in which it operates. An effective way to analyze a company is to study its performance, recent and historical, and then compare it to similar companies. Such companies should be in the same industry or have similar financial characteristics. Besides studying the performance of competing companies, the following need to be determined:

- current condition of the industry to which the company belongs
- expected performance and prospects of the industry during the investor's investment horizon

A method of tracking the current performance of any industry group is to note its "group rank," which is provided by *Investor's Business Daily* (*IBD*) every Friday. It indicates how well the company's industry group has performed compared to 197 other groups tracked by *IBD*. Group rankings are reported on a scale from A (best) to E (worst). *IBD* also reports on "Groups with the greatest percentage of stocks making new highs" as shown in Table 1. *The Wall Street Journal* (*WSJ*) also reports, in a limited manner, the performance of various industry groups.

Table 1: Groups with the greatest percentage of stocks making new highs

Retail-Major Dis Chains	50%
Food-Confectionery	43%
Medical-Drug/Diversified	33%
Aerospace/Defense	20%
Machinery-Const/Mining	10%
Building-Hand Tools	10%
Retail/Wholesale-Bldg Prods	9%
Retail/Wholesale-Office Supplies	9%
Insurance-Life	8%
Retail-Consumer Elect	8%
Commercial Svc-Engineering/Rd	6%
Household-Audio/Video	6%
Medical-Generic Drugs	6%

Source: *Investor's Business Daily*, May 21, 1998

TECHNICAL ANALYSIS

Technical analysis is based on observing a stock's behavior with the primary focus being on price and trading volume. It attempts to forecast stock price movements primarily through the use of:

- stock price charts
- some technical indicators

The cornerstones of technical analysis are the following principles:

- behavior of any stock, or the stock market, can be related to trends that develop over time; a trend refers to the main underlying direction of a stock (or the overall market)
- price movements are not random; they occur in patterns that can be analyzed to predict the future price movements of the stock (or the market)

In order to understand technical analysis, an investor needs to become familiar with a number of key technical analysis principles and terms. These are described, along with the typical stock price cycle, in the following sections.

Support

When a stock stabilizes after a big drop or a decline in price, technicians (technical analysts) say that it has found "support" or made a bottom. According to technical analysis, a stock's price should stop falling at the support level because supply will no longer exceed demand. A bottom can be recognized by a sharp sell-off (on heavy volume) or by successive price lows (on decreasing volume).

A line drawn across the low points, or bottoms, on a stock price chart is called a support line (Figure 1). Technicians view this as a level at which a stock will find "support" during a downward price move, which will prevent it from declining further. A stock may have several support levels. If a support level is breached to the downside, it is considered to be a bearish sign. When a support level is breached decisively, support is expected to be provided at the next support level.

A stock's underlying trend is represented by its moving average line, which effectively is its average price in the recent past. Typically, this period is 30, 50 or 200 days. Supply tends to diminish, and demand to rise, whenever a stock price decreases to the underlying trend (moving average line) or to levels located within a few percentage points, typically 3%, on each side of that trend. When a support level is reached, a large number of traders come in to buy, which causes the stock to rebound. In particular, buying at the support level is done by large institutional buyers. They use predetermined level(s) as their entry point.

A support line can be reached, and rebounded from, many times. A support level becomes more solid, acting like a "floor," as the frequency with which support is provided by that level increases. Consequently, that level becomes attractive as an entry point, to more and more traders, as it is expected to provide a floor beneath which a stock will not slide easily, and from which a rebound can be expected. If the support line is broken, it may become a resistance level.

Figure 1

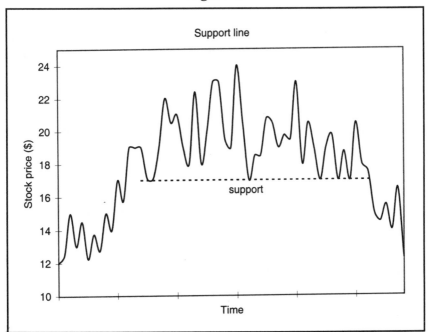

Resistance

A top, or resistance, is a mirror image of a bottom. According to technical analysis, it is the price at which a stock price should peak because supply will tend to rise while demand will fall off. A line drawn across the top points on a stock price chart is called a resistance line (Figure 2). In contrast to a "floor" for a support level, a resistance line provides a "ceiling" through which a stock cannot penetrate easily during its upward move. If it does, it is considered to be a bullish sign.

Resistance generally occurs when the price rises to the underlying trend (moving average) or to levels located within a few percentage points, typically 3%, on each side of that trend. Many investors use a resistance level as their exit point for that stock. When a resistance level is reached, a large number of sellers come in to unload their shares, which causes the stock to reverse direction. This can happen many times, with large numbers of investors dumping shares at the resistance level every time the stock price approaches that level.

A resistance level becomes more solid and important as the number of approaches and failures to pierce it increase. Consequently, that level becomes attractive as a selling point to more and more traders as it provides a ceiling above which a stock will not rise easily, and from which a reversal is expected. Therefore, technicians do not recommend buying near a resistance level. However, a powerful breakout through a resistance level on heavy volume is considered to be a very attractive point for getting into a stock. After a resistance level is breached, it usually becomes a support level.

Generally, stocks that have traded at a higher price for a long time, and with heavy volume, have the maximum resistance. Until selling dries up, a stock is unlikely to penetrate its resistance line. This can happen when some changes come into play, such as improved earnings or revenues, gain in market share, new product cycle, improving market or group, improving economy, etc.

Figure 2

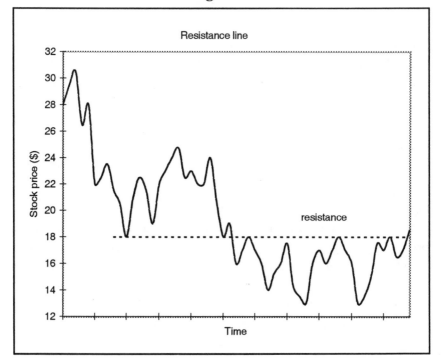

Basing

<u>Basing characteristics</u>

When a stock trades within a narrow price range, often on low volume, it is said to be basing (Figure 3). During a basing period, resistance and support lines come close to each other. During this period, neither buyers nor sellers have an upper hand since they are more or less evenly matched. A basing pattern can occur for weeks, months or even longer. During this phase, neither supply nor demand becomes one-sided. A basing period can occur:

- during an uptrend, when a stock pauses and rests, digesting prior gains
- quite often after a price decline, especially precipitous drops

Figure 3

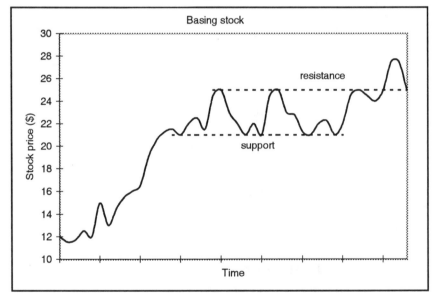

After a consolidation period, a stock will eventually move out of its trading range. This is known as a "breakout", which can occur either to the upside or the downside. An upward breakout occurs either when there are few sellers left or new buyers start coming in. A downside breakout occurs when there are few buyers left and selling predominates. A guideline to confirm the validity of a breakout is for the stock to move over the top of its base by 3%.

<u>Using the "breakout" strategy</u>

Technicians use the "breakout" strategy to find strong stocks. However, buying a stock based on this strategy does not guarantee success. Many stocks breakout but still fail to make any significant upward move. Therefore, one should not use this strategy in isolation from other factors. When buying a breakout stock, make sure that it meets three criteria: is in a major uptrend, has based over 7 weeks (preferably 3–5 months), and has strong earnings.

The following are some guidelines to determine the strength, or weakness, of a stock's breakout:

- basing duration: the longer the basing period, the more powerful is the expected breakout
- if most of the stock's basing has occurred above the 50-day moving average, it is the sign of a strong stock
- the larger the breakout (especially with heavy volume), the more bullish is the sign
- higher the trading volume when breakout occurs, more bullish is the sign; it is preferred that breakout volume be 2 to 3 times the average daily trading volume
- a stock breaking out of a base and quickly climbing 10% can be a very powerful mover
- a pullback of 3% from the top of the base is a failure indication (for example, from a 100 base top to 97)
- breakouts into new highs are less risky because they have less overhead resistance
- relative strength should be higher than 70, preferably in the 90s

Understanding the stock price cycle

There are four major phases in a typical stock price life cycle. These are:

- phase 1: basing
- phase 2: rising
- phase 3: topping
- phase 4: declining

These four phases are shown in Figure 4. Technical analysts try their best to identify each phase as early as possible because of the potential

Figure 4

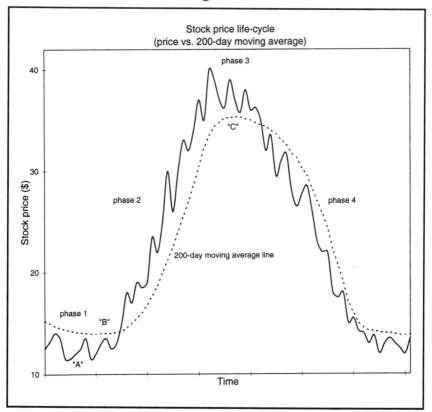

for increasing, or protecting, profits through early recognition. However in many cases, these phases are not very obvious until after the fact to those viewing stock charts.

<u>Phase 1</u>

In this phase, the stock develops a "basing" area where buyers and sellers are more or less evenly matched. It trades sideways—up and down (in a range)—between the support and resistance levels. The following are important characteristics of this area:

- basing can continue for weeks, months or years
- swings between the upper level (resistance) and lower level (support) are routine
- buying at the low level (Point A) can ensure good trading profits

A breakout over the top of the basing area and the 30-week moving average, Point B, signals the start of phase 2. If a stock is bought just when it starts basing, it entails the risk of tying up money for a lengthy period without any significant price appreciation occurring until a breakout occurs.

Phase 2

In this phase, the stock starts to make "higher highs." This is the most profitable phase in the stock price cycle and is considered to be the best time to buy a stock. In this phase, buyers are in control and maximum price appreciation occurs. The following are some characteristics of this phase:

- a breakout on heavy volume indicates a strong stock (even though fundamental news may not reflect that)
- the 30-week moving average starts moving up after the breakout
- as the stock moves up, successive highs are higher
- lows on pullbacks are higher than the prior ones
- if the stock drops below the 30-week moving average, it is a bearish sign

At some point, months or years down the road, the stock price moves closer and closer to its moving average line, which starts to curve down. When this happens, it signals the end of phase 2.

Phase 3

In this phase, the stock begins to level out again. Buyers and sellers are more or less evenly matched, and the stock does not make any appreciable progress. A characteristic top (Point C) starts to shape up, as in phase 1 basing, and the stock bounces up and down. While this action is mostly sideways, the stock may whipsaw across its moving average, which remains quite flat. This situation is a precursor to the start of phase 4. Hence, an investor needs to become more alert at this point and seriously evaluate exiting from the stock. No buying is recommended in this phase.

Phase 4

In this phase, the stock starts its decline and selling rather than buying is recommended. This phase is characterized by:

- moving averages that move lower
- successive highs in any rally are lower than the prior one
- successive lows are lower than the prior ones

Figure 5 shows two examples of a stock price cycle for Alliance Semiconductor and Central Sprinkler. For Alliance, one complete cycle is shown. However, the Central Sprinkler chart shows two cycles, with the second one being shorter than the first.

Trends

Trend characteristics

Stocks do not move from one price level to another in a straight, unbroken line. Instead of moving in an uninterrupted manner to the next price level, they move in a characteristic jagged manner. A typical sequence of movements can be a slow rise up, down, up with a surge, sideways, and up again. These movements in different directions can occur either during an overall up, or down, price movement.

Over time, if the net price movement is up, the stock is said to be in an uptrend (Figure 6). If a stock's price is charted during an uptrend, it will be noticed that successive bottoms are higher than the preceding bottoms. Conversely, if the net movement is in the downward direction, the stock is said to be in a downtrend. In this case, successive bottoms will be lower than the preceding bottoms.

A trend can be either long-term or short-term. An established uptrend indicates that, for the time being, demand forces are stronger than supply forces. A major factor in establishing a trend is when institutions, who account for most trading activity in the stock market, take positions in a stock or get out of it. Once a trend is established, either up or down, it remains in place for some time due to momentum.

Identifying trend reversals

An investor's ability to identify an uptrend in an early stage provides an excellent opportunity to realize big gains. Usually, stocks in uptrends can be held until a reversal occurs. Trend reversal can occur

Figure 5

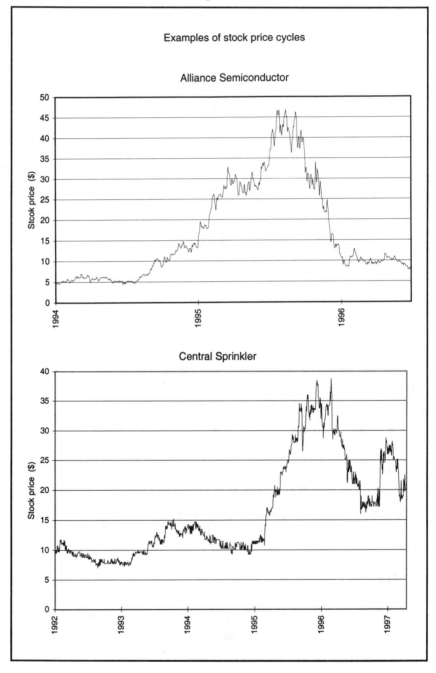

Figure 6

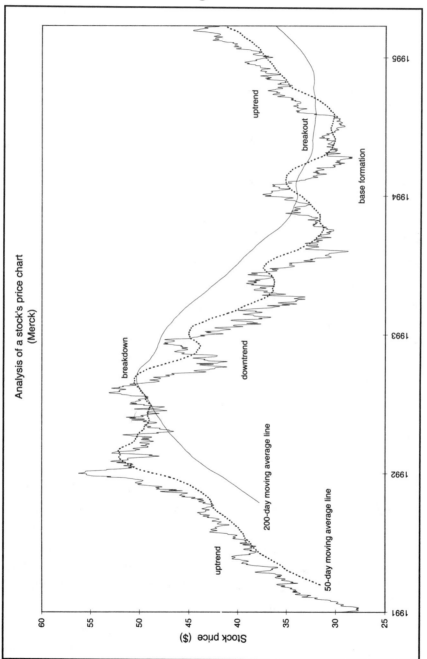

Analysis of a stock's price chart
(Merck)

after weeks, months or even years. These trend reversals take place when there remain only a few buyers (during an uptrend) or sellers (during a downtrend). A trend can end, ultimately, in one of the following ways:

- a downward reversal following a rise
- an upward reversal following a decline
- bottoming; move into a basing pattern, especially after a decline
- climatic rapid drop (after a decline)
- climatic rapid rise (known as a blowoff)

Technical analysts consider an uptrend to have ended, that is, the breakthrough to be valid, when the penetration of an uptrend line extends below the line by 5%. For example, a price decline to $95 from the uptrend line which is at $100, equivalent to a 5% drop, at the day's close is considered a valid breakthrough and a sell signal.

From a trading perspective, it is ideal to buy when trend reversal takes place at the bottom, or sell when trend reversal occurs during an upward move. For long-term investors, however, the ability to pinpoint trend reversal points does not have the same importance. For those who plan to hold stocks for six months to many years, technical timing is not crucial. However, they can still benefit if they can determine when a trend reversal takes place, because they can sell or buy at more profitable exit/entry points. For this purpose, technical analysis can be a useful tool because it can help determine the points where an existing trend is likely to reverse or find support.

Tools for identifying trends

Investors use a number of tools to identify trends and trend reversals. The easy and most widely used tools that an individual investor can use are described in detail in the following chapters. Sophisticated investors who want to get a handle on complicated indicators such as the moving average convergence/divergence (MACD) and the stochastic index should refer to a number of excellent books that are available in most bookstores.

Investors can also use a number of software tools for identifying trends and trend reversals. These range from quite simple to very sophisticated and proprietary software packages. A number of these tools are listed in Chapter 6 of Volume I.

CONCLUDING REMARKS

There are two philosophies for investing in the stock market: fundamental and technical analysis. The vast majority of investors use fundamental analysis for investment evaluation of a company. Fundamental analysis is based on performing an in-depth analysis of the company and its environment. It includes analyzing the company's industry, financial statements, business prospects and other related factors.

Technical analysis is based on the study of stock price movements and is favored by those with a short-term horizon—short-term traders. Investors using the fundamental analysis approach can use technical analysis as a tool to determine the appropriate time for buying a stock—after a buy decision has already been made.

Stock market investors are always attempting to determine the current trend of a stock, the market, and any potential trend reversal. For those able to do this accurately, the gains can be magnified while any potential losses can be reduced appreciably. For identifying trends and trend reversals a number of tools are available to investors. Many of these are covered in the following chapters.

CHAPTER 2

STOCK MARKET INDICATORS

UNDERSTANDING INDICATORS

A large number of forces, cross currents, and variables are at work in the stock market at all times. The effect of these variables, also called indicators, can vary significantly. The magnitude of the impact of any indicator depends on the time (recession, bull market, bear market, earnings season) as well as the presence or absence of other variables. The relative importance attached to various indicators varies according to an investor's investment philosophy, experiences, and objectives. Most of these indicators, of which there are hundreds, are derived from the following main sources:

- activity taking place in the stock market
- actions and activities of market players (the investors)
- economic and business data
- coincidental factors (which may be unrelated)

Important indicators

With hundreds of indicators to choose from, an investor needs to carefully pick and choose indicators. The indicators picked should be compatible with the investor's investment approach. Among the most widely monitored indicators are:

- earnings per share (EPS)—quarterly and annual
- earnings estimate revisions
- earnings per share (EPS) rank
- revenues (sales) growth
- P/E ratio
- moving averages
- trendlines, trend channels and trading bands
- market breadth
- advance/decline (A/D) line

- number of new daily lows and highs
- relative strength (RS) rank
- relative strength (RS) line
- accumulation/distribution
- trading volume
- float - supply of stock
- institutional ownership
- number of analysts
- buy/hold/sell recommendations
- industry specific indicators

With the exception of the P/E ratio indicator, all these indicators, as well as some related ones are described in Chapters 2 and 3 of this Volume. The P/E ratio has been comprehensively discussed in Volume I.

Indicator combinations

Many indicators are available to stock investors for analyzing the overall market and individual stocks. These indicators can be combined into hundreds of permutations and combinations. However, if the wrong indicators are combined, they can give very conflicting signals. The number and the types of indicators tracked by market professionals varies significantly. For example, one analyst closely tracks six indicators: specialist shorting, put-to-call ratios, mutual fund cash, technical pattern of Treasury bills and bond yields, A/D line, and the bullish/bearish consensus numbers. Elaine Garzarelli, the stock market strategist who correctly predicted the DJIA crash of October 19, 1987, uses 14 indicators. She weighs monetary, economic, valuation, and sentiment indicators equally in her model.[1] The 14 fundamental factors used in her proprietary methodology for forecasting stock market movements are:

- earnings
- industrial production momentum
- coincident/ lagging ratio
- free reserves
- 3-month bill rate

- bill rate vs. discount rate
- interest rate momentum
- money supply
- money supply vs. economy

- earnings yields to interest rates
- P/E equations
- cash levels
- number of bullish advisors
- yield curve

[1] *The Garzarelli Edge*, 1996, pg. 3

As is obvious, analyzing so many indicators is beyond the capability of individual investors who have limited time and resources available to them. These investors should go for a simpler approach, which can be quite effective. Such investors should use only a few indicators that can be monitored and analyzed easily. Tracking too many indicators is not recommended because, besides being difficult to monitor and analyze, their effect is not cumulative.

Choosing indicators

With many indicators to choose from, it is not easy to decide which ones to monitor and the relative importance to be assigned to each indicator. In general, an investor should use an assortment of indicators from different perspectives: monetary, psychological and valuation. This combination gives greater depth than looking at one or two indicators only. Examples of indicator combinations for analyzing individual stocks are shown in Chapter 10.

Investors should realize that determining which indicator to use is an art rather than a science. Only over time, after making mistakes and gaining experience, do investors learn to pick and choose the right combination of indicators to meet their investment objectives and goals.

EARNINGS PER SHARE (EPS)

One of the most important factors determining the success or failure of a stock is the company's ability to consistently earn profits. An analysis of past winners clearly shows that excellent profitability, or earnings, was a common factor in the success of most winners. Even companies whose earnings rose modestly but consistently, year after year, proved to be excellent investments.

To measure, compare and analyze earnings, an indicator called earnings per share (EPS) is used. EPS is the net income earned by each share of common stock. Net income is equal to the after-tax income from continuing operations plus (or minus) discontinued operations and any extraordinary items.

Calculating EPS

EPS is calculated by dividing a company's net income by the total number of its outstanding shares. It is reported in two ways: annually and quarterly. Annual EPS is calculated by dividing the net annual income by the total number of outstanding shares. Quarterly EPS is calculated by dividing the net income for the quarter by the total number of outstanding shares.

Suppose a company's net annual earnings are $2 million and it has 4 million outstanding shares. Its annual earning/share can be calculated as follows:

annual EPS = $2 million/4 million shares = $0.50/share

If the company earns $600,000 for the quarter, its quarterly EPS will be calculated as follows:

quarterly EPS = $600,000/4 million shares = $0.15/share

A company's annual EPS can also be calculated by adding its EPS for the prior 4 quarters. For example, if a company had EPS of $0.90, $1.0, $1.15 and $1.25 in the prior 4 quarters, its annual EPS will be:

$0.90 + $1.0 + $1.15 + $1.25 = $4.30/share

EPS growth rate

To analyze a company's profitability, investors thoroughly analyze earnings because higher earnings translate into a higher EPS and a higher stock price. The two earnings components that receive the maximum attention from investors are:

- current quarterly earnings (EPS) and its rate of increase
- annual earnings (EPS) growth rate

The EPS growth rate is calculated as follows:

EPS growth rate =

   (EPS in current year - EPS in prior year)/EPS in prior year

For example, if the annual EPS in the current year is $2.50, while it was $2.20 in the prior year, the annual EPS growth rate will be:

($2.50 - $2.20)/$2.20 = 13.6%

An important factor in the success of stocks is the acceleration in earnings growth. This refers to the rising percentage change in profit, as measured from one period to the next. Accelerating earnings growth is one of the most potent factors in the success of a stock. For example, starting in the third quarter of 1995, Ascend Communications increased its operating earnings in the following sequence: 133%, 300%, 325% and 380% (Figure 7). During this period, the stock rose from 17 to over 70. Table 2 shows examples of some other winners in recent years. It lists the characteristics of some recent leaders who had a phenomenal runup despite poor market conditions at the time they made their big moves. As can be observed, all of them had high EPS rank (90+). Therefore, considering this potent factor, investors should monitor a company's EPS growth rate and earnings acceleration rate very closely.

EPS as a comparison tool

The EPS number helps in comparing companies of different sizes. It puts profits in perspective by comparing them with the same yardstick. For example, a company earning $100 million annually, with 100 million outstanding shares, will have an EPS of $1/share. However, if a smaller company earns $25 million/year, and it has 10 million outstanding shares, its EPS will be $2.5/share—a far higher number. Obviously, the latter is a better value for the shareholders, even though its profits are $75 million less, since it provides them with a better rate of return.

Effect of earnings on P/E multiples

There are three important factors that can make a stock price rise:
- increased earnings; any rise in earnings get translated into a higher price—assuming that the P/E remains steady
- investors bid up the stock to a higher P/E, while earnings remain unchanged
- both earnings and P/E rise

Investors' changing perception of a company's future earnings potential can result in their awarding its stock a higher P/E than it currently commands. Any P/E increase over the current level combined with

Figure 7

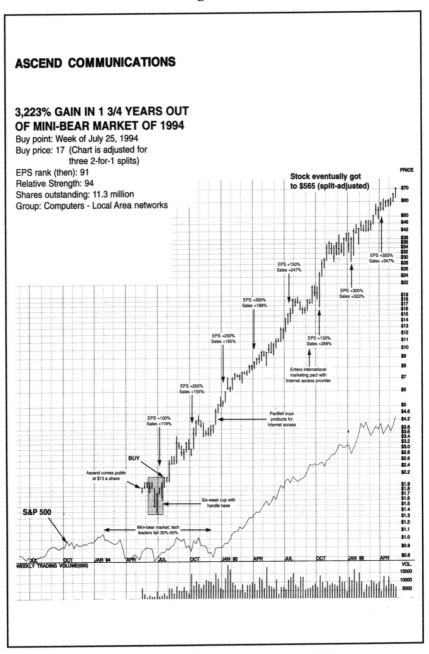

Reproduced with permission of *Investor's Business Daily.*

Table 2: Characteristics of winners

Company	Buy point	Percent increase	Period weeks	5 yr. EPS growth % (at buy point)	Last quarter EPS change %	EPS rank %	RS rank %	P/E ratio	Industry
Cisco Systems	11/2/90	2,687	175	257	155	99	97	30	Comp./LANS
Micron Technology	1/20/95	294	33	312	132	99	94	10	Elec Comp Semiconductors
International Game Technology	2/1/91	1,510	143	81	39	93	94	19	Leisure & Recreation/Gaming
Home Depot	8/20/82	462	42	new issue	386	97	98	58	Bldg Products-Retail/Wholesale
Amgen	3/16/90	658	94	losses	700	94	90	281	Med-Biomedical
Wal-Mart Stores	6/15/79	961	215	31	35	NA	74	12	Retail-Discount & Variety
Surgical Care Affiliates	2/24/89	1,410	146	losses	267	92	89	28	Medical Products
Ascend Communications	7/29/94	3,223	93	new issue	100	91	94	49	Telecom Equipment
Microsoft	10/17/86	305	49	99	75	98	80	22	Computer-Software
Franklin Resources	9/7/84	1,294	126	102	115	99	96	13	Finance-Investment Management

Source: *Investor's Business Daily*

accelerating earnings can cause a stock price to increase tremendously. An example is Informix, which in May 1994 was trading at a P/E half that compared to other companies in its group. When investors realized that the company would release its products on time, and its earnings would grow at a healthy pace, its price was bid up from $16.06 to $32.125 within 7 months. Its P/E doubled during that period, rising to a level in line with other companies in its group.

If a company's earnings start to accelerate, as they did for Ascend Communications, it starts beating earnings estimates. This causes analysts to start revising their earnings estimates, which fuels it upwards. This typically occurs at the start of a strong product cycle, when a company enters a strong and rapid growth phase.

How earnings are reported

A stock's price rises or falls, over the long term, in tandem with the company's earnings, dividends and financial health. Therefore, since investors are aware of how earnings influence a stock's price, they wait for a company's earnings announcements with anticipation. These earnings, accompanied with financial highlights, are released every quarter. The reporting months can vary from company to company; however, most companies follow the calendar year and report the quarterly earnings in April (1Q), July (2Q), October (3Q) and January (4Q).

Earnings are reported by the major newspapers, Online services, and a number of sources on the Internet. The most comprehensive earnings data are reported by *IBD*, *WSJ*, and *Barron's*. These publications provide tables listing companies with the highest percentage change in earnings (up or down). In its stock tables, *IBD* also provides a company's estimated earnings for the next quarter and for the fiscal year as well. Estimated earnings can also be obtained from the sources listed in Table 3.

Table 3: Internet sources for earnings estimates

Analyst Center ....http://www.schwab.com
First Call..http://www.firstcall.com
IBES ....http://www.ibes.com/

Table 3: Internet sources for earnings estimates (cont'd.)

Individual Investor Online ....http://www.iionline.com/

InvestTools ....http://www.tabula.com/

Nelson's ....http://www.irnet.com/pages/Nelson.stm

SchwabNow ....http://www.schwabselect.com

Standard & Poor's ....http://www.stockinfo.standardpoor.com

Research Wizard ....http://www.reswizard.com

Yahoo ....http://quote.yahoo.com

Zacks ....http://aw.zacks.com

Analyzing earnings

Earnings releases from companies are accompanied by high sounding and glowing descriptions of their performance. However, an astute investor will look closely at the results to discern the true picture. For example, while the reported earnings may be "record ones," they may not show up favorably when compared year to year in percentage terms. The company's earnings growth could actually have decreased despite higher revenues.

An investor should study earnings reports closely and be on the lookout for "write-offs" and restructuring charges, which can distort earnings. Also to be noted are "non-recurring" or "extraordinary" items because they too can distort earnings. One should always observe signs of acceleration or deceleration in earnings, which is a good indicator of potential gains or losses.

If it is observed that earnings decreased or failed to grow as expected, the cause(s) should be investigated. For example, earnings can be temporarily affected due to an acquisition which, while temporarily depressing the present earnings, has the potential to provide excellent growth and profits in the future. An example is the acquisition of a number of companies by Platinum Technology in 1995 and 1996, which depressed its earnings and stock price. However, the acquisitions positioned Platinum strategically for the future and, as expected, it rebounded strongly and the share price more than doubled in 1997.

Quarterly EPS (current quarterly earnings per share)

The earnings per share reported for the latest quarter is a very good indicator of the current profitability of a company. It shows the magnitude and trend of its recent earnings, which is the fundamental basis for stock valuation.

What to look for

Analysts look for a company's EPS to be increasing consistently. The EPS chart in Appendix C shows the consistent stock price rise for Oracle Corporation in tandem with the rise in its quarterly and annual EPS. More than seeing a simple increase in EPS, investors prefer to see an accelerating rate of increase in EPS (i.e., the percentage increase). For example, if a company's earnings have been growing at 20% per year and accelerate to 35% or even higher, it is a sure sign that its stock is poised to make a significant upward price move.

The greater the rate of increase in EPS, the greater is the price appreciation potential for the stock. This is borne out by the behavior of past winners whose profits increased 60–90% prior to their significant and rapid price advance. Consequently, one of the most important factors in stock selection is the percentage increase in EPS compared to the same quarter of the previous year. In general, the current quarterly EPS should have a high percentage increase (20–30% over the previous year's comparable quarter). Examples of winning stocks rising in tandem with accelerating quarterly EPS are shown in Figure 7 and Table 2.

Periods to analyze

When analyzing EPS, both the quarterly and 6 to 9 month periods should be analyzed separately. Analyzing EPS for only a combined 6 or 9 month period can cause an important trend to be missed. Suppose that the total EPS for the last 9 month period (current fiscal year) was higher than the corresponding period of the previous fiscal year. The limitation of this combined 9-month EPS number is that it will be unable to show whether the last quarter was worse compared to both the:

- prior quarter (of this year)
- comparable quarter (of last year)

Specifically, a combined EPS for the first 9 months of 1998 will be unable to show that the EPS for the third quarter (3Q) of 1998 was lower than both the:

- EPS of the second quarter (2Q) of 1998
- EPS of the third quarter (3Q) of 1997

Such a situation is considered bearish because it indicates decelerating earnings and, hence, it would definitely need to be investigated.

Guidelines and tips for analyzing quarterly EPS

- analyze EPS for at least 2 or 3 prior quarters; analyze the quarterly trend, not a consolidated period
- EPS in the last quarter should be compared to the same quarter of the previous year. For example:
  - EPS for the 1st quarter of 1998 should be compared to the 1st quarter of 1997
  - EPS for the 1st quarter of 1998 should not be compared to the 4th quarter of 1997
- the current quarterly earnings increase, in percentage terms, should be compared to the same quarter a year ago
- the higher the percentage increase in EPS, the better it is
- select stocks with accelerating quarterly earnings growth
- favor companies with 20 to 30% increase in earnings in the last reported quarter (versus the comparable quarter of the previous year)
- winning stocks with accelerating earnings usually see a very heavy increase in trading volume prior to their price breakout to the upside
- comparison can be misleading if earnings in the previous year were low or there was a loss; in such a case, a poor current EPS can appear good compared to the previous year's earnings
- notice any unusual factors, extraordinary charges, one-time items, an increase/decrease in number of outstanding shares, etc., which can distort earnings
- compare earnings to other stocks in the same group/industry; if earnings at similar companies are growing at 30%, and the company being analyzed is growing at 20%, it is not a positive sign and should be investigated
- analyze current earnings in conjunction with anticipated future prospects (based on fundamentals and news)

Annual earnings per share

An indicator of consistent profitability

Investors should analyze both the quarterly and annual earnings per share. While recent quarterly earnings results are a good indicator of a company's current profitability and momentum, its annual earnings provide another useful perspective. It enables investors to confirm a consistent and healthy earnings history, which is the sign of a winning stock. The EPS chart in Appendix C shows the consistent price rise for Oracle in tandem with the rise in its quarterly and annual EPS.

Investors want to see a company's annual EPS show an increasing trend for the past 5 years. A down year can be ignored if a quick earnings recovery was made in the following year, and the upward earnings trend continued. This 5-year growth criteria is used by many analysts as a screening criteria in the stock selection process. When used as a screening method, the 5-year earnings growth criteria can easily screen out 75% of stocks.

Use projected annual earnings

A widely used valuation method employed by investors to determine if a stock is overvalued or undervalued is based on analyzing its P/E ratio. These investors consider a stock to be undervalued if its P/E is low and overvalued if its P/E is high. Typically, using the under/overvalued criteria, such investors decide whether a stock should be bought or sold.

As is quite obvious, the magnitude of the P/E ratio is directly dependent on the annual earnings number used in the P/E calculation. Typically, this ratio is calculated using the trailing earnings figure. However, using this backward-looking number does not make much sense. Instead, it is more appropriate to use projected future earnings, which are more relevant to a stock's future price movement and achievable level.

How to forecast earnings

Estimating future earnings, which depend on a company's future earnings growth, is not an easy or simple task. Investors who are able to forecast future earnings growth of companies manage to get a head start in predicting its stock price appreciation. Consequently, they are able to reap excellent financial gains. One way to predict this growth rate is to analyze the growth prospects of the industry group to which the company belongs, as well as the company itself. There are a number of sources from which estimated earnings growth rates for the company and the industry can be obtained. These include reports from First Call (Appendix A), S&P (Appendix B), Zacks (Appendix C), Value Line, S&P Industry surveys, and *IBD* stock tables.

Guidelines and tips for analyzing annual earnings
- the annual compounded earnings growth rate should be 20 to 50% or higher for the prior 3 to 5 year period
- if growth rate decreases, say from 35% to 20%, seriously evaluate selling the stock even if it has been a leader
- faster the earnings growth, the greater are future earnings and stock price to be expected
- both annual and quarterly EPS should be growing at a healthy pace
- consistent earnings growth in the past few years, combined with strong current earnings in recent quarters, are the ingredients of an outstanding stock
- P/E ratios reported in newspapers are typically based on trailing (past) earnings, which have little bearing on future performance; use projected earnings

EARNINGS ESTIMATE REVISIONS AND EARNINGS SURPRISES

Earnings estimates

The level of earnings affects stock prices significantly. Therefore, analysts try to forecast a company's earnings for the current quarter and year. These forecasted earnings are called earnings estimates. Some analysts conduct their own research, while others publish the average of what has been estimated by stock analysts tracking the company. The earnings estimates published by S&P Corporation (Appendix B) and Value Line are based on the research conducted by a single organization.

Other estimates reported by First Call (Appendix A), Zacks (Appendix C), and *IBD* stock tables are based on data provided by a large number of analysts working for different organizations. These earnings estimates are called consensus earnings estimates. Besides the average estimate, First Call and Zacks also report the high and low range of earnings estimates. The consensus earnings estimates generate more confidence than estimates from single sources because a single wrong estimate in a large number of estimates cannot distort the average (consensus) estimate significantly.

When analyzing earnings estimates, the range of earnings estimates should be checked. Suppose two companies have the same mean earnings estimate of $1.50 per share—with the first company's earnings in the $1.40 to $1.60 range and the second company's earnings in the $1 to $2 range. The reaction by investors to an earnings surprise of the same magnitude from these two companies will be different. A 10¢ shortfall or positive surprise will have a greater impact on the company with the more narrow band ($1.40–$1.60) compared to the company with the wide earnings estimate spread ($1–$2).

Earnings estimate reports can be purchased for a small fee through a broker or from investment sources on the Internet and Online services (Appendixes A–D). A number of web sites, including http://quote.yahoo.com, provide free earnings estimates.

Understanding earnings estimates

The market usually prices a stock based on its expected future earnings. Since the market is quite knowledgeable and efficient, earnings estimates are already reflected in a stock's price. Simply stated, current expectations are already reflected in a stock's price and any change in expectations brings swift market reaction. For example, if the market is used to a company beating earnings estimates, and it announces earnings that do not beat Wall Street expectations, its stock price will drop in most cases. Also, if a company does not meet estimates, its stock will invariably be punished.

Earnings estimates should be used with care. The following are some important factors to keep in mind when using earnings estimates:

- one-time gains/losses can distort earnings estimates
- only operating earnings should be considered
- many 5-year growth projections for relatively young firms can be completely unrealistic due to excessive bullishness; this results in higher P/E ratios
- estimates for companies made by only a few analysts should be viewed with extreme caution
- analysts typically underestimate earnings when they are rising and overestimate them when they are falling

Earnings estimate revisions

What revisions indicate

Usually, estimates revised upward indicate that something positive is happening in the company or its industry. The positive factors could be accelerating revenues, introduction of successful new product(s), gain in market share, cost cutting, etc. All these tend to increase the bottom line profitability. Consequently, the upward revision of an earnings estimate is one of the best indicators for predicting a rising stock price. Therefore, investors should seek stocks whose earnings estimates are being revised upwards, rather than downwards.

Investors should watch earnings estimate revisions very closely. When a company's earnings estimates are being lowered, the probability of the stock outperforming the market is considered slim.

Effect of revisions

While the earnings estimate figures are important for analyzing stocks, the key is earnings revision rather than the estimates themselves. As earnings expectations change based on the changing prospects for the company or the economy, analysts following the company translate the information and news they collect into numbers. These are used to revise the current earnings estimates upwards or downwards to reflect the positive or negative developments. Any upward earnings revision is considered positive, which causes the stock price to rise. Any downward revision is considered negative, which tends to drive the stock down.

Investors use revisions in earnings estimates to gauge the direction and magnitude of the improving or deteriorating fundamental health of a company. Based on the new estimates, their expectations for price appreciation or decrease change proportionately.

How revisions are reported

Upward and downward earnings revisions, which indicate the average revision in each estimate, are typically reported for the past 7, 30 and 60 days. The higher the one-month change in earnings estimate, the better it is. A significant upward revision in earnings estimate can occur if several analysts raise the estimate simultaneously or if a single analyst raises the estimate by a large amount. Appendix A shows the earnings estimate revisions made for Oracle Corporation.

The effect of revisions can be gauged from the case of Project Software and Development Company. In its July 1996 earnings estimate report, issued by First Call, the following revisions were made for fiscal years 1996 and 1997:

• 5 upward revisions, with no downward revision, in the past 7 days
• 6 upward revisions, with 1 downward revision, in the past 30 days
• 6 upward revisions, with 1 downward revision, in the past 60 days

After these revisions were made, the stock rose from $29.75 on July 30, 1996, to $42 ³/₈ by December 31, 1996.

Earnings surprises

Effect of earnings surprises

A company's earnings results are viewed positively if its quarterly result compares favorably against the previous year's comparable quarter. A stock is viewed even more favorably if it exceeds earnings expectations. When a company reports better than expected earnings figures, it is known as an "earnings surprise." As quarterly earnings are reported by companies, any earnings surprises reported on a particular day are highlighted by the *WSJ*, *Barron's* and *IBD* as shown in Table 4.

Companies beating estimates are well rewarded with price apprecia-tion. However, those failing to meet investor expectations are severely punished. Even small disappointments can cause big price drops. If the leading stock in a group (such as Intel in the semiconductor group) reports better than expected earnings, it almost invariably moves the whole group positively. The converse also holds true. Sometimes beating estimates is not considered good enough by the market because such an increase may have resulted from cost cutting, aimed at boosting profits, rather than from increased revenues.

Table 4: Earnings News

Company	Symbol	Last Qtr Change	Last Qtr Earnings ($/sh)	Last Qtr Sales	After Tax Margin
Best Ups					
Westco Bancorp Inc.	WCBI	+1075%	0.47 vs. 0.04	+0%	+0.0%
Mays J W Inc.	MAYS	+575%	0.27 vs. 0.04	+17%	+21.7%
General Cigar Hldgs Inc.	MPP	+160%	0.39 vs. 0.15	+83%	+16.1%
Signature Eyewear Inc.	SEYE	+88%	0.15 vs. 0.08	+18%	+6.5%
Motorola Inc.	MOT	+59%	0.54 vs. 0.34	+13%	+3.6%
Printronix Inc.	PTNX	+55%	0.45 vs. 0.29	-6%	+9.2%
Helen of Troy Corp.	HELE	+40%	0.21 vs. 0.15	+21%	+9.7%
Orange Nat'l. Bancorp	CGNB	+39%	0.43 vs. 0.31	+0%	+0.0%
Lance Inc.	LNCE	+35%	0.23 vs. 0.17	+2%	+6.3%
Excel Tech. Inc.	XLTC	+33%	0.20 vs. 0.15	+12%	+14.0%
First Empire State Corp.	FES	+31%	6.62 vs. 5.05	+%	+.0%
Most Downs					
Weider Nutrition Intl.	WNI	-46%	0.07 vs. 0.13	+14%	+3.2%
Molecular Devices Corp.	MDCC	-22%	0.14 vs. 0.18	+16%	+14.4%

Source: *Investor's Business Daily*, October 8, 1997

Effect on smaller companies

Small growth companies are affected more dramatically than large cap companies by earnings surprises. The reason is that fewer analysts cover them and, therefore, any unexpected positive earnings news attracts other analysts and investors, creating additional buying. Conversely, any negative earnings surprise initiates heavy selling, which usually causes small, low-trading volume stocks to decline considerably due to the proportionately large selling volume.

A reason for the disproportionate price effect, relative to positive or negative surprises, is communications. For investors who want to, earnings information is available the moment it is released. So when they see a disappointing result, they react and exit from the stock immediately. These days, when a bad report comes out, selling takes place instantaneously, rather than slowly. This availability of instant information amplifies the price change due to earnings surprises, both ways, though more so on the downside.

Company executives know how a stock is affected due to any failure to meet earnings expectations. Therefore, they typically try to downplay their earnings prospects so that, later on, they can beat analysts' estimates and give their stock a boost.

How investors should react to earnings disappointments

Short-term traders are significantly influenced by earnings results and surprises. Therefore, they react accordingly—selling at the first sign of any weakness. A long-term investor should not buy or sell stocks based solely on quarterly results. Serious investors should perform fundamental research and be confident with the long-term prospects of the company. The focus should be on analyzing on how well the company will perform in the next 12 to 18 months.

A long-term investor should stick with his investment style. He should not be overly swayed by short-term trading fluctuations and the opinion or actions of other investors or traders. If an investor's stock falls due to a temporary earnings shortfall, but the fundamentals remain solid, he should buy more. The price decline should be viewed as an opportunity. However, in such a case, an investor should buy more shares only if he knows the company very well. If an earnings disappointment comes in and the company's outlook is not bright, it should be sold without hesitation.

EARNINGS PER SHARE (EPS) RANK

Calculating the EPS

EPS rank is a yardstick for comparing a company's profit growth with all other companies in the stock market. It measures a company's earnings growth and the stability of that growth over the past five years with emphasis being placed on the last two quarters.

To calculate EPS rank, the percentage earnings change in the two most recent quarters (compared to the same quarters of the previous year) are combined and averaged with the 5-year figure.[2] The number thus obtained is compared to the results of all other companies and ranked on a scale from 99 to 1. An EPS rank of 99 indicates that the company's profits have been better than 99% of the companies in the stock market. An EPS rank of 75 means that the company's earnings and growth place it in the top 25% of all companies. EPS rank is reported daily in *IBD's* stock tables, which is the only daily newspaper reporting this data.

Relating EPS rank to stock and market performance

Stocks with high EPS rank tend to perform better than other stocks. Cisco Systems and International Game Technology are examples of companies with high EPS ranks, which had superior price appreciation. Cisco, with an EPS rank of 99, had quarterly profit gains averaging 150% during its first three years as a public company starting in 1990. During the same period, its stock made a twelvefold move. International Game Technology, with an EPS of 99, made a tenfold move from 1991 to 1992. In the previous five years, its annual profit growth had been 112%.

---

[2] *Investor's Business Daily*, February 27, 1998.

An *IBD* survey in 1997 covering 6,000 stocks also provides confirmation that stocks with the best price performance in the prior 12 months, that is with an RS rank over 95, have had superior earnings.[3] The survey found that 54% of these stocks had EPS rank greater than 70. Only 32% of the stocks had an EPS rank below 50.

When the market is trending higher, companies with high EPS rank tend to outperform. For example, one study of the market revealed that there were 75 stocks with an EPS rank of 99, priced above $4/share, out of 7,000 stocks that were analyzed. Three months later, after the market improved, 57 stocks had moved higher for an average gain of 29%. Even after including stocks that had moved lower, the 75 companies with 99 EPS rank had moved up for a 19% gain. During the same period, the S&P500 rose a meager 1.5%.

Using EPS rank for stock selection

Many investors use EPS rank for stock picking. They realize that companies with high EPS rank have strong momentum. They also tend to produce fewer earnings disappointments, which can decimate a stock. An investor can realize tremendous gains by picking low EPS rank stocks that will ultimately rise to a 90+ EPS rank. However, this requires sound fundamental analysis in order to ensure that a basis exists for the selected company's earnings to rise in the future. This is imperative because only rising earnings can make the EPS rank rise.

Investors should not focus only on the EPS rank when evaluating a company as a buy candidate. A better approach may be to buy a company whose EPS rank is trending higher. Such companies are also favored by trend-following momentum investors.

Risk of EPS rank

High EPS rank does not guarantee profits and safety. Since such companies generate high valuations and expectations, any sign of a disappointment is enough to decimate their stock. A good example is Micron Technology. In November 1995, after a fantastic runup that took it to a high of 94$\frac{3}{4}$ from its January low of 22, Micron was

---

[3] *Investor's Business Daily,* January 29, 1997.

trading with an EPS of 99 and RS of 90. However, as investors realized that a slowdown was occurring in the semiconductor industry, which would impact earnings, Micron started to decline rapidly and give up almost all its gains. By January 1996, it declined to 29 and by mid-1996 its shares had reached a low of $16.62 (Figure 8). To avoid such disasters, investors should closely monitor such stocks. They should always be alert so that they can pick up signs or any subtle hints of slowing earnings momentum.

Figure 8

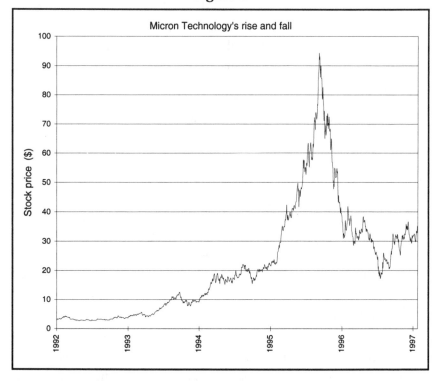

Micron Technology's rise and fall

A word of caution

It should be noted that EPS rank has its limitations. It is calculated with earnings that have already been reported. It does not indicate any potential earnings slowdown in the future. Also, it cannot be a substitute for sound fundamental analysis. An investor should never buy a stock based only on its EPS rank. For an investor, the EPS rank should be just one of many tools in his arsenal.

REVENUE (SALES) GROWTH

One of the most important items that an investor needs to analyze is a company's revenues. Revenue or sales is the dollar value of goods and services that a company brings in by selling its products or services during a quarter or the year. Revenues along with net income are a very good barometer of a company's health. For a company to increase profitability consistently, revenues should show consistent growth. Revenue growth indicates a growing demand for products and services that customers want or need. Rising sales also mean that the product(s) can be produced at a lower cost per unit, which can improve profit margins.

Analyzing sales

Sales growth drives everything on the income statement and balance sheet. Every analysis should determine whether sales increased or decreased since focusing on the gross sales number alone is inadequate. The reason(s) for any decrease or increase in sales should be determined. For example, analysis can reveal that gross sales changed due to an decrease/increase in the number of units sold, unit prices, or currency fluctuations. Since sales are less volatile than earnings, an investor should closely analyze sales trends. If it is noticed that the rate of increase in sales is declining, a warning flag should go up.

Sales growth must translate into earnings at the bottom line. If sales are increasing but earnings are not keeping pace, the reasons should be determined. For example, costs and expenses may be rising faster, which could be a temporary phenomenon. As part of the analysis, one should look closely at margins (operating profit, pretax profit and net profit). Improving operating margins indicate that the company is becoming more dominant in its industry. Net margins are reported in the company research reports published by Zacks, S&P and Value Line.

Return on sales

This is another indicator that is analyzed by investors. It is the percentage of sales that a company converts into profits. It is equal to net income divided by sales. The higher the return on sales, the more efficiently the company is converting sales into net income and managing its business.

Comparing sales

To put sales numbers in perspective, they should be compared where possible to those of other companies in the same group or industry. A number of benchmarks are available for this purpose. For example, the retailing industry uses the "same store sales" number for comparison. This is the percentage increase in sales generated by stores that have been in business for at least one year. The price/sales ratio relates market valuation to total revenues (sales). It is a useful ratio that is also used for comparison purposes (Appendix C).

Company research reports can be used for comparing performance data and ratios with other companies in the same industry. Financial statements also contain valuable revenue information. Some useful information can be gleaned with a simple comparison to other companies. For example, analysis of a software company's sales showed that when its far larger but less efficient competitor had comparable revenues a few years earlier, it had four times as many employees. The competitor had maintained poor control of its expenses and sales force and, as expected, ran into serious financial problems. Therefore, in this case, it was quite obvious that the company being analyzed was operating quite efficiently.

MOVING AVERAGES

Besides fundamentals and psychological indicators (market sentiment indicators), investors use "mechanical" technical tools to analyze the stock market and individual stocks. Among the widely used tools in this category are the various moving averages, which determine trends.

A moving average is essentially the average price of a stock for a specified period. The objective of moving averages is to get a smooth directional trend by eliminating random, irregular, fluctuations and noise. A moving average (MA) is an important tool because it helps determine whether a stock is in an uptrend or downtrend.

Moving averages can be plotted for any time period. However, the most widely used ones are the 30-day, 50-day and 200-day moving averages. Some analysts use a 60-day instead of the 50-day moving average. Moving averages can be plotted for individual stocks or for any stock market index. The same basic interpretation principles and analysis guidelines apply in both cases. However, differences do exist, which are listed and explained in the following sections.

What a moving average indicates

The use of a moving average is based on the assumption that if a stock pushes through its moving average line, such as the 30-day or 50-day moving average line, it will continue moving in the same direction, for some time, due to momentum. If penetration is to the upside, momentum will make it continue its upward move, rather than let it move in the downward direction (Figure 9). Similarly, if penetration through the moving average line is to the downside, it is expected that the stock will continue to move downwards, rather than reverse direction upwards. Therefore, when a stock trades above its moving average line, or pushes through it, investors view it bullishly and consider it a buy signal. On the other hand, selling is indicated when a stock trades below or slides below its moving average line.

The explanation for this behavior is investor sentiment and psychology. Consider a stock that is trading above its 50-day moving average line. The majority of its recent buyers will have bought their shares at a lower price. Therefore, they will view their investment positively. Conversely, if a stock is trading below its 50-day moving average, most of its recent buyers will have bought it at a higher price. Therefore, they will view their investment bearishly, which will become a further drag on the stock. This helps explain the basic technical analysis rule of investing: buy stocks in uptrends and sell them in downtrends.

Figure 9

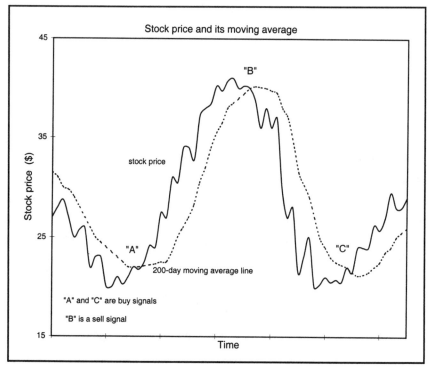

Calculating a moving average

A 50-day moving average is essentially the average price of a stock over the past 50 days. It is calculated by:

- adding a stock's closing price of the day to the closing prices of the previous 49 days, and
- dividing the resulting sum by 50

This number is plotted daily, which generates a line that becomes a "moving average," which shows a smoothed trend of past prices. Typically, a moving average line is plotted against the stock price with the aim being to clearly show their relationship.

Once created, a moving average line is maintained, or made to "move," by using a simple procedure. Every day, the newest closing stock price is added to the 50-day sum after the oldest value (the stock price 50 days ago) is dropped (subtracted) from the 50-day sum. The new sum is then divided by 50 to get the current moving average. This procedure ensures that the 50 most recent days are always used in the calculations.

The 50-day moving average is shown in most stock and market charts provided by various sources. For individual stocks, *IBD* is a good source for determining a stock's current price relative to its 50-day moving average. On Wednesdays, *IBD* stock tables include a column under the heading "% vs. 10 wk avg." This data shows how much percentage-wise a stock's current price is above or below its 10-week average price.

Which moving average to use

A study of a stock's pattern can be revealing when deciding which moving average to use. In general, the time span to be used for a moving average depends on the investment time frame. A long-term investor uses a moving average based on a longer period, typically 200 and 50 days, while a short term trader uses a shorter period. The 21-day moving average is commonly used by short and intermediate term players. Day traders use the 5-day moving average. The 30-day moving average is very widely followed. Since it is so widely used and monitored, any price move below this line causes a rather high negative sentiment and reaction.

The time period for a moving average also varies according to a stock's volatility (beta). Because a stock with a high beta can have wide and sharp price swings, it is analyzed with a moving average based on a longer time period.

Moving averages and buy/sell timing

The main objective of using a moving average is to determine its position relative to the stock and market index prices, as well as its direction. When a stock or an index (like the DJIA or the S&P500) is above its moving average line, it is viewed bullishly. On the other hand, if it is below its moving average line, it is considered to be a bearish sign. If an index or a stock is moving decisively above or below its 200-day moving average, it is usually considered to be a buy or sell signal respectively. However, one should be very careful in using the 30-day moving average line as a buy or sell indicator because a stock can move back and forth across this line quite frequently.

Moving averages are "lagging" indicators. If used as tools to generate buy and sell signals, they can be rather late with associated consequences. It should be realized that a moving average is just one of many tools that technical analysts use for analyzing trends. This indicator must not be used in isolation while ignoring other factors. It is preferable to use it as a signal that something has changed, rather than using it purely as a timing device—a sell or buy signal for getting out of, or into, a stock or the market.

Moving average as a forecasting indicator

A downward breach of a moving average line is a bearish sign that often precipitates massive selling. Perhaps one of the best known instances of the stock market plunging after a moving average line was breached occurred in October 1987. Until then, for the prior three years, the S&P500 had been trading above its 200-day moving average line. On October 15, 1987, the index cut below its moving average line, sending a warning signal. On October 19, Black Monday, the stock market crashed 22.6%.

In April 1997, the NASDAQ's 200-day moving average line was breached. After trading below this line for approximately a month, the NASDAQ rebounded and continued to climb strongly. By early October, the index had risen to 1,700 from its April low of 1,194—a gain of 42%

An investor should realize that penetration of the 200-day moving average does not guarantee a change in the market's direction. In January 1998, the NASDAQ slipped below its 200-day moving average line. However, it stayed below the line for only two days and then started a powerful move upwards. From a low level of 1,465 on January 12, it climbed powerfully to a level of 1,770 by the end of February.

An index can crisscross its moving average line for months without any meaningful change in direction. For example, from October 1997 through January 1998, the DJIA moved below its 200-day moving average line four times. However, the long-term upward trend remained intact.

In recent years, due to the instant availability of information, the number and impact of momentum players has increased considerably. Because so many investors are simultaneously monitoring the stock market and taking almost collective action when a "technical" sell signal is generated, a strategy based on moving averages tends to end up being self-fulfilling.

Rules and tips for using moving averages

Though all moving averages help determine the price trend, their interpretation can be somewhat different depending on the moving average period. Some common rules do exist, however, for using moving averages for both individual stocks and the market. These rules are:

- moving averages like all indicators are not infallible
- no definitive way exists to interpret the violation of a moving average line
- analyze technical patterns in conjunction with fundamentals

Rules and tips for stocks

- stock is in an uptrend if it has been trading above its moving average line for some time
- stock is a downtrend if it has been trading below its moving average line for some time
- if a stock is moving decisively above or below its 200-day moving average line, it is considered as a strong buy or sell signal respectively
- stock is vulnerable to a correction if it is overextended above its moving average line
- stock that breaks below its moving average line:
  - may be headed lower
  - is viewed bearishly if accompanied with heavy volume
- stock breaking out above its moving average line is expected to make good price gains
- if a moving average line is breached to the upside on heavy volume, and:
  - fundamentals are positive, it is considered a buy signal
  - fundamentals are negative, do not rush to buy; if penetration of the moving average line is significant, a comprehensive review and analysis is in order
- if a stock moves above its 30-day moving average line when it is trading above its 200-day moving average line, it is considered bullish; a move in the opposite direction is considered bearish

Rules and tips for the market

- if major market indexes (such as the DJIA or the S&P500) remain above their 200-day moving average, an upward trend is indicated

- note divergences between important market indexes and their moving averages:
  - if major market indexes are above their 200-day moving average and one suddenly drops below it, the other market averages will often follow
- if an index is moving decisively above or below its 200-day moving average line, it is considered a strong buy or sell signal respectively
- if an index moves above its moving average line:
  - it is a bullish sign
  - after staying below it for a long time, it indicates an upward change in direction
- if an index cuts below its moving average:
  - it is a bearish sign
  - after staying above it for a long time, it indicates a downward changing trend for the market
- if an index cuts below its moving average, it is a:
  - sell signal if you are bearish
  - sign to be cautious if you are bullish
- observe the slope of the moving average line:
  - if the average is rising sharply and the index is well above it, it is considered bullish
  - if an index is below a sharply declining moving average, it is considered bearish

Using moving averages in conjunction with trendlines

Some analysts use a moving average line in conjunction with a trendline to interpret stock charts. They use an uptrend line and a rising moving average to provide dual confirmation that an uptrend is in progress. The following are the basic points for using this technique:

- an uptrend continues to be valid even after the uptrend line is penetrated to the downside if the moving average line has not been penetrated to the downside
- an uptrend continues to be valid even after the moving average line is penetrated to the downside if the uptrend line has not been penetrated to the downside
- an uptrend is considered to have ended if both the uptrend and the moving average lines have been penetrated to the downside

Monitoring moving averages

Moving averages of the major market averages as well as a number of individual stocks are provided daily by *IBD*. Among the market averages shown every day in *IBD*, to monitor the trend of the overall market, are the 200-day moving averages for the DJIA, S&P500 and the NASDAQ Composite. The 10-week moving average is plotted in the charts of companies shown in *IBD's* "NYSE and NASDAQ Stocks in the News" section. It is also shown for 28 stocks, showing strong characteristics, which are displayed in the "Your Weekend Review" graphs on Fridays.

The moving averages of individual stocks are shown in the stock charts provided by a number of Internet and Online sources. Typically, the 30-day, 50-day and the 200-day moving average lines are shown. A large number of sources that provide investment research, including moving averages, are listed in Chapter 6 of Volume I.

200-DAY MOVING AVERAGE

Long-term trend indicator

The 200-day moving average is an excellent long-term trend indicator. It is calculated by averaging the closing prices of the past 200 trading days. This average smooths out daily price fluctuations and erratic gyrations to give a better view of the long-term trend of a stock or the overall market.

A stock trading above its 200-day moving average is considered to be in an uptrend and, therefore, in bullish mode. A stock trading below its 200-day moving average is considered to be in a downtrend and has bearish significance. In contrast to the other short term averages, which are favored by short term traders, the 200-day moving average is closely monitored by long-term investors.

Stocks and the 200-day moving average

Guidelines and tips

- if a stock trades above its 200-day moving average line, it is in an uptrend
- if a stock holds above its 200-day moving average line, it is a bullish sign
- if a stock trades below its 200-day moving average line, it is in a downtrend
- if a stock breaks below its 200-day moving average, it is a bearish sign

- a stock trading 50% or more, above its moving average line, is considered "overextended"; profit taking is suggested if it is overextended by 70 to 100%
- most professional investors want to:
  - buy a stock trading above a rising 200-day moving average line
  - sell a stock before it goes under the 200-day moving average line (because it is usually a late signal)

Understanding "gaps" across the 200-day moving average

If a stock "gaps" below its 200-day moving average, it is considered by many market players to be a reliable sell signal. A gap occurs when a stock skips a price, either up or down from the previous day's close, at the start of a trading day. This jump or drop can be significant and can extend to many dollars/share.

When a stock gaps, its trading range is either above or below the trading range of the previous day. This is usually triggered by some unexpected news, which significantly affects the stock positively or negatively. A gap to the upside indicates strong demand, especially for a liquid stock that has a large supply. Some analysts will view a gap as a sell signal if a stock cuts below its 200-day moving average and wait 2 to 3 days to give the stock a chance to rally. If it does not rebound to a position above the 200-day moving average line, then they sell the stock.

Market and the 200-day moving average

The 200-day moving average, shown for the DJIA in Figure 10, is one of the most closely monitored market indicators. During bullish periods, the 200-day moving average acts as a floor under the market averages. However, when the market is under pressure and the DJIA is trading below its moving average, this line acts as a resistance.

Analyzing the 200-day moving average lines for the DJIA, S&P500 and the NASDAQ can indicate where the current action and price momentum are centered. For example, if the DJIA is below its 200-day moving average line, with the S&P500 just above its 200-day moving average line, and the NASDAQ way above its 200-day moving average line, it clearly indicates that the action is at NASDAQ, the home of small cap growth stocks. It indicates that small cap stocks are outperforming the large cap stocks.

Relating the 200-day moving average to the market health

Market analysts closely observe the percentage of stocks trading over their 200-day moving average line. This number indicates the overall health and trend of the market. The higher the percentage of stocks trading over their 200-day moving average, the more healthy the market.

In 1995, when the stock market had a tremendous runup, the percentage of stocks trading over their 200-day moving average line peaked at 79% in mid-September, when the rally in most stocks ended. By late October, the percentage had fallen to 61%. By December, the percentage had risen to 69% following a rebound in the market.

In April 1997, when the market was in a correction, the percentage of NYSE stocks trading over their 200-day moving average line was 50%. This meant that half of the NYSE stocks were in a price decline. By October, when the correction was over and the market was rising strongly, the situation had reversed and 85% of NYSE issues were trading above their 200-day moving average line.

For a bullish scenario, the percentage of stocks trading over their 200-day moving average line should be trending higher. The number of stocks trading over their 200-day moving average on the NYSE is reported daily by *IBD*. For the NYSE, the percentage of stocks trading above the 200-day moving average has historically ranged from a high of 80 to 90% (at the peak) to a low of 10 to 20% (at the market bottom). This percentage fell below 20% at market bottoms in late 1990, December 1987, late 1981, and late 1974.

As a market direction change indicator

The 200-day moving average line has been known to signal important changes in the market's direction. When the DJIA declines below its 200-day moving average line, it is a bearish sign for the market. In August 1990, when the market underwent a bear market, both the DJIA and the S&P dropped below their 200-day moving average. In 1987, both these averages dropped through their 200-day moving average two days prior to the October crash.

A drop through the 200-day moving average does not necessarily indicate a trend change. In July 1996, both the DJIA and the S&P500

Figure 10

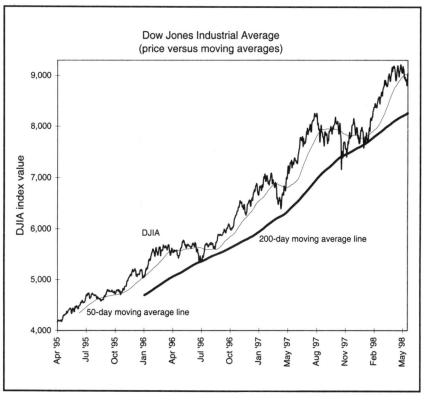

Dow Jones Industrial Average
(price versus moving averages)

cut through their 200-day moving average. However, they rebounded quickly within a few days.

In the following months, both the indexes rose to new record highs. In January 1998, the NASDAQ and the DJIA 200-day moving average lines were breached. However, both the indexes rebounded quickly and continued their climb to new highs.

Guidelines for interpreting the number of stocks trading above their 200-day moving average line

- if the majority of stocks are:
  - above their 200-day moving average line, the market is in an uptrend
  - below their 200-day moving average line, the market is in a downtrend

- if the percentage of stocks trading over their 200-day moving average:
  - is trending higher, it is a bullish sign
  - is trending lower, it is a bearish sign
  - is over 80% and starts to decrease, it may indicate that the market is correcting
  - drops below 20%, it is almost certain that a market bottom has been reached
  - moves over 90% and remains there, it indicates a powerful market with the potential to generate more gains

Shortcoming

A criticism of the moving average is that it is a lagging indicator. Typically, by the time it indicates a change in direction, most investors already have reached the obvious conclusion. Besides, according to these critics, there is nothing special about the 200-day average. After all, it is valid to ask: "Why not use a different period such as a 210-day or 170-day moving average?"

In response, it can be said that the 200-day moving average is almost invariably used by investors using long-term moving averages. This group of investors is very large. Consequently, a lot of the market action and event triggers are determined by the 200-day moving average. By ignoring this and using a different period such as 180 days, an investor can miss an important market trigger.

TRENDLINES, TREND CHANNELS AND TRADING BANDS

Trendlines

Trendline analysis is a very important foundation of technical analysis. It is used to analyze and forecast the future direction of a stock based on its behavior in relation to its trendlines. The basic concept is that a trend once established, remains in effect for some time. Trend analysis primarily aims to determine if there are signs of a weakening, or change, in the established trend.

A trendline, Figure 11, is a line drawn by connecting the

- low (bottom) points on a stock chart for a rising trendline
- high (top) points on a stock chart for a falling trendline

Figure 11

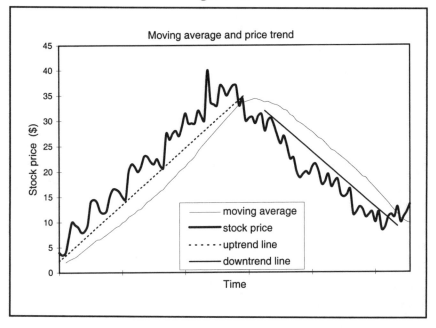

Technicians believe that a rising trendline acts as a support to a stock during its upward move, while a falling trendline acts as a resistance to any attempt to move up through it. The following are some key signs that analysts look for when analyzing trendlines:

- frequency with which a stock touches a rising trendline: the more frequently a rising trendline is touched, the greater is the support and trend validity considered
- change in trading volume on a trend break: a break with heavy volume is considered more significant

The following are some guidelines and tips suggested by technical analysts when using a trendline as a buying indicator:

- never use a trendline in isolation; use it in conjunction with other indicators and fundamental analysis; buy a stock only if other indicators confirm the buy signal
- during a rising trend:
  - a trend change can take place; a support can fail
  - after a support line is hit ("tested") and rebound has started (in the upward direction), buying may be done
  - avoid buying if a stock is too far above the rising trendline

- a falling trendline decisively penetrated to the upside is viewed as a buy signal; buy only if other indicators are in confirmation

The following are two points that should be kept in mind when using a trendline as a selling indicator:

- never use it in isolation; use it in conjunction with other indicators and fundamental analysis
- rising trendline: a drop below it signals an end to the upward trend and, therefore, is bearish

Trend channels

Some technicians analyze stocks by studying their trend channels. A trend channel is created by drawing a straight line connecting the stock's price lows, which can be rather tricky, along with a parallel line for its price highs (Figure 12). Trend channel followers expect that a stock will remain within a channel, bouncing up and down between the top and bottom of the rising channel. It is important to understand that a trend does not mean going from a trough to a peak; rather, it means going from peak-to-peak and trough-to-trough.

If a stock is in an uptrend, it will move back and forth within the extremes of its rising trend channel. This action will continue until the stock breaks below the bottom of the trend channel, which is a sign that the trend may be ending. Trend channel followers buy a stock when it is in the lower area of a rising trend channel. They sell if it breaks below the channel. Short-term traders sell when a stock moves to the top of a trend channel. If a stock breaks out of the top of a channel, however, the expectation is that it can move significantly higher.

About three out of every four stocks move within trend channels, but many market players do not use trend channels. Instead, they prefer to use trendlines.

Trading bands

It has been observed that stocks tend to trade in the short term within a fairly narrow and predictable range around their moving average line. This range is called a trading band (Figure 13). When a stock moves to either end of its trading band, it unleashes forces pulling in opposite directions. These forces are created by the short-term traders

Figure 12

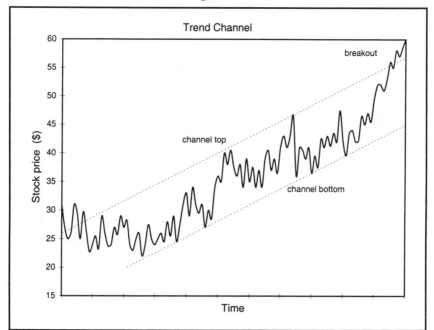

Trend Channel

and long-term investors. When a stock reaches the top of its trading band, short-term traders start selling for profit taking, which pressures the stock and slows its upward move. Typically, the stock will reverse direction without touching the top band. This is known as a failure swing. A failure swing can occur at the bottom also, when reversal takes place without touching the bottom band. This happens when buyers step in and the stock rebounds. A failure swing at the bottom is considered to be a positive sign.

If a stock's rebound continues until it pushes through its 30-day moving average line, it indicates continued strength. When a stock penetrates its top band with sufficient strength, it indicates that buyers have the upper hand over sellers and, therefore, it has strong momentum to the upside. This is considered a good buying point by momentum investors.

Figure 13

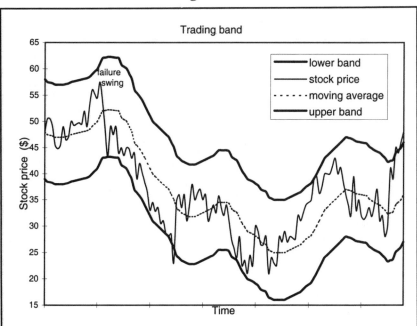

In general, technicians consider the following to be positive signs: failure swing at the bottom band, penetration of the top band, and rebound off the 30-day moving average after the top band has been penetrated.

CONCLUDING REMARKS

There are literally hundreds of variables, or indicators, that influence the stock market and individual stocks. The influence of each indicator varies, depending on the:

• company
• industry
• state of the economy
• health of the stock market
• presence or absence of other indicators
• combination of indicators existing at any given moment
• investor psychology

It is not possible for any investor to monitor more than a limited number of indicators. Besides being difficult to monitor, too many indicators can give conflicting signals. Therefore, only a few indicators reflecting the philosophy, approach and risk level of the investor should be picked. The most important indicators, which should be monitored very closely include earnings/share (quarterly and annual), EPS rank, P/E ratio and the 200-day moving average (which indicates the long-term trend of the stock).

CHAPTER 3

MORE STOCK MARKET INDICATORS

MARKET BREADTH

To determine the overall market trend, investors track "market breadth," a comparison of the total number of stocks that decline and advance each day. If the number of advancing stocks outnumbers declining stocks by a big margin, the market is said to have "good" breadth. If advances outnumber declines by a slim margin, breadth is said to be weak. During a correction, decliners outnumber advancing stocks by a big margin. For example, when the DJIA declined 4.8% during the week of January 5, 1998, decliners swamped advancers as follows:

	Advancing Stocks	Declining Stocks
Jan 5, 1998	1,659	1,417
Jan 6, 1998	1,039	1,997
Jan 7, 1998	1,213	1,800
Jan 8, 1998	1,120	1,892
Jan 9, 1998	552	2,540

If the market breadth is negative for many straight sessions, typically 10 or more, it usually signals an end to upside momentum. This occurred in July 1996, when the market had over 10 days of negative breadth and was followed by a market correction.

If the DJIA moves higher, analysts like to see market breadth improve simultaneously. Such an improvement indicates that most stocks are participating in the upward trending market. They also like the other indexes to be moving in the same direction as the DJIA. The term "confirmation" is often used to describe the market phenomenon of various indexes being in sync.

A technical tool for measuring breadth, which is very widely used by market analysts, is the advance/decline (A/D) line for the NYSE. It is the simplest of all breadth measures.

ADVANCE/DECLINE (A/D) LINE

Plotting the A/D line

The A/D line is produced using a simple procedure. Every day, the total number of stocks falling in price (daily declines) are subtracted from the total number of stocks rising in price (daily advances). The positive difference, of daily advances minus daily declines, is added to a cumulative total. If the difference is negative, in other words, if declines outnumber advances, this number is subtracted from the cumulative total. Stocks that remain unchanged in price are not included. This cumulative A/D number is then plotted which, over time, yields a trend line.

A weekly A/D line is also widely used by analysts. It is based on a weekly, rather than a daily, price change. The weekly A/D line has an advantage in that it eliminates some of the volatility and noise associated with daily trading.

What the A/D line indicates

The A/D line gives a broader view of the market's condition than the well-known averages (DJIA and S&P). If more stocks advance than decline, the A/D line moves upwards. However, when more stocks decline than advance, the A/D line moves downwards. The basic idea for using the A/D line is quite simple. If the number of stocks rising in price is more than the number of declining stocks, the market is improving and, consequently, this is bullish. However, if more stocks are declining, it portrays a weakening or bearish market.

The A/D line for the market is shown in most major newspapers. While the A/D line for the NYSE is the one most widely used, some analysts use the A/D line for the NASDAQ and the AMEX to get a broader view of the stock market.

Divergence

What divergence indicates

The DJIA and the broader market, as represented by the A/D line, do not always move simultaneously in the same direction. If both are moving upwards, it is considered to be a bullish sign. If the DJIA is making new highs (or moving up), while most stocks are declining as indicated by the A/D line, it is a bearish sign. It is analogous to the "generals" advancing while the "troops" are retreating. When the DJIA and the overall market move in opposite directions, or move in the same direction (up or down) at different rates, a "divergence" is said to occur.

Divergence can exist between any pair of indexes. For example, if the utilities index is headed lower, the DJIA transportation index could be moving up in the opposite direction. Divergence indicates that most stocks (or some major sectors at least) are deteriorating while the DJIA is rising or vice versa. An explanation for this phenomenon is that some sectors are forward looking and, therefore, are often the first to react to forthcoming negative news such as a weakening economy or rising interest rates.

Divergence and trend change

Divergence between the DJIA and the broader market signals a potentially important change in the trend of the stock market. Therefore, analysts try to forecast whether, the overall market or the DJIA will change course and move in the other direction. Generally, if the NYSE A/D line is headed lower, the DJIA is expected to follow suit. If the A/D line is moving up while the DJIA is declining, it is considered to be a better situation than the other way round. This is based on the expectation that the DJIA will more likely play catch up with the A/D line, to the upside, rather than the other way around.

A divergence near the end of a bull market can be caused by:
- some sectors starting to head lower in anticipation of a weaker economy 6 to 9 months prior to its actual occurrence
- rising interest rates that cause utilities, which are very interest sensitive, to start heading lower

- firmness in the DJIA components, which typically are the last ones to be sold because they are considered more stable

Investors should note that divergences are not necessarily good indicators when it comes to timing. They can emerge weeks and months before the major averages react.

<u>Warning signs associated with divergence</u>
- declining issues outnumber advancing stocks
- a new market high is not accompanied by heavier volume
- stocks rally on declining volume
- the number of stocks setting new highs drops off; there are fewer and fewer highs
- the number of stocks trading above their 200-day moving average declines

A/D line: an early warning system

<u>The record</u>

The A/D line indicates the performance of the broader market. Therefore, it is considered a better indicator than the DJIA of where the market is headed. In the past 18 years, the A/D line has turned significantly lower prior to major market peaks. This happened in 1980, 1983, 1987, 1990, and 1996. In 1987, the A/D line peaked in August. However, the DJIA continued to move upwards, by another 10%, for two more months before it underwent a massive plunge in October. The A/D line also flashed warnings prior to the viscous bear market of 1973/74.

In 1994, the A/D line started to deteriorate sharply after the Federal Reserve started to hike interest rates. It started to turn up only at the end of the year. Even though the S&P500 earnings rose 40% that year, the market's poor performance, when the DJIA and S&P500 respectively gained 1.2% and 2.1% for the year, can be classified as a stealth "bear market." Normally, in a year when the earnings rose so much, the stock market would have risen considerably. In 1996, the A/D line started declining at the end of May. This was followed by the market correction in July.

The A/D line does not always act as a leading indicator. For example, it failed to act as an early warning signal for the DJIA's decline that occurred in April 1997. The A/D line, rather than act as a leading indicator, started to decline simultaneously with the DJIA in mid-March 1997. It followed the NASDAQ, which had started declining earlier after peaking at 1,400 in late January. Both the A/D line and the DJIA reversed direction at the same time, in mid-April, after the market corrected in the first two weeks of April. Again, in October 1997 and January 1998, the A/D line did not act as a leading indicator, starting its decline simultaneously with the DJIA.

Do not be misled by the DJIA

Investors should be wary if the DJIA or the S&500 are making new highs while the A/D line is not improving. When the overall market turns south at the end of a bull market, blue chip stocks are typically the last ones to be sold off by bearish investors. At such times, a steady or higher trending DJIA, or S&P500, can mask the deterioration in certain market sectors. These sectors may already be discounting deteriorating business conditions 6 to 9 months down the road. A typical example is the interest sensitive utility stocks, which can weaken earlier due to an anticipated rise in interest rates.

Lead time

In the past, the lead-time indicated by the A/D line has varied from 10 to 49 weeks, with an average of 24 weeks. However, as has happened many times since 1980, it is not necessary for every divergence to lead to a major market decline. The A/D line can actually reverse direction and follow the upward trending DJIA. In 1986 and 1988, investors using the declining A/D line as a sell signal missed an S&P500 rise of 13% and 16% respectively. Therefore, any divergence should not be used as a precise timing tool for leaving the market.

Using the A/D line

The A/D line can be used as an early warning system since it is a good, though not an infallible, leading indicator of a market top. However, it should not be used in isolation. Instead, it should be used in conjunction with other indicators. When market turning points are suspected, several averages should be checked to see if any significant divergences (different averages moving in different directions) exist.

Additionally, other trend indicators should be analyzed in order to get a better picture of the overall market health and trend.

Guidelines and tips for analyzing an A/D line
- if divergence continues for several weeks, it is bearish
- if the A/D line makes a significant new low, it is bearish
- the A/D line is not a good indicator of a market bottom since it reacts very slowly compared to the DJIA, which can reverse direction faster because it represents only 30 stocks
- the A/D line is more accurate at forecasting market tops
- when analyzing an A/D line, the following need to be observed:
  - an upward or downward trend of the A/D line
  - the pattern of the highs and lows; if each high is higher than the last one, it is bullish
  - it is bearish if:
    - a high does not exceed the last high and/or
    - a low is lower than the last low
  - divergence from the market averages: a tenet of technical analysis is that market divergence precedes weakness

NUMBER OF NEW DAILY LOWS AND HIGHS

If a stock trades at a price that is its lowest trading level in the past 52 weeks, a new daily low is said to have been made. If it reaches its highest level in a year, a new daily high has occurred. The total number of stocks reaching new highs during a day, as well as the total number of stocks reaching new lows, is an indicator that is tracked by stock market analysts. While these numbers are reported for the three major exchanges, the NYSE numbers are the ones most closely analyzed by market watchers.

A market health barometer
The new daily low and high numbers, especially the number of daily new lows on the NYSE, indicate the health of the market. While these numbers have limited use on a day-to-day basis, they are important for discerning trends. For example, if more stocks are making new price highs than new lows, the market is considered to be in an uptrend. In such a positive environment, the market is expected to rise further. Conversely, the outlook is bearish if there are more new daily lows being made compared to new daily highs.

On April 13, 1997, when the market was correcting, the number of new highs was 32 and the number of new lows was 215. At that time, only 50% of stocks were trading above their moving average line. On October 3, 1997, when the market was rising, the number of new highs was 1,035 and the number of new lows was only 15. At that time, 85% of stocks were trading above their moving average line. On February 27, 1998, when the market was rising strongly to new highs after having undergone a correction, the number of new highs was 461, while the number of new lows was only 33.

Forecasting market declines

A rise in the number of new daily lows has been a good indicator of a market decline in the past. This indicator indicated market declines starting in October 1994, February 1994, August 1990, and October 1987.

In November 1995, while the DJIA had been climbing to new highs, the NYSE A/D line had been lagging. This indicated bearish divergence. Actually, the rise in new lows began in September 1995, when the market leading group, semiconductors, started falling apart. Reinforcing this divergence was the rising number of NYSE stocks making 52-week lows. This indicated a market with an undercurrent of problems beneath the surface.

More recently, in the first half of October 1997, the number of new lows ranged between 15 and 33. However, during the second half of October, the number of new lows increased sharply and ranged from 50 to 311. This increase in the number of new lows preceded, by only a few days, the DJIA's decline from 7,938 (on October 16) to 7,161 (on October 27).

Analysis guidelines

The following are some guidelines for analyzing this indicator:

- in a healthy market, the number of daily new lows on the NYSE will not exceed 40
- exceeding 40 new lows should not be a serious cause for concern if it occurs for only a day or two
- it is bearish if the NYSE new daily lows exceed 40 for five consecutive days

- during uncertain times, a rise in new daily lows can result due to a flight from low priced speculative stocks to quality issues

Where to find these numbers

Every day, *IBD* provides price charts of 28 stocks each on the NYSE and NASDAQ. These stocks are highlighted because they met one, or more, of the following criteria:

- hit new price highs
- are near new highs
- had greatest percent increase in volume

IBD also reports the number of new highs and lows on each exchange. For example, the following numbers were reported on February 27, 1998, when the DJIA had risen strongly to 8,545 after declining to 7,391 in January 1998:

	New highs	New lows
NYSE	221	12
NASDAQ	208	17
AMEX	32	4
Total	461	33

Seven weeks earlier, on January 9, 1998, after the DJIA had declined sharply by 4.8%, the market tone was very different and the following numbers were reported:

	New highs	New lows
NYSE	66	137
NASDAQ	37	83
AMEX	17	16
Total	120	236

RELATIVE STRENGTH (RS) RANK

Relative strength (RS) rank is a technical indicator that measures a stock's price performance relative to all other stocks. It measures a stock's price change during the past year compared to all other stocks. More weight, 40%, is given to the most recent three-month period. The ranking ranges from 99 (highest) to 1 (lowest). A 99 rank for a stock means that it outperformed 99% of all other stocks in price appreciation. Figure 14 shows the RS rank as marked by the pointer "Relative price strength rank and line."

If a stock's relative strength rank is below 70, it shows that the stock is lagging the better performing stocks in the overall market. An RS of 75 means that a stock outperformed 75% of all stocks, or 3 out of every 4 stocks, during the same period. Looking at it from another angle, it means that 25% of all stocks performed better than the stock being analyzed. In other words, such a stock is definitely not a leader.

Basic principle

The basic principle underlying RS is momentum. It is based on the belief that a stock that has performed strongly compared to other stocks will continue to do so in the near future. On the other hand, a relatively weak stock will continue to be weak. Analysts using RS believe that the probability of a high RS stock continuing to outperform is very high. The logic is that a trend once begun is very likely to continue. Consequently, they believe that the likelihood of finding winners from among stocks with high RS rank is greater. This is backed by a study that found that many top performing stocks in the past 40 years began their big moves with an average RS of 87. Examples of big winners in the past couple of decades include Microsoft, Wal-Mart and Amgen. All of them showed high RS prior to their big price moves.

The risk

The RS technique of finding a winner is in direct contrast to the value-based technique of buying a stock when it is down in price. The risk with the value-based technique is that a stock may remain out of favor for a long period, with consequential associated risks. The RS rank method also has its critics who point out that buying a high RS stock is a step too late. A preferable technique might be to buy when RS is in the high 80s, prior to a stock making its most meaningful move. Also, one can avoid buying when a stock is at the very top, in the 98–99% rank, when most of the price appreciation may already have occurred.

RS and stock picking

RS rank is one of the basic selection criteria for momentum investors. For stock picking, they try to confine their buying to companies with an RS rank of 80 or higher. This is based on the belief that leaders will have an RS strength in excess of 80. This ensures that laggards are rejected.

If a stock is picked based on its RS rank, its earnings projections should also be checked. If the earnings forecast is not positive, such a stock should be avoided. Buying a stock with a high RS rank but a poor earnings outlook is very risky. If a stock has strong earnings momentum, but low RS in the 50s or 60s, it can be considered as a buy candidate.

It is important that RS rank should not be used in isolation. Instead, it should be used as a final check after a company's earnings have passed the evaluation process.

Using RS with other criteria

RS rank can be combined with EPS rank to create a potent combination. A company whose EPS and RS ranks are greater than 80 demonstrates strong performance. While one is a fundamental measurement, the other indicates market valuation. Such a company is indicated to be a superior one and a potential winner. However, keep in mind that strong historical performance does not necessarily guarantee similar results in the future. An indicator like RS rank should only be taken as a sign, which should be followed by further research prior to buying a stock.

Monitoring RS

If RS rank decreases while a stock is moving sideways, or even while it is moving up, it indicates that the market is rising faster than the stock. This is a warning that the stock may soon start to decline. In a declining market, the RS of leading stocks drops sharply. If a stock's RS rank holds up well in such a scenario, it indicates a potential winner. When the market rallies, such a stock has a greater probability of performing very well. Other factors to note when analyzing RS are:

- RS often starts to go down after a stock price starts declining; it can be an early warning of a potential larger drop in the near future
- RS can decrease due to many reasons including weakening company, or industry, fundamentals
- stocks with RS declining for a couple of months should be watched carefully; the cause of the decline should be determined
- stocks with RS rising for a couple of months are performing more strongly than the overall market and should be viewed bullishly
- check a stock's price pattern to ensure that it has a solid base and is not extended more than 5 to 10% above this base

RELATIVE STRENGTH (RS) LINE

What the tool indicates

The RS line is another tool used to indicate a stock's price trend. It is based on comparing a stock's price to the S&P500 index. Figure 14 shows the RS line as marked by the pointer "Relative price strength rank and line." The comparison can also be made for an index or average. For example, Figure 15 shows the RS line of *IBD* Mutual Fund index, which indicates its relative performance compared to the S&P500. The RS line of a number of sectors and indexes are shown in Figure 30 (Chapter 6).

As with any trendline, it is expected that once an RS trendline gets established, it will continue for some time. Analysts also use a moving average line, in conjunction with the RS line, to confirm a stock's uptrend. When evaluating a stock for buying, it is preferred to pick a stock whose RS line is trending higher. Some analysts recommend buying stocks with strong earnings growth, with an RS above 80, when they emerge from a price consolidation area after at least seven weeks. In general, if a stock's price breaks out of a base, its RS line should also do the same.

Guidelines for analyzing RS lines

<u>Bullish signs</u>

If a stock's:

- RS line breaks out before the price, it is bullish and may lead to a price breakout
- price corrects but the RS line does not pull back much, it is a bullish sign
- RS line remains in an uptrend, it is bullish

<u>Bearish signs</u>

If a stock's RS line:

- fails to make a new high and undercuts a prior low, it is bearish
- fails to confirm a new high in price, it is bearish
- has been rising and the trend is broken, it is bearish

ACCUMULATION AND DISTRIBUTION

What the tool indicates

This is a proprietary tool used to analyze a stock's supply and demand, which tries to determine the direction of money flow. This indicator is based on a stock's daily trading volume and price change, with volume being measured on "up" days (when price rises) and "down" days (when price decreases). The basic idea is that money is flowing into a stock if its trading volume, during the specified period, is heavier on "up" days than on "down" days. This phenomenon, which is referred to as accumulation, indicates positive momentum. Distribution is the opposite of accumulation.

Accumulation indicates professional buying by institutions or that buyers outnumber sellers. Distribution indicates the opposite. Accumulation indicates that there is good demand for the stock. Therefore, the probability is high that it will make further progress to the upside. On the other hand, distribution indicates poor demand for the stock. It occurs when a stock or market index drops in price or closes at the low end of its daily range despite heavy trading volume. Distribution often precedes a stock, or a market, price decline.

Accumulation and distribution are reported in a range, from A through E, as follows:

A & B - stock is undergoing accumulation
C   - neutral
D & E - stock is undergoing distribution

Figure 14

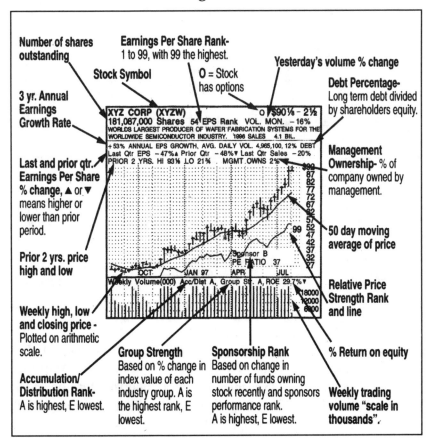

Reproduced with permission of *Investor's Business Daily*

Figure 15

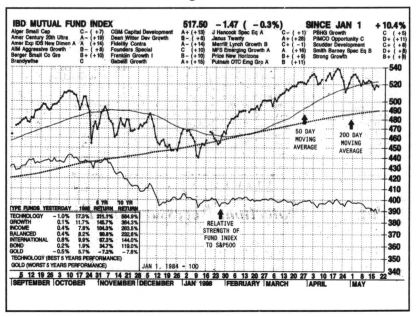

Reproduced with permission of *Investor's Business Daily*

Recognizing accumulation and distribution

A stock is considered to be undergoing accumulation if:

- its price rises when it trades on heavy volume
- it closes at the high end of its daily trading range when it trades on heavy volume

A stock undergoes distribution if:

- its price drops on heavy volume
- it closes at the low end of its daily trading range when it trades on heavy volume
- no price increase occurs despite heavy trading volume
- after an advance, there is no further upside price progress despite heavy volume

Guidelines and tips for analyzing accumulation/distribution

- do not use this tool alone; it must be used in conjunction with other tools
- when evaluating a stock for buying, favor stocks with an A or B rating

- a continuous rating of A is more reliable than one which occasionally slips to a B rating; same applies for E changing to D occasionally
- if a stock moves up, and starts forming a base, it should retain a rating of C or better
- do not expect the market to advance if leaders start showing distribution (C, D or E)
- if a stock shows distribution (D or E), even if it has not suffered a big price drop (which usually comes later), technicians recommend that you evaluate your sell options
- distribution is often covered by a misleading slight price rise
- selloff on heavy volume followed by rallies on low volume is a bearish sign

TRADING VOLUME

Relating volume to trend

A very important indicator, for both individual stocks and the overall market, is trading volume. Savvy investors closely monitor trading volume levels because heavy trading often precedes major price moves. They know quite well that simultaneously rising volume and price often precedes further price appreciation. Typically, rising volume and increasing price momentum indicate the potential start of a trend.

Focusing on percentage change

For analysis, monitoring daily trading volume alone is not enough. One should also monitor the percent change in trading volume. The reason is that the daily trading volume for different stocks varies considerably. Therefore, if the trading volume of only the most active stocks is monitored, it can prevent stocks with meaningful volume changes from being noticed. For example, it is more meaningful to pinpoint a stock whose trading volume swelled to 1 million shares from an average daily trading volume of 250,000 shares, than a stock whose trading volume increased to 1.8 million shares from an average daily trading volume of 1.5 million shares. The 400% increase for the first company is more meaningful than the 20% increase for the second company. The massive volume rise of 400% can alert an investor to some potential news or development. Therefore, if only the daily trading volume criteria is used, the first company may not be noticed despite its more meaningful change.

Guidelines and tips for interpreting trading volume
- during an uptrend, trading volume usually increases and remains higher than average
- during a downtrend, trading volume is usually lower than average
- trading volume increases:
  - whenever a stock breaks out of its trading range (either up or down); this indicates high interest
  - when a breakout to the upside occurs; a large volume increase is a strong buy signal
- price increase on:
  - above average (heavy) volume indicates professional buying by institutions
  - increasing volume is bullish
  - lower volume is not considered bullish
- price breakout to the downside is considered a sell signal whether trading volume increases or not
- falling price on heavy volume is bearish:
  - in a weak market
  - especially in a rising market
- falling price on lower volume indicates a bottom (selling almost, or fully, completed)
- lower price on massive volume indicates a bottom (selling climax)
- heavy volume with no upward progress is bearish
- trading volume should be compared to the average trading volume; traders compare the daily volume to the average of the prior 5 or 10 trading days

Monitoring abnormal trading volume

Most daily newspapers list the most active stocks on the three main exchanges. This information is of limited use because the typical list usually contains the names of very big companies with large trading volumes. A more useful reporting format is provided by *IBD*. It lists stocks that have the "largest percentage increase in volume" above their average daily trading volume. The *IDB* tables list such stocks in the three major exchanges: NYSE (60 stocks), NASDAQ (100-150 stocks) and AMEX (15 stocks). Each list is separated into two parts: stocks making price moves to the upside, and downside, respectively.

These lists only include stocks that are priced over $15/share for the NYSE and $12/share for the NASDAQ and AMEX.

To aid investors, these lists also provide the EPS and RS ranks of each stock. Consequently, if the winners list includes many stocks with EPS and RS rank greater than 90, it indicates that the leaders are the movers. This could signify the start of a major move. On the other hand, if these leaders are in the losers list, it might indicate that they are losing steam and a market decline may have begun.

Unusual volume as indicated by these lists can steer an investor to a potential investment. The basic idea is that heavy volume is caused by unusual interest. Therefore, the chances are good that such a list may contain winners if their EPS and RS ranks are above 80%. Since such stocks have the potential for a major upward move, the best among these should be investigated.

FLOAT - SUPPLY OF STOCK
Supply and demand balance

A very important factor affecting a stock's price and the extent to which it will appreciate is the balance between supply and demand. The greater the number of outstanding shares, the more difficult it is to move such a stock in either direction because a greater amount of supply will be required to create any downward or upward price pressure.

Companies like GE and AT&T have a large number of outstanding shares. Therefore, it is very difficult to make their price change appreciably. Consider the case when the Exxon Valdez was grounded off the coast of Alaska in 1988. Exxon's stock, which has 1.24 billion outstanding shares and a daily trading volume of 1.53 million shares, barely moved despite the very bad news. To appreciably move such a stock, a massive amount of buying or selling far above its normal trading volume is required. In contrast, the price of a smaller company with only 50 million shares and a daily trading volume of 300,000 shares can move up or down significantly with a far smaller increase in trading volume.

A company's "float", the number of shares available for trading, is a factor analyzed by investors when they evaluate a stock for procurement. Besides the available supply, the percentage of outstanding stock held by a company's management is also a factor that they analyze. The reason is that it can effectively reduce the number of shares available for trading.

Institutional factor

Large institutional buyers use somewhat different stock procurement criteria than individual investors, which makes them favor large cap companies. Consequently, they overlook the best growth companies, which typically have small floats. Individual investors are not constrained by the limitations imposed on institutional investors; therefore, they can favor a smaller company over a larger one with a bigger float when selecting a stock. Hence, they can achieve higher returns due to their exposure to smaller companies, which usually achieve far superior returns.

Effect of share buybacks

The supply of stock can also be reduced, especially in small and medium cap companies, due to stock buybacks. This refers to a company buying back its own shares in the open market. Usually, buyback is initiated if a company believes that its stock price does not reflect its true value or it needs to acquire shares for its employee stock option plan. When the number of shares are reduced, the earnings number in the EPS calculations gets divided by a smaller number of shares, which causes the EPS to increase. Therefore, if a company buys back its shares, it is viewed by investors as a positive development and, consequently, they boost the share price.

INSTITUTIONAL OWNERSHIP

Role of institutions

A large percentage of trading in the stock market is done by institutions such as pension funds, mutual funds, insurance companies, and others. If a small company starts attracting their attention, due to its performance, it can become the catalyst for moving its stock to great heights. On the other hand, when a company with institutional shareholders does not perform well and they start dumping its stock, the share price can be severely depressed.

There are thousands of companies available for investment. Yet, most of them are out of bounds to institutional investors. The reason is that they have very restrictive investing criteria. These include minimum trading volume, market capitalization and positive earnings history for five years. Many companies, especially smaller ones, are unable to meet these minimum requirements. However, those companies able to get their attention and investment by meeting their rigorous screening criteria are reasonably assured of a good price boost.

Level of desired institutional ownership

While it is a positive sign to have institutional ownership, the level of such ownership should be limited. In companies that have a high percentage of institutional presence, the potential for upward price appreciation is quite limited. The reason is that additional institutional buying will be unavailable to provide the thrust that can make a stock move to new heights. Therefore, when selecting a company for investment, favor a company with a low percentage of institutional ownership, preferably in the 25 to 50% range. If institutional presence is over this range, the company is already "discovered," and, hence, its price appreciation will be limited. The problem with selecting an undiscovered company is that good companies with low institutional ownership are difficult to find.

A disadvantage for companies having large institutional ownership is that it makes them very vulnerable to wild price swings if they fall out of favor. If there is some negative news, mass institutional exit can cause a small company stock to drop 25 to 50% in a single day. Despite this risk, it is more desirable to have some degree of institutional participation than to have none at all.

NUMBER OF ANALYSTS

Brokerage and investment companies periodically issue investment recommendations for individual stocks for their clients. These recommendations include buy, sell, hold and other slightly different variations. These recommendations are made after intensive research conducted by analysts who are employed by these companies.

Analysts' function

An analyst's job is to study a company and its industry in-depth, understand the business, interview company officials, and analyze business conditions that have the potential to impact the company. Therefore, if an analyst is astute and conducts satisfactory research, he will become an expert on the company. Consequently, any recommendation made by such an analyst will carry weight. Therefore, when such a well-informed analyst makes a statement regarding the company, the market listens. Stocks can rocket up, or nose dive, when an influential analyst changes a recommendation for the better or issues a downgrade.

Typically, an analyst will follow only a few companies. For each company that is being studied, an analyst will issue a comprehensive company research and/or earnings report. Typically, this report will include detailed information such as earnings estimates for each quarter (and the following year), forecast for the company's 5-year annualized earnings growth rate, business prospects, evaluation of competition, etc. Details contained in typical company research and earning reports are shown in the Appendixes (A–D).

Desired coverage

Usually, small and emerging companies will have a few or, in many cases, no analyst following it. On the other hand, a large, well-established company may have 25 to 30 analysts following it. It is desired that at least four analysts should be covering a company. This ensures that the company has been analyzed thoroughly by a minimum number of professionals. It also creates a higher level of confidence in the consensus earnings forecasts made by these analysts, because a single wrong estimate will not significantly distort the reported average.

BUY/HOLD/SELL RECOMMENDATIONS

Understanding recommendations

Stock recommendations made by analysts are typically categorized into buy, sell or hold. A "buy" recommendation means that the stock is recommended to be bought because it is expected to have good price appreciation. A "sell" means a recommendation to get rid of the stock because the company is expected to have poor price performance. A "hold" means to let the current status remain: maintain any existing positions in the stock; however, no additional buying should be done.

There are many variations of stock recommendation categories used by brokerage companies. Examples are strong buy, buy, accumulate, moderate buy, trading buy (for short-term trading), hold (maintain investment status), sell, etc. An investor should clearly determine what each recommendation term means, if he plans to follow an analyst's recommendations, because each term can mean something different at various brokerage companies.

Obtaining current status of recommendations on a company

Some research reports issued by companies such as Zacks and First Call, besides reporting buy/hold/sell recommendations, also provide the mean of all analysts' recommendations (Appendixes A, C and D). These typically range from 1 (buy) to 5 (sell). Changes in these recommendations, better known as upgrades and downgrades, are reported on the Internet and in various publications including *IBD*, *WSJ* and *Barron's*.

INDUSTRY SPECIFIC INDICATORS

Which indicators to monitor

There are a number of indicators that are applicable to specific industries. Investors track these indicators with the aim of monitoring a particular industry. For example, new car sales and new home sales are good indicators of the health of the automobile and housing industries. Similarly, the state of health of the semiconductor industry is indicated by the book-to-bill ratio, which measures the level of bookings (new orders) against billings (actual shipments). Investors should determine which available indicator is the most appropriate for the industry they are analyzing and monitor it closely.

Benefiting from industry specific indicators

Investors who followed the book-to-bill ratio in 1995, and acted on it, were handsomely rewarded. The ratio rose sharply in 1994 and continued to trend higher. The higher trending ratio indicated a booming semiconductor business. Therefore, it was no surprise that the semiconductor companies had a huge stock price runup in 1995. This is exemplified by Micron Technology, which went up from 22 in January 1995 to 94 $^3/_4$ by September 1995. However, as the semiconductor chip sales slackened, as indicated by the book-to-bill ratio, the semiconductor stocks started slipping and Micron declined dramatically to 29 by January 1996.

CONCLUDING REMARKS

Stock market investors track a very large number of indicators. Some of the most important indicators were described in the previous chapter. They are supplemented by some more important indicators described in this chapter. Of these, the most important ones are the advance/decline line, trading volume and the level of institutional ownership.

It should be realized that no indicator can be analyzed in isolation. Each indicator's influence and importance can vary depending on a number of other factors such as the industry/group to which the company belongs, state of the economy and the stock market, presence or absence of other indicators, combination of indicators existing at any given moment, and investor psychology.

CHAPTER 4

SENTIMENT INDICATORS

ROLE OF PSYCHOLOGICAL INDICATORS

The stock market is a place where economics and psychology are intertwined. Investors need to understand both in order to achieve success with their investments. For this purpose, stock market investors use a number of sentiment, or psychological, indicators to monitor the pulse of the market and gauge investor sentiment. These indicators are regularly reported in many newsletters, periodicals and newspapers. The most commonly monitored sentiment indicators, reported daily in *IBD*, are listed on the following page in Table 5.

Basis for using psychological indicators

Psychological indicators are based on supply and demand. The premise is that if there is more investor bullishness, less demand for stocks can be expected because it can be assumed that the bulls have already invested their available cash. Conversely, if there is widespread bearishness, it means that a lot of cash is available for investing in stocks. Therefore, the potential exists for stocks to be pushed higher.

As a leading indicator

When investor sentiment becomes one-sided, too bullish or optimistic for instance, it becomes an early warning signal of trouble ahead for the market. Due to their leading indicator status, and ability to give signals before market tops and bottoms, psychological indicators are widely used as investment tools. These indicators track the bullish/bearish sentiment of those who can influence the market: market specialists in the NYSE, corporate insiders and professional investment advisors.

Table 5: Psychological market indicators

Psychological market indicator	Current	5-Year				12-Month			
		High	Date	Low	Date	High	Date	Low	Date
1. % Investment advisors bearish (50% = bullish; 20% = bearish)[1]	27.6%	59.1%	12/12/94	25.8%	8/18/97	42.5%	4/22/97	25.8%	8/18/97
% Investment advisors bullish (35% = bullish; 55% = bearish)[1]	48.8%	56.0%	12/03/96	23.3%	7/11/94	52.5%	12/16/97	31.9%	4/28/97
2. Odd lot short sales/Odd lot sales	4.85%	21.3%	3/12/96	0.43%	12/16/93	11.9%	4/14/97	0.92%	9/15/97
3. Public/NYSE Specialist short sales (above 0.6 bullish; below 0.35 bearish)	0.68	2.25	6/14/96	0.56	10/31/97	1.39	6/13/97	0.56	10/31/97
4. Short interest ratio (NYSE Short interest/average daily volume prior 30 days)	6.07	7.20	9/05/96	4.12	12/19/95	7.15	1/02/98	5.52	2/13/98
5. Ratio of price premiums in Puts versus Calls	0.89	2.57	7/02/97	0.29	7/15/96	2.57	7/02/97	0.34	4/11/97
6. Ratio of trading volume in Puts versus Calls	0.55	1.23	12/09/94	0.38	8/06/97	0.95	12/19/97	0.38	8/06/97
7. Mutual fund share purchases/Redemptions (X - Money market funds)	1.53	2.41	7/01/93	0.98	11/01/94	1.75	9/01/97	1.14	11/03/97
8. AMEX daily trading volume as a % of NYSE daily volume	3.98%	7.90%	10/07/97	3.02%	3/25/97	7.90%	10/07/97	3.02%	3/25/97
9. OTC daily trading volume as % of NYSE daily volume	117%	196%	5/07/96	64.4%	4/05/93	182%	10/13/97	93.7%	6/20/97
10. Number of stock splits in Investor's Business Daily 6000 (prior 30 days)	112	191	12/29/97	44	11/18/94	191	12/29/97	86	4/14/97
11. New Issues in last year as % of all stocks on NYSE	19.0%	33.7%	3/03/94	18.5%	6/26/95	29.9%	3/14/97	19.0%	3/17/96
12. Price-to-book value of DJIA	5.93	5.94	3/11/98	2.94	3/17/93	5.94	3/11/98	4.62	4/11/97
13. Price-to-earnings ratio of DJIA	22.3	24.3	7/14/93	13.7	10/26/95	22.4	8/06/97	18.0	4/11/97
14. Current dividend yield of DJIA	1.61%	3.06%	4/02/93	1.60%	8/06/97	1.96%	3/13/97	1.60%	8/06/97

[1] Investor's Intelligence

Source: *Investor's Business Daily*, March 18, 1998

Limitations

While psychological indicators are readily available to those who want to use them, their signals are often ignored by investors at market bottoms. This happens because most investors do not have the courage to buy when everything looks so bleak: a decimated market, poor economy, etc. Generally, the market turns positive 2 to 3 months after the psychological indicators turn positive. Analyzed as a group, psychological indicators rarely fail.

Investors should note two factors when dealing with these indicators:
- sentiment indicators work best at extremes
- a significant gap may lie between data collection and reporting times

BULLISH/BEARISH READINGS

Savvy market players try to gauge the level of optimism and pessimism permeating the market. For this, they use a variety of tools including bullish/bearish numbers and consumer confidence levels. These are reported in surveys, which measure the degree of bullishness/bearishness (of investors, investment advisors and market professionals) and consumer confidence. Three of the most closely followed surveys are:
- Investors' Intelligence Survey
- Conference Board's consumer confidence index
- University of Michigan (UOM) index of consumer sentiment

Investors' Intelligence Survey

This is a survey of 130 investment advisory firms that publish market newsletters. It reports the percentage of bullish versus bearish advisors. *IBD* reports these numbers daily even though they change only once a week (Wednesday).

Bullish numbers

If the bullishness percentage exceeds 55%, it is a bearish warning signal. The reason is that these numbers are viewed in a contrarian way by market watchers. They assume that if a vast majority of investors are bullish, it is highly probable that buyers have already made their investments. Therefore, few buyers and little cash is left to move the market higher. Also, investment letter writers, who mostly are trend followers, have a poor track record in forecasting the market's direction.

In the past, market tops have been preceded by excessive bullishness, while bottoms have been preceded by pessimism. For example, in the third week of June 1996, 49.1% of advisors, a high number, were bullish. Three weeks later, the market suffered a sharp correction. In the last week of July 1997, when the DJIA was trading at 8,116, 46.3% of advisors were bullish. By September 1, 1997, the DJIA had declined sharply to 7,622, causing only 37.6% of advisors to remain bullish by mid-September. However, by mid-October, bullishness had risen to 48.8%, which coincided with the market peak. On October 16, 1997, the DJIA started a sharp decline, which culminated in the massive drop of 554 points on October 27.

Bearish numbers

The other side of the coin is the bearishness number. A well-known clichè is that the stock market climbs a wall of worry. In line with that view, a high bearish number is considered positive for the market. For example, 59.1% of advisors were bearish in mid-December, 1994. However, they completely misread the market which, at that time, started its explosive upward move that resulted in tremendous gains for the market in 1995. Again, in late 1990, 55% of advisors were bearish. However, contrary to their expectation, the market turned upwards for a sizable gain.

Generally, a bearish number below 20% is very bearish and a loud warning sign. It indicates that very few advisors are negative on the market. To the contrary, that is bearish for the market. This situation preceded the big crash in October 1987, when only 19% of advisors were bearish and 61% were bullish.

A high bearish number, while considered bullish, is not always bullish. Investors need remember 1974 when the market dropped even though the bearish figure was 59%.

Analyzing bullish/bearish numbers

Both bullish and bearish numbers should be analyzed in conjunction. When both are in dual confirmation, the signal should be viewed very seriously. A combination of 55% bulls with bears dropping below 20% is dangerous, with very bearish implications for the market.

If a high percentage of advisors are bearish with few bullish advisors, after the market has been going down, it is a good indicator of a turning point. In general, if bearish advisors are in the 55 to 60% range during a bear market, it can be concluded that a bottom has been reached.

It is also advisable to use the bullish/bearish sentiment numbers in conjunction with other sentiment indicators such as mutual fund cash, put-call ratio, short interest, insider selling and others.

Conference Board's consumer confidence index

This index, reported monthly, measures the confidence level of consumers (Figure 16). Since consumer spending is such a big component of the overall economic activity in the country, the level of consumer confidence is a good indicator of future consumer spending. The consumer confidence index includes two main components: current conditions and expectations for future conditions six months later.

Investors monitor the consumer confidence index closely because it indicates future consumer spending and can influence both the stock and bond markets. In September 1996, the consumer confidence index fell to 106.2 from the October level of 111.8. This indicated a potential slowing down of consumer spending and, consequently, it led to the expectation of lower inflationary pressures in the economy. This was viewed positively by the bond market, which rose on this news.

In December 1997, the consumer confidence index rose to 136.2 from 121.8 in November. This was a 28-year high and reflected consumers' positive outlook for the economy. The index continued to rise to a 30-year high by February 1998. With confident consumers providing fuel for the economy, the effect on the stock market was positive; it continued to trend higher—reaching an all time high by early March 1998.

Figure 16

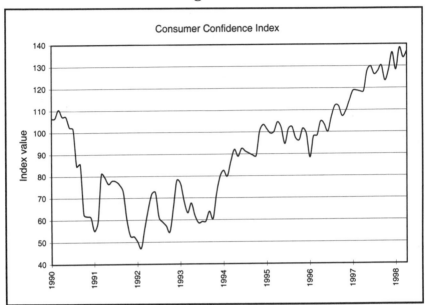

In general, higher consumer confidence is a positive for stocks but a negative for bonds. The reason is that bond traders fear that strong consumer spending can lay the seeds for future inflationary pressures.

University of Michigan index of consumer sentiment

The University of Michigan survey also measures the confidence level of consumers (Figure 17). This is a very good indicator of how consumers, whose spending has a very powerful effect on the economy, view current economic conditions and their own personal financial situation. It also reports consumer expectations.

A report indicating that consumers view their future positively is a bullish sign because it indicates potentially strong consumer spending in the near future. This means that the economy will have one powerful engine of growth in its favor. If consumer confidence numbers go down over a period of months, it indicates a potentially slowing economy, which is a negative for stocks. It has been observed over the years that extreme consumer pessimism usually occurs in tandem with stock market bottoms.

Figure 17

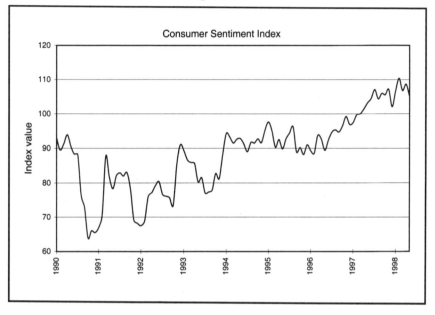

Consumer Sentiment Index

MUTUAL FUNDS CASH

Growth of mutual funds

As of December 31, 1996, mutual funds accounted for 14.5% of the total corporate equity outstanding of $10.09 trillion.[4] The importance of mutual funds can also be gauged from the fact that fund assets were $4.5 trillion, almost as much as the $4.9 trillion held by commercial banks at the end of September 1997.[5]

During 1997, a massive $231 billion flowed into stock funds following the $221 billion that was pumped in 1996.[6] In January 1997 alone, investors pumped $29.34 billion into stock mutual funds.[7] However, cash inflow during January 1998 was only $14.58 billion. The explanation for this decrease is the sharp market decline that occurred in the first half of January 1998, which made potential investors nervous. However, cash inflow rebounded sharply in February 1998, when $24.17 billion flowed into stock funds.

---

[4] *Investor's Business Daily,* December 29, 1997.
[5] *Investor's Business Daily,* March 5, 1998.
[6] *Investor's Business Daily,* January 30, 1998.
[7] *Investor's Business Daily,* February 8, 1997.

Compared to bonds, stock funds have been gaining in importance over the years. In 1987, bonds accounted for 36% of all fund assets compared to 23% for stock funds. In 1997, the situation was the opposite, with 53% of fund assets being held in stocks compared to 23% in bonds.[8] At the end of December 1997, total stock fund assets were $2.4 trillion.[9]

Role of mutual funds cash

When there is a large cash inflow into mutual funds, most of it gets invested in stocks, which helps propels stock prices higher. However, all the cash received from investors is not invested by mutual funds. They always keep aside a certain amount, which is a percentage of their total funds, in cash. This is required for meeting obligations due to potential redemptions, which can be heavy during a rapidly falling market. If mutual funds have inadequate cash and they get hit by heavy redemptions, especially during a weak or panicky market, they can be forced to sell some of their stock holdings in order to raise cash. This can make the market decline worse.

Low cash level—a bearish signal

A 10% mutual fund cash position is considered bullish. A 7% cash level is considered to be a fully invested and, consequently, bearish position because mutual funds need cash reserves for redemptions. The lowest mutual fund cash level in recent years was 4.5% in October 1976. Mutual funds cash level, which is reported by newsletters and newspapers, is a widely monitored indicator (Table 5).

Low cash levels indicate excessive bullishness. As a contrarian sign, this might indicate a market top. The reasoning is that if mutual funds are fully invested, a very important engine for moving the market up will be missing. Low cash levels combined with record money inflow into funds is an indication of extreme bullishness, or euphoria. This is a good indication of a market top.

Low mutual fund cash levels have often preceded market tops. For example, in January 1973, prior to the 1973/74 bear market, cash levels were only 4.5%. In 1996, mutual fund cash levels declined to 6.6% in

---

[8] *Investor's Business Daily,* March 11, 1998.
[9] *Investor's Business Daily,* February 27, 1998.

June from the January level of 8%. This was followed by a sharp correction in mid-July. Again, by October 1996, mutual fund cash levels declined to a bearish 5.9%. This was followed by the market decline of 4.2% in mid-December.

It should be noted that the forecasting record of this indicator has been somewhat mixed since 1973. In the recent past, the level of mutual funds cash has been very low by historic standards, and yet, the market has continued to rise higher and higher. In the 12-month period ending January 1998, the average monthly level of mutual funds cash was only 5.66, while the average for the prior 18 months was 5.82.

High cash level—a bullish signal

When mutual funds get bearish and start increasing their cash percentage, it is an indication that the market is ready to turn upwards. When these funds start deploying their cash, it propels the market upwards. However, if the cash levels drop too much, it is a bearish signal. To some market analysts, mutual funds cash level is one of the most important psychological indicators.

In October 1990, mutual fund cash levels were at 12.9%, an extremely bullish number, which coincided with the bear market bottom. However, this indicator is not infallible. For example, cash levels were quite high prior to the bear market of the 1980s (9.9%) and the October 1987 crash (9.5% in September).

Limitations of this indicator

Some analysts point out that low cash levels do not always portend a problem. For example, the market rocketed up in 1995, despite decreasing cash levels, as well as in the past couple of years. The belief is that so long as investors keep pumping money into mutual funds, low cash levels can be safe. In recent years, a flood of cash has been poured into mutual funds. We can expect this cash inflow to continue due to changing demographics such as the aging of the boomers. Therefore, this indicator may not be the danger signal that it used to be. Also, keep in mind that mutual funds are not the only sources of large-scale investment in the stock market. Others include corporations, pension funds and insurance companies.

INSIDER TRADING

Insider advantage

An insider can be described as a person who has access to important corporate information, which is not available to the general public. Typically, such persons include officers, directors and major shareholders of the company. These insiders are well-informed investors. They have a distinct edge over analysts and individual investors because they are more informed about the day-to-day operations of their companies. Hence, they can use their positions to buy or sell their own company shares in a more timely fashion, before any good or bad news becomes common knowledge.

To keep the playing field level, the Securities and Exchange Commission (SEC) prohibits insiders from trading on the basis of their access to confidential company information. All insider trading has to be reported to the SEC. Some newsletters keep close tabs on insider trading. The *Vickers Weekly Insider Report* publishes a weekly ratio of insider sales to purchases. Also, many newspapers and Internet sites report insider trading activity. However, the reporting by local newspapers is often limited to transactions taking place in local companies.

Insider selling

There can be a number of reasons for insider selling other than the belief that the company's future prospects are bleak. These can be transactions related to the exercise of stock options, personal expenses, children's education, the need to diversify, etc. Therefore, analyzing insider selling is more complex than analyzing insider buying. In general, if insider selling is taking place:

- it is either bearish or neutral
- it does not always indicate that company will under-perform or that it will go down in price

Both insider buying and selling patterns should be studied before any conclusions are drawn. Also, any unusual inside activity should be investigated. If insider selling has been taking place, the following should be taken as serious warning signs:

- unusually heavy insider selling
- abnormal insider selling pattern for the company
- no insider buying; only insider selling taking place
- selling starts after quick price appreciation

Historically, insiders sell stock about twice as much as they buy. So if they are selling at a lower rate than that number, it is a bullish sign. Conversely, if they are selling at a higher rate, it is considered to be bearish. When analyzing insider selling, two points need to be noted:

- historically, insider selling has tended to be a leading rather than a coincidental indicator of market tops
- selling information is available to the public only after a time lag

Insider buying

If insiders are buying their own company's stock, it is considered to be a bullish signal. It indicates their belief that the open market price, of their company's stock, is too low or that the fundamental outlook for the company is very good. In October 1990, insiders were buying at the market lows because they realized that their companies' stocks were undervalued based on anticipated corporate profits.

Compared to selling, insider buying is a more reliable indicator of a stock's future price direction. The explanation is that there exists only one very strong reason for insider buying: believing that the stock is going to perform very well, which typically is due to one of the following:

- high earnings expectations
- upcoming new product(s)/cycle
- belief that stock is undervalued

Sometimes, though not too often, a new executive may buy a company's shares to signal faith in the company or to indicate his team player attitude.

Guidelines and tips for analyzing insider trading

The number of buyers and sellers is more informative than the size of the transactions because less chance exists that the collective judgment of insiders will be wrong. However, one should be on the lookout for any sign that key officers of a company are trading in tandem. Consider the case of Telular Corporation, whose executives were buying heavily in March 1996—three months before the stock took off in June.

The following are some guidelines and tips for evaluating insider trading:

- insider selling:
  - is not particularly meaningful
  - is significant only if there is an unusual or significant amount of selling
- buying is more meaningful than selling; however, large sells or multiple sells are a warning sign
- buy close to insider prices
- companies with more than one insider buying should be favored
- open market purchases are more significant than company sponsored stock option purchases
- do not be influenced by insiders exercising options to purchase stock
- look for patterns—number of shares and number of insiders who are trading
- a stock that has experienced recent insider selling should not be bought

PUT/CALL RATIO

Understanding options

A call is an option that conveys its buyer the right, but not an obligation, to buy the underlying stock at a specific (exercise) price by the expiration date of the contract for the option. A put is an option that conveys the right, but not an obligation, to sell the underlying stock at a specific (exercise) price by the expiration date of the contract. A call buyer is bullish and expects the price to rise. A put buyer is bearish and expects a price decline.

Analyzing the put/call ratio

The volume of puts and calls traded in the market is used to calculate the put/call ratio. This ratio, which is reported in various newspapers, measures the sentiment of option traders who are basically speculators (Table 5). When the put/call ratio is high, it indicates that option buyers are favoring puts because they are bearish. However, they have historically been wrong and contrary to their expectations the market has usually headed higher. The opposite also holds true.

On December 9, 1994, the put/call ratio hit a five-year high of 1.23. However, option traders were wrong as the market emerged from a sideways pattern to begin a new bull market phase. On August 6, 1997, the put/call ratio hit a five-year low of 0.38, indicating that option traders were bullish. However, they were wrong and the market topped the very next day.

The put/call ratio works best at extremes. A high put/call ratio indicates that most, if not all, selling has taken place. At this point, fear is at a peak and the market is ready to rebound.

SHORT INTEREST (SHORT SELLING)

Most investors buy stocks with the objective of selling it at a higher price. However, there also exists a very small group of investors, called short sellers, who buy a stock based on the belief that it will decline in price. Their technique is called short selling or shorting.

Understanding short selling

A short seller borrows stock from a broker, sells it, and then waits to buy back the same stock when it trades at a lower price. When the stock price actually declines, the short seller buys the stock (at the lower price), and then returns the newly bought stock to the broker lender. In other words, a short seller sells first (at a higher price) and buys later (at a lower price). The difference in the sell and buy prices is pocketed by the short seller as profit. However, if the stock price rises against a short seller's expectations, after he has borrowed and sold the stock, he will be forced to buy back the stock at a higher price. In such a case, which is known as covering, the short seller suffers a loss.

Potential loss through short selling

The maximum profit in shorting a stock is 100% if the stock declines to nil value. However, the loss potential is infinite. The reason is that there is no limit to which a stock price can rise before a short sale is covered. Short sales can be profitable in many cases. However, the odds and the system favor those who are stock investors rather than short sellers.

Analyzing short interest

The number of shares that have been sold short on the NYSE as well as the NASDAQ are periodically reported by the major newspapers and on the Internet. Also reported are the total number of shares that have been shorted for each company. Rising short interest is viewed as a growing sign of skepticism.

A useful indicator for monitoring short interest is the "short interest ratio." This is the ratio of short interest to total market volume for the reporting period. A ratio above 2.5% is considered bullish, while a number below 1.5% is considered bearish.

High short interest numbers can give conflicting signals. It can be bearish because it indicates that many investors believe that the stock price will decline. However, it is bullish because the shorted stock must be repurchased some time in the future and, therefore, represents potential buying power. The effect of short selling has been somewhat diminished, in recent years, by the expanded use of options trading.

PUBLIC/NYSE SPECIALIST SHORT SALES

What the smart money thinks

NYSE specialists are responsible for maintaining an orderly market for specific securities traded on the exchange. They have access to both buy and sell orders and are very knowledgeable. Therefore, their actions can give a good indication of where the market is headed. Some of their actions, such as the level of shorting that they perform, can indicate market turning points. When the smart money turns bullish, analysts view it as a signal to start buying. This is in contrast to mutual funds, speculators and investment advisors who typically are wrong and get excited at the wrong time.

Analyzing Public/NYSE specialist short sales

The specialists' opinion can be gauged from the "ratio of Public/NYSE specialist short sales" (Table 5). This ratio shows the ratio of short positions held by specialists compared to the general investing public. In general, when specialists become more confident and start shorting less than the public, it indicates an improving market. A Public/NYSE specialist short sale number above 0.6 is considered bullish, while a number below 0.35 is considered bearish.

OTC/NYSE VOLUME

While a certain amount of speculation in the stock market is normal, an excessive amount raises a warning flag for investors. Being aware of this danger, investors are always watching for signs of excessive speculation, which generally precedes a market top. In contrast, very low speculation occurs at market bottoms, when pessimism is widespread.

Analyzing OTC/NYSE volume

A number of tools are available to investors for determining whether speculation is excessive or minimal. One such indicator is based on a comparison of the volume of shares traded in the OTC market to that on the NYSE (Table 5). If this ratio is high, it indicates increased trading volume on the NASDAQ. Since the NASDAQ is home to small cap, speculative and IPO issues, a high OTC/NYSE ratio indicates more speculation. The reasons why NASDAQ volume increases include:

- rally chasing by institutions who feel they may be missing a powerful upward move
- risk averse individuals getting into the market very late in the cycle

A sharp increase in the OTC/NYSE ratio has coincided with several market tops. Examples are spikes that occurred prior to the October 1987 crash and the 1990 bear market. This ratio also spiked when the small cap stocks topped in mid-1983. A decrease in the OTC/NYSE ratio to very low levels often indicates a market bottom. This occurred in late 1990 (at the end of the bear market) and in mid-1982 (just prior to the start of the super bull market).

Effect of a changing stock market

In 1983, OTC volume exceeded the NYSE volume for the first time. Since then, NASDAQ volume has increased, as a percentage of the NYSE volume. A reason is that many large NASDAQ stocks that in the past would have moved to the NYSE, such as Cisco, Microsoft and Intel, have opted to remain on the NASDAQ. This has caused its trading volume to swell. Therefore, due to the distortion caused by the presence of these heavily traded stocks, the OTC/NYSE ratio has lost some significance in recent years.

Using the OTC/NYSE ratio

When trading becomes speculative, an investor should become wary, rather than follow the frenzied crowd who often happen to be wrong at critical junctures. While the OTC/NYSE ratio should be monitored, it should not be used in isolation. It should be used in conjunction with other sentiment indicators. The OTC/NYSE volume ratio is reported by *IBD* and a number of newsletters.

CONCLUDING REMARKS

Psychology is a very important component in the stock market where greed, fear and hope are in ample supply. Their influence on the behavior of individual stocks and the overall stock market cannot be ignored by an investor without taking high risk. Psychological indicators are very important tools because they help to analyze stock market behavior, which cannot be explained through numbers alone.

Psychological indicators are based on a contrarian idea: if investors are bullish, it actually means the reverse. The logic is that it is highly probable that bullish investors have already invested their cash and, therefore, a fuel source for pushing the market higher does not exist.

Extreme sentiment readings indicate a market top (too bullish readings) or market bottom (too bearish readings). An extremely bullish sentiment indicates problems for the market and should be taken as a warning sign. The most valid confirmation of bullishness or bearishness occurs when both bullish and bearish numbers are in sync.

CHAPTER 5

ECONOMIC INDICATORS

MONITORING ECONOMIC INDICATORS

The state of the economy and the business cycle have an important bearing on the earnings prospects and the price trend of individual companies and the overall stock market. Therefore, variables affecting the business cycle should be closely monitored by stock market investors. These include general economic conditions, interest rates, local and international developments, currency rates, labor rates, and others.

Key indicator reports to be monitored

The most important economic indicators that can help stock market investors gauge the performance and health of the economy are:

- Inflation
- Employment
- Gross domestic product (GDP)
- National Association of Purchasing Manager's index (NAPM)
- Factory orders
- Housing and construction spending
- Retail sales
- Personal income and consumption expenditures
- Industrial production and capacity utilization
- Leading economic indicators
- Money supply

Every month, the government and associated agencies like the Federal Reserve Board release economic reports. Each of these reports, based on the status of various economic indicators, indicates the performance and health of some sector(s) of the economy. Therefore, investors review these reports very closely in order to pick up signs of an accelerating or slowing economy, inflationary pressures, changes in consumer spending or manufacturing activity, etc.

These reports are very eagerly awaited and many times are the catalysts that move the market up or down. This typically happens if the contents of a very important report, such as inflation or employment, are not in line with investor expectations. The highlights of these reports, along with their comprehensive analysis, are reported in *Investor's Business Daily, The Wall Street Journal* and a number of Internet sites. These reports are also reported and discussed with experts on CNBC TV as soon as they are released. These analyses can be very informative and revealing.

Other important indicators to be monitored

Besides the monthly economic reports and the quarterly GDP report, investors should also keep themselves informed regarding the following important factors, which can significantly affect the investment climate for stocks:

- Federal Reserve actions on interest rates
- interest rate trends, with the most important indicators being the 30-year bond rate and the prime lending rate
- changes in the tax rates
- level of government spending and the deficit, which has a significant effect on interest rates due to the level of government borrowing

Effect of economic indicators on the markets

The February 1996 employment report, released on March 8, 1996, is a good example of the importance that investors attach to economic reports. The report indicated that 705,000 new jobs had been created in a single month, which was more than double the expected rise of approximately 317,000 jobs.

The surprisingly strong job number made investors fear that an explosively growing economy would ignite inflation and cause interest rates to rise, which make stocks less competitive with bonds. Higher interest rates also have the potential to eventually slow the economy, hurting corporate profits. Therefore, investors dumped inflation sensitive stocks, causing the DJIA to lose 171 points, or 3.04%. The

NASDAQ Composite index plunged 2.7%. This also turned out to be the worst day for bonds in nearly 6 years. The 30-year Treasury bond's yield, a gauge of expectations for economic growth and inflation, shot up to 6.72% from 6.47%. It lost 3 points (or $30 per $1000 bond), a very significant loss.

UNDERSTANDING ECONOMIC INDICATORS THAT CAN INFLUENCE THE MARKET

Inflation

Inflation decreases the value of money due to rising prices. It influences the business cycle and in turn is affected by the business cycle. The inflation rate in the economy has a direct impact on the investment environment. Any rise in the inflation rate makes interest rates rise and negatively impacts stocks. Rising interest rates also influence the way investors allocate bonds, stocks and other investment vehicles. The two most important indicators of inflation are the producer price index (PPI) and the consumer price index (CPI).

<u>Producer Price Index (PPI)</u>

The PPI is an index of commodity prices (Figure 18). No services are included in this index, which is a gauge of prices paid to factories, farms and other producers. The PPI measures price changes at three production levels: crude goods like raw crops, intermediate goods like lumber and paperboard, and finished goods like clothing and furniture. The PPI measures inflation at the wholesale (producer) level. It is the first inflation report of the month and can considerably affect the stock market because the inflation rate, whether measured by the PPI or the CPI (consumer price index), influences everything from Federal Reserve policy to consumer and auto loans. Any change in the inflation rate as indicated by the PPI should be investigated to determine its cause.

Two PPI numbers are reported each month: the overall rate and the core rate. The core rate is calculated after excluding the PPI's two volatile components: food and energy. The core rate is the one investors usually focus on. In general, an annualized PPI rate below 3% is desired. In 1997, the PPI actually declined 1.2%, the biggest annual decline since 1986 when oil prices dropped. The core PPI rate rose only 0.1% during 1997, its smallest gain ever. This indicated that inflation was under control—a positive for the stock market, which loves a benign inflation scenario. The 1997 trend continued in early 1998, when the PPI fell 0.7% in January, the largest one-month drop since August 1993.

If the PPI rate rises, it negatively effects bonds and stocks. On the other hand, if it decreases or is maintained at a low level, it boosts the market. For example, in September 1996, the PPI was reported to have risen 0.2%, which was slightly below the forecasts. This caused the bond and stock markets to move higher since the report confirmed the view that inflation would remain low.

Figure 18

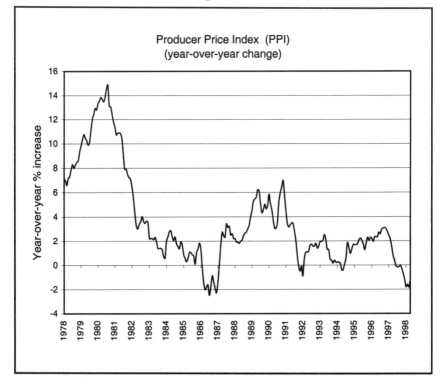

Consumer Price Index (CPI)

The CPI is widely regarded as the most important measure of inflation at the retail level (Figure 19). It measures the prices of both consumer commodities and services for a fixed basket of goods and services. Again, two CPI numbers are reported: overall rate and the core rate (excluding food and energy). As with the producer price index, investors should focus on the core rate. Also, it is advised that the CPI average of several months should be analyzed to get a better idea of the price trend.

Over time, the CPI is closely correlated to the PPI. On a monthly basis, however, they can vary measurably. During 1997, the CPI index increased only 1.7%—the best inflation performance since 1986. This was a considerable improvement over 1996, when the CPI rose 3.3%. The decrease in the PPI during 1997 coupled with the economic crisis in Asia has led to talk of deflation in recent months. The perception is that inflation has been tamed and, therefore, this index is not causing Wall Street the concern that it used to in the past.

If the CPI rate rises, it negatively effects bonds and stocks. On the other hand, if it decreases or is maintained at a low level, it boosts the market. For example, it was reported that the overall CPI rate, as well as the core rate, increased by 0.3% in September 1996 after a 0.1% rise in August. The numbers were still considered good because the year-to-date core CPI was 2.8% compared to 3.0% for the comparable period in 1995. This caused the bond market to move higher, lowering the yield, which was positive for the stock market.

Commodity Research Bureau Index (CRB)

The CRB index, which indicates the commodities price trend, is another indicator tracked by investors (Figure 20). It represents an unweighted average of 17 prices grouped into energy, grains, industrials, livestock/meats, precious metals and softs. Since 1996, the CRB has been in a downtrend.

Declining commodity prices are a positive for the economy, consumers and the stock market. Low commodity prices help keep inflation and interest rates low. Changes in the CRB index can affect the stock and bond markets. For example, when the CRB index of raw material prices fell in September 1996, bonds surged because it reinforced expectations that inflation would not increase in the near future. The CRB index does not affect the markets like the CPI or the PPI. However, it is monitored by stock analysts because it can indicate potential inflationary pressures in commodities, which ultimately can work their way into the PPI and the CPI.

Figure 19

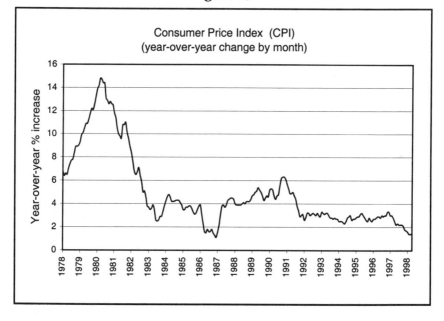

Employment report

What it includes and indicates

The employment report is the most important and closely monitored report pertaining to the health of the economy (Figure 21). While the GDP report provides better insight than the monthly employment report, it is only published quarterly. Therefore, investors look to the unemployment report to fill the two month gap when the GDP report is not published. The employment report includes both the goods- and service-producing sectors. It provides very useful information for various sectors of the economy and is a very good measure of the economy's health and future direction. The report's various components are closely scrutinized by economists and investors.

Figure 20

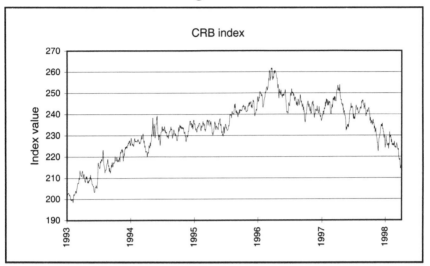

Figure 21

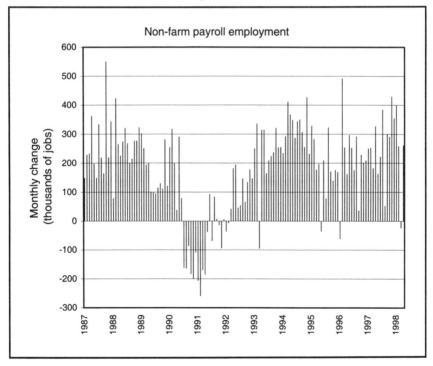

The employment report contains numbers for non-farm jobs created (in goods producing, services and government sectors), the jobless rate, weekly hours and hourly earnings (in manufacturing). Each of these is analyzed and reported in newspapers to gauge the health of the economy in a particular area. The two numbers most closely watched in this report are:

- non-farm jobs growth (number of new jobs created)
- unemployment rate

In general, if payroll employment increases at a healthy pace, the stock market considers it to be positive, while the bond market views it negatively due to its potential inflationary effect. While investors desire steady growth, any sign of excessive jobs growth creates jitters in the markets, because investors fear that the economy may overheat and consequently cause inflationary pressures. However, a weak jobs growth number indicates that the economy is slowing and is therefore viewed positively by the bond market.

The Labor Department also reports the "Employment cost index (ECI)" every month. Employment costs include wage and salary costs as well as the cost of providing employee benefits. The ECI is considered to be a leading inflation indicator because labor compensation is the single biggest cost of production. Therefore, analysts like to see the ECI trend remain steady.

Jobs growth: an important number to analyze

A monthly jobs growth of 200,000–300,000 is generally considered good since it indicates a steadily growing economy. Any number above, or below, this figure indicates an economy growing strongly, or slowly, respectively. The overall jobs growth number can vary depending on the state of the business cycle: whether the economy is coming out of a recession, is in a recession, or has been expanding for a while.

The main driving force for any reaction by the market to the jobs report is expectations. The reported numbers have to be within the range of estimates made by economists, which usually are in tune with the state of the economic cycle. The jobs growth numbers estimated by economists are reported in major publications (including the *WSJ*, *IBD* and *Barron's*), prior to the release of the employment report.

Care should be used in analyzing these reports. Besides being on the lookout for one-time factors skewing results, one should not read too much into a single report. Instead, one should look at a few reports before jumping to any conclusion regarding the direction of the economy.

Market reaction to the employment report

On July 5, 1996, it was reported that 239,000 new jobs were created in June, about 50% more than economists had expected. The result was that the DJIA dropped 114.88 points. Both the DJIA and the NASDAQ lost about 2% of their value that day. On the other hand, the September 1996 report showed a surprising drop of 40,000 non-farm jobs. Economists had been expecting a gain of 170,000 jobs. This indicated that the Federal Reserve would not raise interest rates in the near future since the economy appeared to be slowing rather than overheating. Therefore, the benchmark 30-year bond gained about 1 1/8 points, or $11.25 per $1,000 bond. The yield fell 9 basis points to 6.74%. The stock market moved up 60 points, or 1.01%, to a new high of 5,992.

In October 1996, 210,000 new non-farm jobs were created, in line with most estimates. The market hardly yawned. Compare this to the similar job growth number in June 1996, which had so negatively affected the market. The different reactions to the two reports were due to different expectations. In October, more job growth had been expected because 35,000 jobs were lost rather than created in September. When analyzed in conjunction with the 35,000-job loss in September, the average for the two months (September/October 1996) showed anemic jobs growth. The three-month average growth slowed to 152,000 jobs. Hence, the market did not react.

Recently, strong job growth numbers have not spooked the stock market as they did in the past. In February 1998, 310,000 new jobs were created after an increase of 375,000 jobs in January. The February report indicated that the economy was healthy and growing.

Therefore, continued growth in corporate profits could be expected. The release of this report caused the DJIA to rise 125 points (1.5%). The positive reaction, in contrast to the reaction to a similar report in June 1996, was due to the different inflation scenario in 1998. During 1997, inflation as measured by the CPI was only 1.7% and consequently investors were not worried about the inflationary effects of a tightening labor market.

Gross domestic product

The Gross domestic product (GDP) is the total value of goods and services produced in the country during the year (Figure 22). It is reported every quarter and is a good indicator of how fast the economy grew during that quarter. The GDP is the broadest measure of aggregate economic activity in the country. This report also contains the GDP deflator, which is believed to be a more precise inflation measure than the CPI.

If the GDP increases at a healthy pace, stocks tend to rise due to the potential for higher profits resulting from a healthy business climate. On the other hand, anemic or negative GDP growth affects the stock market negatively. In 1997, GDP growth was 3.8% following a rise of 2.4% in 1996, 2% in 1995 and 3.5% in 1994. This healthy growth in the economy translated into healthy corporate profits and a rising stock market.

The release of the GDP report does not impact the stock market significantly. Most of the components used to calculate the GDP are already known when it is released and, therefore, major surprises are rare. The stock market reacts strongly to the GDP numbers only if they are significantly above or below the advance estimates made by economists.

National Association of Purchasing Manager's Index (NAPM)

What it includes and indicates

The NAPM index provides an indication of economic growth (Figure 23). If the NAPM overall index is above 50, it indicates that the manufacturing sector is expanding, while a reading below 50 indicates that it is contracting. This index, which provides a comprehensive view of

Figure 22

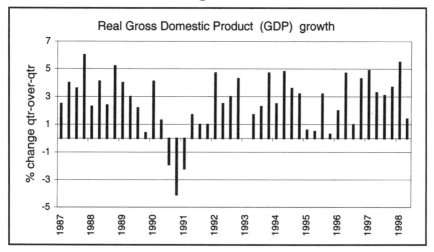

the manufacturing sector, tracks the economy's ups and downs fairly well. In general, if the NAPM rises, it tends to move the stock market up while pushing bonds down. If the NAPM decreases, especially below 50, the effect is the opposite.

The overall NAPM index includes many components with each providing valuable insight into a specific area. These components are new orders, order backlog, production, supplier deliveries, inventories, prices paid, employment, new export orders and import orders. Each component indicates what is going on in a particular sector. For example, the "supplier deliveries" component is considered to be a barometer for inventory investment and capacity utilization. It is one of the numbers monitored by the Federal Reserve for making a decision on whether or not to tighten money supply, which can effect economic growth.

Effect on the market and economy

In September 1996, the NAPM index decreased to 51.7, down from 52.6 in August, which was lower than had been expected. This suggested that manufacturing was growing at a slower pace, and therefore was viewed positively by the market and bonds rallied. The

Figure 23

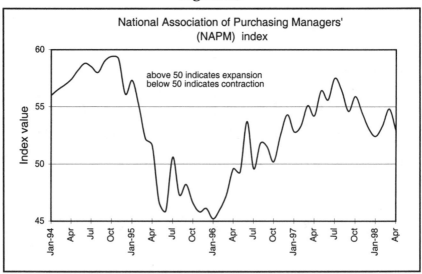

December 1996 report showed that the index rose to 54 from 52.7 in November, reversing the declines in the previous two months. The prices paid component also surged in December to 51.5 from 45.9 in November. This triggered inflation fears and the DJIA dropped 100 points in early trading. The 30-year bond lost $11.875 for a $1,000 face value. The bond yield, which moves in the reverse direction compared to the price, rose from 6.64% to 6.74%.

Bonds and stocks do not always react in the same way to the NAPM index. For example, in February 1998, the NAPM index rose to 53.3 from 52.4 in January, ending a three-month decline. This was higher than expected and indicated that the economy was stronger than expected. The DJIA did not react to this news and rose 4 points for the day. However, the reaction of the bond market was very negative. The 30-year bond fell 1 $\frac{1}{4}$ point or $12.5 per $1,000 face amount.

Investors and economists pay more attention to the direction and steadiness of the numbers than to the NAPM index numbers themselves. For example, the index ranged around 50 for most of 1993. However, in 1994 it climbed 10 points within a few months, which indicated increasing bottlenecks and cost pressures. At the same time, the NAPM prices paid component rose significantly—from the 50s into the low 60s. This indicated a strong and potentially overheating economy, which became a factor in the Federal Reserve's decision to raise interest rates. In the past 10 years, the Federal Reserve has hiked interest rates when the NAPM index was around 56 and the vendor performance index was about 57.[10] Vendor performance indicates how fast companies fill their orders.

Factory orders

What it includes and indicates

Each month, the Commerce Department releases the "Factory Orders" report. This report is another indicator of how certain sectors of the economy are performing. The components of this report include new factory orders (durable and non-durable goods), inventories, factory shipments (measure of current demand), and unfilled orders (measure of longer-term pent-up demand and backlogs). A positive factory orders number indicates growth, while a decline in factory orders indicates a slowing or contracting economy.

Monthly factory orders are volatile and need to be analyzed as such. For example, in September 1996, factory orders rose 2.7%, the largest increase in more than two years. This was followed by declines in November and December. In January 1997, factory orders rose a robust 2.5%, which was followed by an increase of just 0.8% in February.

Durable goods

The durable goods component indicates the new orders placed for big-ticket items expected to last three years or more (Figure 24). Tracking these orders helps investors anticipate changes in production activity in the country. Typically, orders tend to decline 8 to 12 months ahead of a cyclical downturn and rise about a month ahead of the trough of a recession.

A report with a strong rise in orders is expected to spur manufacturing

---

[10] *Investor's Business Daily,* January 3, 1997.

activity to meet rising demand and indicates a stronger economy in the months ahead. On the other hand, a drop in orders indicates a weakening in the manufacturing sector in the following months. In general, if the durable goods orders are up, bonds tend to go down while stocks tend to rise.

Figure 24

Durable goods report volatility

This component tends to be volatile from month-to-month. In August 1996, orders for durable goods fell a surprising 3.1%, the biggest drop in more than a year. This indicated an economic slowdown, which raised the question about future corporate earnings. The result was that investors started to sell economically sensitive stocks. Stocks less tied to swings in the economy fared better. Bond traders also liked the news and its implications of a weaker economy. They pushed the 30-year Treasury up 17/32, bringing down the yield from 6.92% to 6.88%.

The volatility range of this indicator can be gauged from the reports issued in the last four months of 1996. In September, durable goods orders rose a very strong 4.6%, followed by a meager rise of 0.1% in

October. However, orders declined by 1.7% in both November and December 1996, only to be followed by a robust rise of 3.6% in January 1997.

Inventories

Any increase or decrease in inventories has a direct effect on orders placed, which can affect the production of goods and, in turn, the economy. Hence, the buildup or depletion of inventories is tracked by investors. These numbers are analyzed in conjunction with other indicators. For example, wholesalers' inventories, which are reported monthly, are tracked in conjunction with sales. If sales of autos, lumber and metal products decrease, while inventories increase, the combination might indicate that businesses could be having problems selling their products.

Housing and construction spending

The housing sector, one of the biggest sectors of the economy, is a leading indicator of economic activity. Investors view it as an extremely important indicator because it helps forecast the direction of the economy. It is the first indicator to turn down when the economy goes into a recession. It is also the first one to rise when the economy rebounds. Changes in the housing sector are primarily triggered by changes in mortgage rates, which in turn are affected by inflation and interest rates. Historically, changes in consumer spending patterns have first appeared in the housing and auto sectors.

Housing starts

A gauge for measuring the health of the housing market is the "housing starts" number (Figure 25). An increase in this number is considered a positive for the economy. This is due to the large effect that the housing industry has on construction spending, building activity and associated sectors of the economy. When housing starts increase, stocks tend to rise while bonds tend to go down, and vice versa. Housing starts figures can be volatile from month-to-month. For example, in December 1997, they declined 0.7% following a rise of 0.3% in November. Month-to-month volatility is also affected by the weather due to its affect on construction activities.

An associated number monitored by investors is the number of building permits issued, which is a gauge of future construction spending (Figure 25). Building permits and housing starts are leading indicators of future spending in the housing sector, usually by many months.

Figure 25

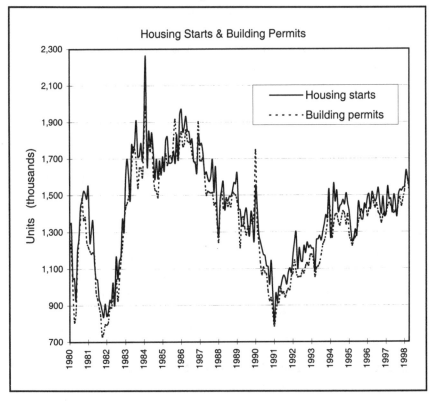

Sales of new and existing homes

Also reported and closely monitored are monthly sales of new and existing homes (Figures 26 and 27). Strong "new home sales" indicates strength in the key housing sector. Sales of new homes, as well as existing homes, are negatively impacted by higher mortgage rates. Therefore, rising interest rates tend to slow down an important sector of the economy. A rule of thumb is that a one point drop in interest rates adds 100,000 onto existing home sales and 50,000 new homes.[11]

In general, when new home sales increase, stocks rise and bonds decline. Existing home sales, which account for 80% of the total housing market, are considered a more accurate indicator of the housing market than housing starts. The reason is that they measure actual rather than expected closings, which is what the housing starts number indicates.

Figure 26

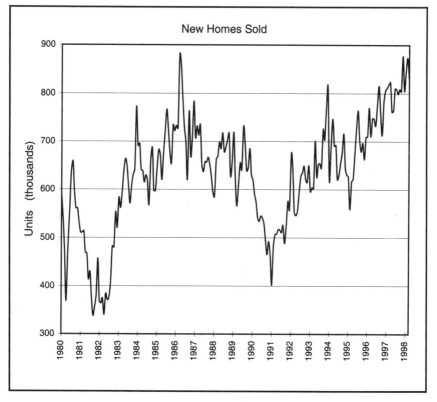

Construction spending

This is another report that reflects housing activity. It includes residential and non-residential new construction, as well as public construction spending. The level of construction spending is influenced by higher

[11] *Investor's Business Daily*, January 8, 1998.

Figure 27

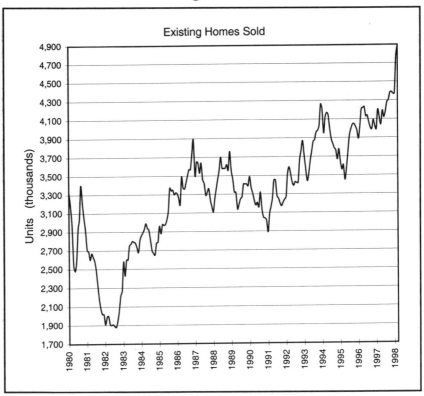

mortgage rates, which impacts both home sales and construction. The monthly construction spending report, typically, does not have any significant effect on the stock market or the bond market. Since these numbers can be volatile from month-to-month, it is advisable to consider three months data in order to determine the trend.

Retail sales

Retail sales are reported every month by the Commerce Department. Its main components are durable and non-durable goods. An increase in retail sales indicates good consumer spending. Since consumer spending makes up two-thirds of the overall economy, it is closely monitored by analysts.

A good indicator of consumer spending is monthly sales at the nation's major retailers. Comparable store sales, for stores open a year or more, are reported as "chain-store" sales. These sales, which do not include the effects of recent store opening, closings and expansions, indicate the level at which consumers are spending their money. A component of retail sales is auto sales, which can be volatile from month-to-month.

Retail sales are the first good indication of the strength or weakness of consumer spending in a given month. These figures can affect the market. If retail sales rise, it is a positive for retailers because it indicates good business. This tends to cause bonds to decline and stocks to rise.

Personal income and consumption expenditures

Personal income represents the compensation individuals receive from all sources. An increase in personal income provides fuel for consumer spending. Therefore, if personal income increases, stocks tend to rise and bonds tend to decline.

Consumption expenditures represent the market value of all goods and services purchased by individuals. Tracking these expenditures is important because consumer spending makes up a very large component of overall economic activity.

Industrial production and capacity utilization

The industrial production index is a measure of the physical volume of output of the nation's factories, mines and utilities (Figure 28). A healthy rise in industrial production indicates a growing economy. Therefore, when this index rises, stocks tend to go up and bonds tend to decline. A slackening in this indicator is viewed as a sign of a potential slowdown in the economy. This occurred in February 1998, when industrial production remained unchanged from a month earlier—the first time this happened in over a year. This was attributed to the effect of the Asian economic crisis, which was expected to slow down the U.S. economy.

Figure 28

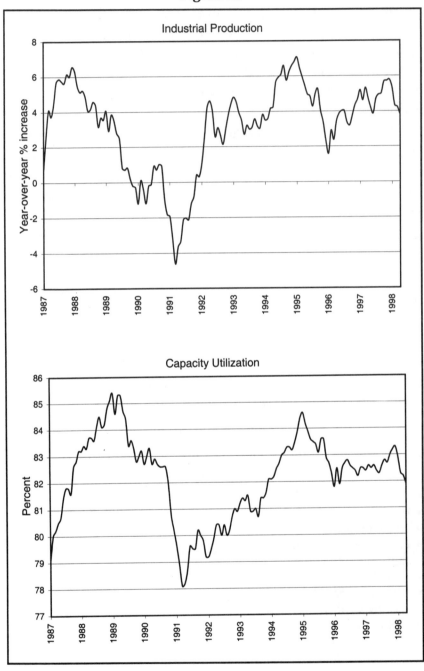

Capacity utilization indicates the extent of usage, or the "employment rate" of the nation's manufacturing capacity. It is an indicator of potential bottlenecks and, consequently, inflationary pressures building up in the manufacturing sector. The reason is that high utilization rates can be inflationary. At the end of the expansion peak in 1989, capacity utilization rate was 85.3%. In late 1994, it stood at 84.5%, which was among the factors that led the Fed to increase the Federal Funds rate through early 1995. An 85% rate is viewed by some economists to be the point when inflationary pressures tend to rise.

If capacity utilization rises, stocks tend to go up and bonds decline. However, if capacity utilization is very high, it becomes a negative for stocks as well. The reason is that the stock market starts anticipating inflationary pressures, which can impact the stock market negatively. However, if capacity increases faster than production, it is expected that inflation will remain in check.

Index of leading economic indicators (LEI)

The LEI, reported monthly by the Conference Board, is a composite of 10 different indicators (Figure 29). It is used to predict future aggregate economic activity. The LEI indicates the direction of the economy 6 to 9 months down the road through the use of a group of leading economic indicators. It is designed to give advance warning of turning points in the business cycle. Three consecutive monthly changes in the LEI in the same direction signal turning points in the economy. The ten components of the LEI, each of which has its own predictive value are:

- average work week
- consumer orders
- equipment orders
- stock prices
- consumer expectations
- new jobless claims
- vendor performance
- building permits
- money supply
- yield spread

The yield curve replaced the material prices and unfilled factory orders components in November 1996, to better measure changes in the business cycle. The yield spread measures the spread between the yield on the 10-year Treasury note and the Federal Funds rate. When this spread narrows, the expectation is that the Federal Reserve will either keep interest rates unchanged or reduce them in the not too distant future.

The LEI peaks and troughs about 6 to 9 months earlier than the economy and consequently is widely used as a forecasting and planning tool. While the LEI is a good indicator of the future direction of the economy, it is not infallible. Since 1952, the LEI predicted 10 recessions out of which only seven occurred. Since the individual components of the LEI are released prior to the monthly release of the overall index, it does not affect the stock market in any significant way.

Figure 29

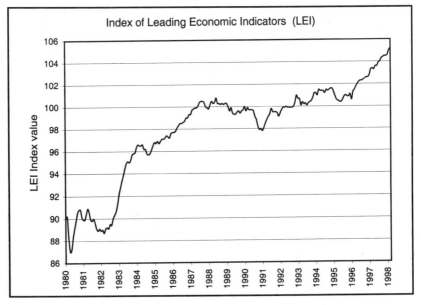

Money supply

Money supply is the total of all money held by the public. It includes total cash and checking account balances at commercial banks held by everyone in the country except the government and other banks. Many investment professionals believe that a correlation exists between the nation's money supply and stock prices. When money supply is expanding at a steady rate, with low inflation, stock prices tend to rise. However, when money supply contracts or inflation increases, stock prices are negatively affected.

The growth and size of money supply are influenced by the reserves at member banks and the discount rate, which are controlled by the Federal Reserve. In the 1970s, money supply grew at an average of 10% annually while inflation averaged 7% per year.[12] As the negative effects of inflation became apparent, a tighter monetary policy was applied by the Federal Reserve. The result was that in the past ten years, money supply increased at an annual rate of only 4%, a period when inflation averaged only 3.5%. With low inflation, the stock market prospered during this period.

CONCLUDING REMARKS

The price appreciation of a stock depends on its profitability, which to a large extent depends on the business cycle and the health of the economy. Therefore, it is very important that an investor continuously monitor the state of the economy, discern trends and identify forces that may affect the profitability of individual stocks and the overall market. For this purpose, the periodic reports issued by the various government departments and agencies are very useful.

The best sources for the timely monitoring of various economics reports and statistics, that are usually released monthly, are *Investor's Business Daily*, *The Wall Street Journal* and the CNBC TV station. *IBD* and the *WSJ* provide analysis and comprehensive comments on the various economic reports the day after they are released. On CNBC, the highlights of these reports are reported as soon as they are released, along with analysis and comments from experts in the field.

---

[12] *Individual Investor,* November, 1996. pg. 34.

CHAPTER 6

UNDERSTANDING STOCK MARKET BEHAVIOR

DETERMINING MARKET TREND

Need to determine market direction

Long-term the stock market rises about 75% of the time, which sets a positive tone for most individual stocks. Similarly, when the market declines in a correction or a bear market, it takes down with it three out of every four stocks. During a declining market, an excellent stock may either hold its own or rise modestly. In a bull market, such a stock will outperform admirably. However, practically no stock can be assured that it will remain unaffected when the market is declining during a correction or a bear market.

In view of this effect on individual stocks, it is important that an investor learns to determine the overall market's direction and trend. An investor needs to understand the state of the market (bear market, bull market, choppy market trading in a narrow range—with or without appreciable volatility) because each one of these factors can affect any stock.

What needs to be monitored

Market behavior and trends can be monitored through the major stock market averages and indexes. These indexes are groupings of individual stocks, ranging from 30 to almost 7,000, which track market and sector behavior. Their primary purpose is to highlight the underlying trend. Investors also use them as a benchmark against which they can measure the performance of their stock or portfolio.

To keep abreast of what is happening in the stock market an investor should monitor and observe, as applicable, the following:

- market averages: DJIA, S&P500, NASDAQ, AMEX, Russell 2000
- trading volume levels
- trend reversals
- market tops and bottoms

Various daily newspapers reporting daily stock prices also provide data on some selected indexes and averages. However, the most comprehensive data on these indexes and averages are reported by *Investor's Business Daily* and *The Wall Street Journal.*

What needs to be done: follow-up action

The level to which an individual stock ultimately rises depends on the company's fundamentals. However, it pays to study the behavior of the market and the forces that impact it such as the inflation trend, economic cycle, investor confidence and alternative investments. Serious investors should master the art of recognizing market extremes and changes in market direction, to realize maximum benefit. For example, when a market peak or a downturn is recognized, an investor can begin to:

- decrease holdings (25 to 50%)
- sell the weakest stocks first

Conversely, when plenty of bargains are available at a market bottom, an investor can start increasing his investment in stocks.

MARKET AVERAGES AND INDEXES

Each of the three big exchanges (NYSE, NASDAQ and AMEX) has a primary index for indicating the collective price movement of their stocks. Figure 30 shows three major averages (NASDAQ Composite, S&P500 and the DJIA) as well as some sector indexes. The most widely quoted and monitored stock market index is the Dow Jones Industrial Average (DJIA), which was created over a 100 years ago.

Figure 30

May 21, 1998

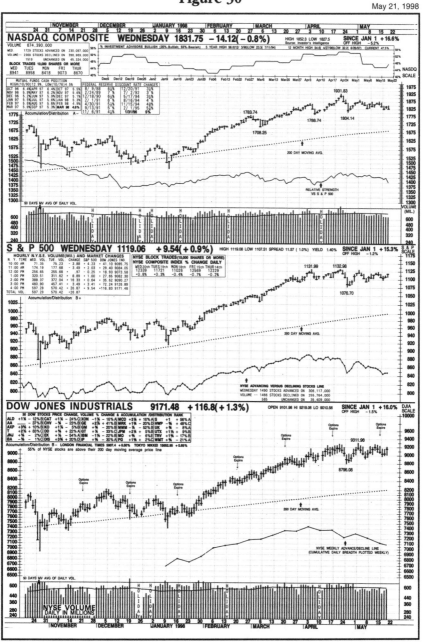

Reproduced with permission of *Investor's Business Daily*

Dow Jones Industrial Average (DJIA)

Many investors incorrectly think that the DJIA, also called the Dow, is the stock market. The DJIA's daily movements are reported in the media to reflect the performance of the market as a whole. This is quite misleading because even though the DJIA includes the largest American companies, it contains only 30 stocks and therefore does not reflect the action of the overwhelming majority of stocks in the stock market.

The DJIA price moves are reported in points, rather than dollars, in terms such as " the Dow went up 20 points." The DJIA moves are calculated in such a way that for each one dollar rise in an individual DJIA stock, the overall DJIA moves up about 2 points. Therefore, if GE's stock rises $2, the DJIA will rise approximately 4 points.

DJIA components

The 30 DJIA stocks are Allied-Signal, Alcoa, American Express, AT&T, Boeing, Caterpillar, Chevron, Coca Cola, Disney, Du Pont, Eastman Kodak, Exxon, General Electric, General Motors, Goodyear, Hewlett-Packard, IBM, International Paper, Johnson & Johnson, McDonald's, Merck, 3M, Morgan JP, Philip Morris, Proctor & Gamble, Sears, Travelers Group, Union Carbide, United Technologies and Wal-Mart.

Indicator of market health

The DJIA is closely monitored due to the belief that the performance of the country's largest companies reflects the state of the overall stock market. However, while this is correct to some extent, it does not adequately reflect the performance of the overall market, which includes thousands of small- and medium-sized companies. Because of this inadequacy, investors use other indexes to get a better overall view of the stock market's health. These indexes give investors a feel for underlying currents that the more widely followed DJIA index may miss.

Other important market indexes

The DJIA is very good at reflecting the market behavior over the long term. However, on a short-term basis, it can often be misleading.

Among the most important indexes tracked by market watchers, to get a comprehensive view of the overall market, are the following indexes:

- NYSE indexes (Composite, Industrial, Transportation, Utilities and Financial)
- S&P500
- NASDAQ (Industrial, Insurance, Banks and Composite)
- Russell 2000
- Wilshire 5000
- *IBD* Mutual Fund index

NYSE Indexes

The NYSE Composite indicates the aggregate market value of all stocks listed on the NYSE. The sum of the individual market values is expressed relative to the market value, 50, of the base period year (1966). The market value is calculated by multiplying the price/share by the number of outstanding shares.

To get a more comprehensive view of the market, one needs to look at the Dow Jones Transportation and Utilities average as well. Each of these averages reflects the performance of a specific market sector. While the industrials are a blend of growth and cyclical stocks which tend to respond to prevailing moods of the market, the transportation average is composed of cyclical stocks that respond to economic and earnings forecasts. The utilities average is driven by interest rates and dividend yields, while the financial average also is interest sensitive.

S&P500 Index

The S&P500 index, which measures the performance of the 500 largest companies in the U.S., gives a broader view of the market than the DJIA. It includes stocks traded on the NYSE, AMEX and in the OTC market. The index includes 400 industrial companies, 40 financial, 40 utility and 20 transportation companies. The S&P500 index was introduced in 1957. It is a benchmark against which mutual funds and portfolios are compared for performance. The median market capitalization of companies in the S&P500 is $4.5 billion, with the largest being $225 billion (GE).

NASDAQ Index

The NASDAQ index primarily consists of smaller, lesser known, companies. However, some big names like Microsoft and Intel are also included in this index. The NASDAQ index is weighted according to market capitalization. Because of their larger market capitalization, bigger companies have a disproportionately large effect on this index. Any big movement in such a stock causes a large change in the NASDAQ index.

Russell 2000 Index

The Russell 2000 index is a good gauge for monitoring the performance of small company stocks. Small stocks are also tracked by a relatively new index, the S&P600.

Wilshire 5000 Index

Another broad-based index is the Wilshire 5000. It tracks about 6,900 stocks and is considered a good measure of the total value of wealth contained in the stock market.

IBD Mutual Fund Index

Investor's Business Daily's mutual fund index, (refer to Figure 15 on page 74), is a useful measure for tracking the overall performance of mutual funds. It is a benchmark against which money managers and many individual investors measure the performance of their portfolios.

Industry and sector indexes

A number of industry and sector indexes, some of which are shown in Table 6, are available to investors for monitoring specific stock sectors and groups. These indexes can be analyzed to check the relative performance of individual sectors. Also, before buying a stock, an investor can determine how the industry to which the company belongs has been performing. The best source for analyzing these indexes is *IBD*, which ranks them according to their performance. Sectors and indexes reported in *IBD* include the high technology sector, junior growth sector, consumer sector, defensive sector and the new issues index.

Table 6: Market Sector Indexes

% change since Jan 1, '97	3 month % change	Index	Index value	Change	% Change
+44.08	+15.57	Dow Jones Transportation	3249.95	+42.16	+1.31
+40.84	+14.06	High-Tech index	416.36	- 2.63	-0.63
+40.64	+10.06	Consumer index	457.11	- 0.34	-0.07
+39.36	+11.90	NYSE Finance	489.40	+5.36	+1.11
+39.06	+15.52	Bank index	668.55	+10.36	+1.57
+38.37	+15.44	U.S. Defense index	353.08	+1.69	+0.48
+35.61	+ 6.22	Insurance index	469.81	+5.07	+1.09
+33.37	+17.08	NASDAQ OTC Composite	1721.91	+6.04	+0.35
+32.32	+15.04	S&P Midcap 400 index	338.18	+2.18	+0.65
+32.28	+12.72	Value Line index	903.00	+4.02	+0.45
+31.36	+ 9.06	Medical/Healthcare	1937.50	+15.94	+0.83
+29.93	+ 7.18	NYSE Composite index	509.70	+4.01	+0.79
+29.39	+10.80	IBD 6000 index	621.40	+4.27	+0.69
+28.91	+16.08	Junior Growth index	426.45	-1.35	-0.32
+26.80	+ 0.28	Senior Growth index	622.52	+2.25	+0.36
+25.53	+19.79	New Issues index	423.24	+2.88	+0.69
+25.24	+13.42	AMEX Composite index	716.80	+6.88	+0.97
+25.15	+ 3.80	Defensive index	971.61	+6.66	+0.69
+ 5.03	+ 5.62	Dow Jones Utility	244.23	+1.42	+0.58
- 6.66	+15.73	Gold index	60.92	-1.22	-1.96

Source: *Investor's Business Daily,* October 7, 1997

The high technology sector index includes Altera Corp., Arrow Electronics, Cognex Corp., Cisco, Electronics Imaging, HP, IBM, Intel, Kent Electronics, Linear Technology, Motorola, Microsoft, Maxim Integ., Oracle, Project Software, Sun Microsystems, Silicon Valley Group, Texas Instruments, Vicor Corp. and Xilinx.

The defensive sector index includes Albertsons, Colgate Palmolive, Campbell Soup, CPC Intl. Inc., Central S W, Con Edison, Edison Intl., Entergy Corp., General Mills, Homestake Mining, Kellogg, Philip Morris, Quaker Oats, PepsiCo, Procter & Gamble, UST Inc., Winn-Dixie and Wrigley Wm.

PRACTICAL APPLICATION OF AVERAGES/INDEXES

Using indexes for comparison

Indexes can be used to compare the market or sector's rise and fall with prior years. For example, on October 12, 1989, the DJIA dropped 190 points. While this was a pretty bad day, it was not as disastrous when compared to the October 19, 1987, drop of 508 points. Another advantage of indexes is that the performance of a portfolio can be compared to an appropriate index or average. If the comparison is unfavorable, it may indicate that the investment strategy or tactic(s) being followed needs to be changed.

The best source of information for tracking various market indexes is *IBD*. Besides comprehensive data, it also provides charts for individual stocks and selected stock sectors for key sectors of the U.S. economy. These include the high-tech, junior growth, consumer and defensive sectors. These price charts also include RS lines that compare the performance of these sectors against the overall market represented by the S&P500.

Which average/index to use

With so many averages and indexes to choose from, one needs to be careful in selecting the right one. An investor should pick the correct index for comparing its performance against his own stocks, or the results will be misleading. For example, the performance of a small growth company should not be compared to the DJIA or the S&P500. Similarly, if an investor wants to monitor the overall market, he should not focus only on the DJIA. By doing so, he will miss major movements in the overall stock market. Instead, he should also monitor broader measures like the S&P500 and the NASDAQ.

In 1996, for example, if an investor had monitored only the DJIA, he would have missed the significant under-performance of the small cap stocks. They had a very poor year while the DJIA was making new highs. Again, the NASDAQ Composite fell by more than 10% in 1992,

1994 and 1996, while the DJIA did not have a correction of any major significance until July 1996, when it declined 7.47%.

It should be realized that even if different sectors are moving in the same direction, the magnitude of their moves can be significantly different. In early 1997, the Russell 2000, a small cap benchmark, lagged the S&P500 appreciably. Starting in July, it exploded on positive earnings news while the S&P500 and many blue chip stocks lagged. Therefore, one should not monitor only one or two sectors or indexes and assume that they represent the overall behavior of the stock market.

BULL AND BEAR MARKETS

Bull and bear market characteristics

The stock market is a very dynamic place characterized by perpetual price movements. The direction of these movements can be up, down or sideways. Like the economy, the stock market climbs steadily upward in its characteristic jagged manner for a few years. This period is known as a "bull market." This is followed by a period in which the market moves steadily downward, interspersed with small rallies, for an extended period. This period, typically less than a year, is known as a "bear market."

The state of the stock market, bull or bear, directly impacts the profitability of companies. Therefore, market analysts are continuously engaged in an exercise of trying to forecast the market's future direction. During bull markets, investors try to be fully invested. During bear markets, they reduce exposure to stocks.

Defining bull and bear markets

Market players use different definitions for bull and bear markets. A bull market is commonly defined as a market in which there is a 20%, or greater, rise in stock prices. Another defines a bull market being characterized by a 30% price rise. In this century, there have been 20 bull markets with an average duration of 3.1 years. The current bull market run started in October 1990, when the DJIA stood at 2,365.

A bear market is defined as one in which the stock market declines 20%.

Some of the recent market lows were made in 1990, 1982, 1978, 1974, 1970, 1966 and 1962. A market low also occurred in 1987, which missed the pattern by one year. In 1990, the NASDAQ fell 31%, while it declined 13.7% in 1994. In 1996, it declined 16.5% on an end-of-day basis.

Bull and bear cycle

When the stock market undergoes a significant price decline, it generates a climate of fear. When a market bottom is reached, extreme pessimism reigns. At that time, a bull market starts. As price gains are made, fear starts to recede. As further gains are made, caution sets in. However, as significant price appreciation takes place with the bull market continuing, investors tend to forget the pessimistic bear market days. At that time investor attitude can be described as confident and euphoric.

By the time a top is reached, most investors remain convinced that the market will keep going up indefinitely. At that point, the bear market starts. As the market starts declining, the same emotions characterize the market but in the reverse direction—confidence, caution and fear. Finally, when the bottom is reached, the feeling is widespread that prices will continue to decline even further. At that time, the next bull market is ready to start.

Bull and bear statistics

If we consider an *IBD* survey in which a bull market was defined as any upward move greater than 22% which lasted longer than one year, there have been 25 bull markets in this century. Their average duration was two years and three months, with an average gain of 84.4% in each. Of these 25 bull markets, only three were less than 30%, while seven bull markets soared more than 100%.

IBD's survey also reported that there have been 26 bear markets during this century. The average bear market lasted 17 months with an average drop of 30.8%. The market declined more than 40% eight times, including 1968, 1973 and 1987. The worst bear market, which followed the market collapse of October 1929, lasted 35 months. During that debacle, the DJIA declined to 40 from a peak of 390. In 1973–74, the DJIA dropped 45%, with many high-flying stocks plunging 70 to 80%.

Table 7, reported by the *WSJ*, shows the frequency and severity of stock market declines in this century.[13] Compared to the *IBD* survey, which indicated 26 bear markets, Table 7 shows that 29 bear markets took place this century. These differences can be attributed to different criteria being used for defining a bear market. Table 8 lists the major bull markets of this century, along with their duration in days and their percentage gains. The longest bull market has been the current bull market, which started in October 1990 and is still going strong after a phenomenal 361% gain (as of February 1998).

Table 7: Stock market declines since 1900

	Routine declines (5% or more)	Moderate correction (10% or more)	Severe correction (15% or more)	Bear market (20% or more)
# of times since 1900	318	106	50	29
Frequency	about 3 times/year	about once/year	about once every 2 years	about every 3 years
Last occurrence	July 1996	August 1990	August 1990	October 1990
Average loss before decline ends	11%	19%	27%	35%
Average length	40 days	109 days	217 days	364 days

Source: *Ned Davis Research Inc.* (*WSJ* - July 19, 1996)
Note: This table does not include statistics for the corrections that occurred in 1997.

The following table lists the major prolonged bull markets of this century.

Table 8: Top bull markets

Period	% gain by DJIA	Duration in days
10/11/1990–	234	2,698[1]
6/13/1949–4/6/1956	222	2,489
10/27/1923–9/3/1929	344	2,138
4/28/1942–5/29/1946	128	1,492
7/24/1984–8/25/1987	150	1,127
10/19/1987–7/16/1989	72	1,001
7/26/1934–3/10/1937	127	958

[13] *The Wall Street Journal*, July 19, 1996, pg. C1.

Table 8: Top bull markets (cont'd.)

Period	% gain by DJIA	Duration in days
10/22/57–1/5/60	63	805
11/09/03–1/19/06	144	802
10/07/66–12/03/68	32	788

[1]duration till February 28, 1998, when the bull market was still in progress

Source: *Ned Davis Research Inc. (IBD* - January 20, 1998)

UNDERSTANDING BULL MARKETS

Birth of a bull market

Great bull markets

Many bull markets start during recessions. In fact, one of the greatest bull markets started during the Great Depression in July 1932. In just 20 months, it rocketed the DJIA from 40 to 110, a gain of 175%. Another roaring bull market, which realized a gain of 160%, took place during the 1920s before the October 1929 crash. The current bull market, one of the greatest ever, started in 1990 with the DJIA at 2,365. By February 1998, it had propelled the DJIA over the 8,500 level.

What starts a bull market

The explanation for a bull market starting in a recession is fairly simple. When the economy contracts, the Federal Reserve attempts to stimulate it by reducing interest rates. This has a very powerful effect on the market as it eases credit and improves liquidity in the system. This helps corporations and businesses, whose borrowing costs decrease, which helps their bottom line—net profits. With the prospects for corporate profits improving, investors start bidding up stock prices, which start moving up sharply.

Federal Reserve's tools

Among the two most powerful tools that the Federal Reserve uses to stimulate the economy and sow the seeds of a bull market are the discount rate and bank reserve requirements. Reducing either one strongly affects the market. This happened during 1990–1991, when the economy was in a recession and a bear market had set in. The discount rate was reduced to $3\frac{1}{2}$% by December 1991, from a $6\frac{1}{2}$% level in December 1990, in a series of cuts that powered the bull market.

End of bull markets

When the reasons for high valuations no longer remain intact, bull markets end. Typically, the stock market starts having trouble when recession worries disappear and get replaced by concern about inflation. When short-term interest rates start rising, stocks start getting competition for investment dollars and they start to be negatively impacted.

Bull market phases

Typically, bull markets can be divided into two phases (Figure 31). The first phase begins when the economy is in a recession and corporate profits are falling. As interest rates decline and liquidity is increased, stocks start rebounding in anticipation of improved corporate profits. In this initial bull market phase, when the economic recovery and expansion has just begun, stocks show the largest price appreciation.

During the second phase, when the economy is in full gear, expanding corporate profits drive the price appreciation of stocks, even though interest rates either remain steady or start moving up. Figure 31, based on an analysis of 11 bull markets since 1953, indicates that the following gains were realized for the S&P500 in the two bull market phases:[14]

- Phase I: prices rose an average of 28.2% while profits fell 1.1%
- Phase II: prices rose an average of 31.1% while profits rose 26.2%

The following are points to keep in mind when analyzing bull markets:

- a typical bull market lasts more than two years, with gains exceeding 80%
- in a bull market, buy and hold until signs appear that the bull market is nearing its end

---

[14] *The Argus Update*, January 1993.

Figure 31

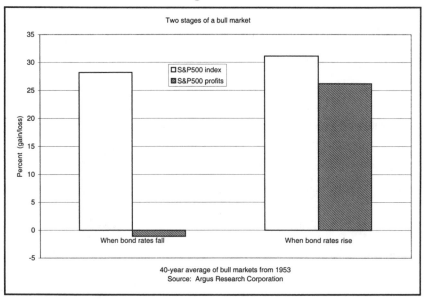

Two stages of a bull market

40-year average of bull markets from 1953
Source: Argus Research Corporation

Riding the bull market

To get the maximum benefit from a bull market, an investor should have the nerve and courage to buy stocks when the economic picture looks very bleak. This occurs during the latter part of a recession, when gloom and doom is pervasive. An investor should be fully invested when a bull market starts, which is its strongest phase and generates huge gains for those who are invested at that time. For example, after bottoming in October 1990, the DJIA climbed 650 points to 3,000, a gain of 28%, in only 5 months.

Stocks should not be bought indiscriminately during the early stage of a bull market. Instead, one should try to identify its potential leaders— those who will be its big winners. One should try to identify and buy leaders because they are the first ones to rise when the bull market makes its powerful move, and the first ones to make new price highs.

Recognizing bullish signs
• favorable interest rates; lower interest rate trend
• low inflation

- moderate economic growth coupled with low inflation and a low, or falling, discount rate
- fiscal responsibility
- excessive pessimism
- market moving to new highs without widespread bullishness (such a market contains a lot of power)
- high level of mutual fund cash
- number of stocks on the NYSE making new lows is very small
- NYSE A/D line starts improving—starts trending upwards
- decreasing flow of new stock issues (new issues can adversely affect the market's supply/demand balance)
- more buyers than sellers
- accumulation taking place (as indicated by high volume on up days and low volume on down days)

UNDERSTANDING BEAR MARKETS

Birth of a bear market

A bear market is every investor's nightmare. Many bear markets begin when the economy is steaming ahead and catches many investors by surprise. When it does arrive, a bear market creates panic and pessimism. However, for those who are able to forecast the onset of a bear market and lighten stock investments on time, it presents a great opportunity. Such investors can pick up bargains and reap significant profits.

Ignoring bear market signs

There are many signs of a bear market. However, many investors ignore them. These signs typically are at market tops, when there is a tendency to ignore bad news and warning signs. Investors start believing that the market will continue to go up and up. A very good example is what happened in 1987 when, between January and August, the DJIA rose an astounding 40% while the S&P500 rose 30%. During this period, bond yields rose from 7.5% to 9%, which by any standard were very high. By October, when the crash occurred, bond yields had risen to 10%. In 1987, the DJIA crashed because while stocks rose to lofty levels, the Federal Reserve tightened money supply and interest rates rose. In just two months of the 1987 bear market, the DJIA fell 41%.

Every investor fears a repeat of the 1929 and 1987 crashes. Any such decline can wipe away all profits made even in the best bull market. Therefore, investors need to recognize bear market characteristics and remain prepared for such events. This is not too difficult as bear markets do not arrive overnight. When signs point to a market top and an impending bear market, it is advisable to take appropriate action such as reducing exposure to stocks.

Recognizing bearish signs
- similarities with prior market rises: both 1987 and 1929 markets had parabolic price rises
- rising long-term interest rates plus an economic recession: this is one of the worst case scenarios
- markets rising when interest rates are rising
- excessive economic growth coupled with rising inflation and a rising discount rate
- more corporate earnings reports coming in below expectations
- overvalued P/E multiples which, historically, have traded in the 12–15 times earnings range; market rises too much from normal "valuation" levels such as the P/E of the S&P500 rising above 20
- excessive enthusiasm and euphoria, especially by professionals, occurs near the end of a bull market and the start of a bear market
- individual investors stop shorting since they turn bullish
- excessive speculation; signs include:
  - increased trading volume on the NASDAQ versus the NYSE
  - more new issues and secondary offerings (from existing public companies) which can adversely affect the market's supply/demand balance
  - high flying IPOs (in price and volume)
  - increasing number of stock splits
  - low quality and low-priced stocks start to appreciate in price
- investors seek shelter in blue chips (either DJIA stocks or NASDAQ blue chips such as Microsoft and Intel)
- leadership warning signs:
  - market leadership changes to speculative issues
  - new leadership emerges from the defensive group, which performs well
  - leading stocks falter: distribution in the bull market leaders
  - original bull market leaders undergo distribution for days, or even weeks, prior to the market break

- NYSE A/D line deteriorates; starts trending lower
- greater number of new lows versus new highs; the number of stocks on the NYSE making new lows is 40 or more
- advancing market unable to make further progress while volume is heavy (called churning)
- distribution as indicated by high volume on down days and low volume on up days
- rallies fail and are on lighter volume

UNDERSTANDING CORRECTIONS

Correction characteristics

An individual stock or the stock market does not rise in an uninterrupted manner when it is in an uptrend or a bull market. While the overall upward trendline is jagged, which indicates minor price pullbacks along the rising path, it is not unusual for a correction to occur during the overall upward movement (Figure 32). A correction is a price drop during a bull market whose magnitude is typically only a few percent. However, it can be as high as 10%.

Market declines and corrections tend to come unexpectedly, just when most investors least expect them. When investors decide they can no longer afford to hold cash and miss any more gains in a rising market, the market surprises them with a correction.

During the life of a bull market, there can be many minor corrections of 5% to 8%. In some cases, there can be an intermediate-term correction of 15%. However, after every correction, the market reverses direction and resumes its rise.

Reasons for corrections

There are a number of reasons for corrections including:

- asset allocation by investors (from stocks to bonds and/or cash)
- increasing interest rates
- higher than normal stock valuations
- change in the state of the economy and business cycle
- stock group rotation
- external factors (news, political events, etc.)

Figure 32

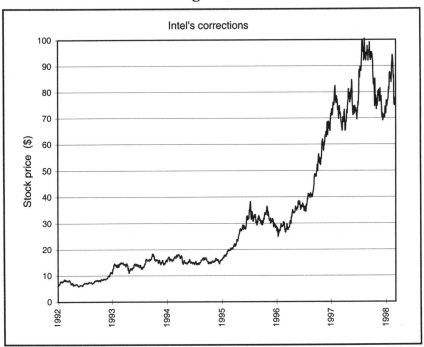

Intel's corrections

Examples of corrections

The most recent market correction occurred in January 1998, when the DJIA declined 8.4% (Figure 10) while the NASDAQ declined 8.55% (Figure 33). In 1997, there were three corrections in April, August and October. In April 1997, the DJIA declined 10.7%, while the NASDAQ lost 14.2%. From August to September, the DJIA lost 9.4%. This decline was followed by a rally that propelled the DJIA 8.76% higher by October 7 However, this was followed by another correction in October and the DJIA lost 12.8% in just three weeks.

While corrections occurred periodically between July 1996 and January 1998, there had been a dearth of corrections between 1990 and 1996. In a sharp correction in July 1996, the NASDAQ lost 16.5% of its value on an end-of-the-day basis, while the DJIA lost 7.47%. On an intraday basis, the DJIA declined 10.59%. When it finally underwent the July 1996 correction, the DJIA had gone more than 5 years without a 10%

Figure 33

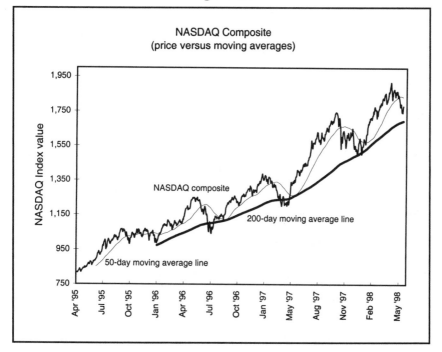

correction. The previous longest stretch was 3 ½ years. However, while the DJIA did not correct during this very long period, individual stocks as well as many sectors (like technology) suffered significant corrections. Some groups were decimated and underwent a bear market, rather than a correction. During this period, the NASDAQ suffered only one correction that caused it to decline 13.7% in 1994.

While corrections and price declines are typically spread out over weeks or months, they can also occur in a shorter period. For example, on November 15, 1991, the DJIA dropped 120 points, a 3.92% fall. On March 8, 1996, the DJIA dropped 171 points, equivalent to a 3% decline, while the NASDAQ plunged 2.7%. Again, on December 18, 1995, the DJIA dropped 101 points to 5,075—a 2% decline.

Corrections: a healthy phenomenon

A correction should be viewed as a healthy phenomenon that allows the market to get on solid footing and reduce investor expectations. A price correction of several percentage points helps put a damper on excessive speculation, which can increase stock prices beyond reasonable valuation levels, especially during a quickly rising market.

Even the best individual stocks suffer corrections. Typically, such stocks rebound and rise to new highs. For example, Intel declined 33% from July 1995 to January 1996 (Figure 32). However, it rebounded and more than tripled to 165 between March 1996 and January 1997. In 1994, it declined 24% while in 1993 it suffered two corrections: a 26% decline (between March and April 1993) followed by a 23% decline (from September through November 1993). Another outstanding stock of the decade, Cisco, has also suffered periodic declines as shown in Figure 34.

Timing to avoid corrections

Long-term investors should not try to time the market in order to avoid a market correction. By the time most investors realize that a correction is under way, it is often too late to bail out. Also, if one exits the market, it is difficult to know when exactly to move in. By moving in and out of the market, one increases the risk of missing the short powerful moves characterizing the market, which are very difficult to predict. For example, in late 1994, many leading market watchers predicted a mediocre, or even worse, market performance in 1995. By sitting on the sidelines, they missed the extremely powerful move that the market made in 1995. Again, in 1997, the DJIA rose 29% between April and July. In just one month, between April 11 and May 11, the DJIA gained 883 points—a gain of 13.8%. Investors who bailed out due to the April correction missed a very powerful market move.

What a long-term investor should do is to look beyond these corrections and avoid being preoccupied with short-term uncertainties. There is no doubt that some years will be good and some mediocre or worse. However, using a horizon of five years or more, and by remaining invested using the buy and hold strategy, investors can expect to post fairly healthy gains in the long run.

Figure 34

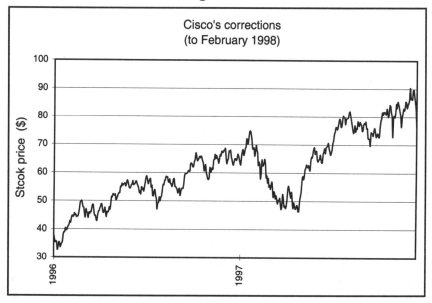

Cisco's corrections
(to February 1998)

Sector rotation

<u>Rolling correction phenomenon</u>

Sometimes, corrections taking place in certain market sectors or groups can be masked by the major market indexes, which may be trading normally within a narrow range or even rising. This phenomenon of rolling corrections when only a group or sector corrects, rather than the entire market, is called sector rotation.

In 1994, the market averages barely moved. Yet, this was a rotating bear market. The market experienced a rolling sector by sector correction. The major averages hid extensive damage among individual stocks. Also, since earnings during this period increased by 30%, the effect was that P/E ratios decreased because prices remained steady. This drastic reduction in multiples was, in effect, a silent correction.

<u>Reason for sector rotation</u>

In the 1990s, sector rotation has been quite pronounced. The reason is that investors have been reluctant to pull out of stocks completely. The explanation for this is their realization that stocks are the best investment choice coupled with their fear of missing major market moves. However, at the slightest sign of reduced expectations, or trouble with a group, they have had no hesitation in moving on to more attractive sectors.

In the past three years or so, approximately every six months or so, investors have been stampeding with a herd mentality into one or more stock groups. After bidding up their prices to high valuation levels, they stampede off to greener pastures. This has typically occurred when the sector/industry fell out of favor with institutional investors, who account for almost 75% of all trading activity.

Recent sector rotations

One of the most severe sector corrections occurred during the latter part of 1995. While the DJIA was rising 10.6% from 4,630 to 5,182, from August to December, high technology stocks were being decimated. During this period, the high-technology index declined 7.8% from 229 to 211. Due to worries caused by the peaking of technology companies' earnings, slowing computer sales and fears of a slowing economy, investors fled to defensive stocks. The largest U.S. mutual fund, Fidelity Magellan, reduced its technology stock holdings from 43% in October to 24.5% by November 1995. To the casual observer, no correction was taking place. However, the "stealth" correction was camouflaged by the sector rotational action of the market, which was not reflected in the DJIA.

The following are some more examples of sector corrections in the past few years:
- 1994 to early 1996: retail apparel sector lost 26%
- September 1993: utilities lost 25% in one year
- early 1992 to the end of 1994: biotech sector lost half its value
- IBD's chip (semiconductor) index lost 50% in the 10-month period starting in September 1995[15]

Opportunities in the ruins

Two central emotions drive the stock market: greed and fear. During corrections and bear markets, fear is pervasive, but these are also times

---

[15] Investor's Business Daily, February 7, 1997.

of opportunity for investors who will be severely tested. Savvy investors who are able to understand the stock market cycles can pick up bargains while others are dumping stocks. And during market tops, such investors can sell while others are still buying.

During corrections, try to pick the potential leaders of the next upside move. Typically, these leaders make the most significant moves when the market rebounds. Besides conventional methods for picking winning stocks and leaders (based on fundamentals), investors should focus on stocks with an EPS rank over 90. These stocks have a greater probability of outperforming when the upside move finally takes place.

Care should be taken in picking up stocks that have fallen sharply during a correction. Stocks that fall sharply during a bull market correction reveal their inherent weakness. Many investors mistakenly believe that if a stock falls more than others, it will rebound more, which usually does not happen.

RECOGNIZING A MARKET TOP OR BOTTOM

Importance of recognizing a top or bottom

It is very important for investors to learn how to select stocks and, after buying, monitor their performance. They should also develop the ability to read the status of the overall market. This is important because the health and performance of the market influences the performance of individual stocks in the short term. It is well known that when the market is in trouble, due to a bear market or correction, about 75% of stocks drop in price. At such times, even good stocks suffer declines. Therefore, an investor should be able to recognize a market top, or bottom, which can lead to making more profitable decisions in one of two ways: by delaying buying to a more favorable time or by selling before investors start dumping en masse.

The following sections enumerate signs associated with market tops and bottoms. However, it needs to be recognized that some conventional signs of a market top have had a poor forecasting record in recent years.

Market top signs

In the 1990s, a period characterized by low interest rates, a continuous flood of cash has poured into mutual funds. An important factor causing this phenomenon has been a shift in the attitude of the population at large, which has made stocks the investment vehicle of choice. They realize that in the current low inflation and low interest rate environment, stocks can provide reasonable and higher returns, compared to money market funds, CDs and bonds. So while, by many conventional criteria, this attitude would have indicated speculation and a market top in the past, the paradigm has shifted. This attitude shift has been a factor in the market moving a lot higher this decade. Those who recognized this shift and invested in the stock market have participated in the great bull market, which started in 1990.

In general, the following signs can be recognized as indicators of a market top:

- high valuation levels
- dividend yield on the DJIA and S&P500 falling below 3% (this has been a poor indicator in recent years)
- widespread bullishness:
  - belief that the present scenario is different and history will not repeat this time
  - making heroes of money managers
  - trumpeting enormous gains to be made in the stock market (by the media)
- rising interest rates:
  - especially short-term rates (as indicated by the discount rate)
  - long-term interest rates (as indicated by the 30-year Treasury bond)
- stocks no longer react positively to strong earnings
- NASDAQ volume expands significantly
- DJIA:
  - rallies but on contracting volume
  - stalls but trading remains heavy
  - declines on expanding volume
- excessive speculation, especially among low-priced stocks
- distribution and topping takes place among the market leaders
- breakdown of a large number of secondary stocks, even as the DJIA and S&P500 make new highs

- market unable to move higher despite increasing volume; typically, the total market volume will increase over the previous day's high volume with little or no upward progress
- downward trending A/D line

Market bottom signs

When the market declines either in a correction or a bear market, an investor should be able to recognize the "bottom." This is the level where all sellers have dumped their shares and the market finds support. It is at this level that the market stabilizes before starting its rebound. This first phase of the rebound is the most profitable and, therefore, it pays to be able to recognize a market bottom. Signs of a bottom include:

- intense selling on heavy volume
- successive lows on decreasing volume
- increase in market price, with increasing heavy volume on successive days of a rally
- pessimism is extreme; bearish numbers are very high and bullish numbers are low

FORECASTING MARKET DIRECTION

Forecasting record

The track record of most money managers, newsletter writers and Wall Street market strategists in forecasting market gains has been fairly mediocre. A study of the market's performance in 1995 will show how far off they can be. At the end of 1994, a year when the bond market had a miserable performance, the DJIA closed at 3,834. At the start of 1995, the bulls had an optimistic DJIA target of 4,300 for the year, with a high forecast in the 4,500 range. The bears were forecasting that the DJIA could retest the April 1994 low, of 3,539, and perhaps drop even further.

The actual result was quite off the mark. The DJIA gained 33.5% and rose to 5,117. What went wrong? After the battering the bonds received in 1994, most market analysts did not believe that interest rates would decrease. Therefore, they based their valuation forecasts on higher interest rates. Other reasons put forward by the various strategists, for expecting a mediocre performance, were the following:

- divergence of stocks and bonds
- poor market internals
- mutual fund speculation
- political gridlock
- overvalued stocks
- low dividend yield

However, contrary to expectations and forecasts, interest rates decreased in 1995, profit growth of companies was sustained and inflation remained in control. Since the basic assumptions were wrong, the forecasts were inaccurate.

In 1995, according to *Timer's Digest*, 36 market timers made forecasts on where the DJIA was headed by the end of 1996. Their forecasts ranged from 3,550 to 6,600. In 1996, the DJIA actually closed the year at 6,448 after reaching an intraday high of 6,606 in November. However, only 7 timers had predicted a DJIA of 6,000 or greater. Only two had forecast a DJIA greater than or equal to 6,200. However, only one predicted a DJIA of 6,600. This should be an eye opener for those who give too much credit to the forecasting ability of professionals.

The market sentiment index, which measures the bullishness and bearishness of market newsletter writers, is another example of how incorrectly these professionals read the market. When they are bullish, the market turns south and vice versa. Therefore, investors should not be overly swayed by their opinions and forecasts, which are often shown to be quite inaccurate.

Forecasts can change

Forecasts are based on many assumptions. Over time, as more economic and market data becomes available, they are refined and changed. Usually, this happens gradually because the economy and the market rarely change overnight. Typically, the magnitude of the forecast changes is minor. However, at times, these changes can be drastic. This happened in 1994 when the Federal Reserve started increasing interest rates after years of easing and an accommodative policy. As a result of the change in the interest rate trend, the basis for valuations and market forecasts changed immediately. Consequently, new forecasts had to be made.

Overall, market strategists have a mixed forecasting record at best. Adding to the confusion caused by inaccurate forecasts are the sudden and drastic changes in forecasts that analysts sometimes make. Take the case of the Garzarelli forecast. In July 1996, she forecasted that the DJIA would rise to 6,400. Two days later, she reversed her forecast and predicted that both the DJIA and the S&P500 would fall 15 to 25% from their highs. For the NASDAQ, she predicted a fall of 35%. The reason for her changed forecast was a bearish change in one of the indicators that she tracked, which indicated that cash flow was not keeping up with reported earnings. The actual market performance was quite different. The DJIA managed a 6,547 closing high for the year, which was reached on November 25, 1996. For the year, the DJIA gained 26%.

Groups to watch for market direction

Investors use a wide range of indicators and groups to forecast market direction. Among those monitored for this purpose include the NYSE A/D line, utilities index and the brokerage index. The A/D line and the brokerage index top out six months before the overall market. The utilities have also led the market in both directions. For example, in 1987, the utilities plunged just prior to, and with, the 1987 crash. It also led the market by six months in 1990, when the market underwent a bear market.

A group to watch for market direction is the technology sector. This sector is a good indicator for the health of the market. Stocks in this group are relatively volatile and have a high beta. Therefore, when the technology sector is performing well, it means that institutions are investing in this sector. Hence, it indicates that they have confidence in a relatively risky sector, which sets a positive tone for the market. Therefore, an investor should closely watch this sector, even if his investments are in other sectors.

SEASONAL FACTORS

A number of seasonal factors have a bearing on the behavior of the stock market and industry groups. For example, it is well known that semiconductor companies have a slow summer season. Typically, just before the start of summer, these stocks get dumped somewhat indiscriminately. By fall, they are back in favor. Therefore, if a purchase decision is reached in spring, a knowledgeable investor tends to put off a planned purchase of a semiconductor stock to a more favorable time (a few months later). On the flip side, many investors holding semiconductor stocks tend to lighten their holdings at the start of the summer season.

January effect

Stock prices have been observed to surge in January. In particular, small stocks have shown a tendency to outperform large cap stocks during this period. This phenomenon is known as the "January effect." Historically, small cap stocks have outperformed the large cap stocks by 5.5% during January.[16] Since 1953, the S&P has beaten small cap stocks in January only five times.[17]

From 1980–1997, January has been the best performing month for the DJIA. During this period, it has shown an average monthly gain of 2.78%. Even for a longer period, from 1950 through 1997, January has been the best month with an average monthly gain of 1.74%.

The seeds for the January effect are sown in the previous months. At year end, usually from October through December, investors sell their poorly performing stocks for taking a tax loss. Institutional investors, such as mutual funds, also sell their laggards in order to make their portfolios appear better. Additionally, there is large money inflow into IRAs and company retirement plans. Therefore, when the cash generated from these sources and year-end bonuses pours into the stock market, at the beginning of the year, it boosts stock prices. In recent years, this "effect" has been missing. In the past three years, from 1996–1998, the January effect was noticeably absent.

[16] *Investor's Business Daily,* January 14, 1998.
[17] *Investor's Business Daily,* November 17, 1997.

October jitters

As October gets closer, investors start getting nervous for good reason. For the DJIA, it has been the most frightening month due to the great stock market crashes of October 1929 and October 1987. Six of the twelve largest daily percentage drops in the DJIA, including the three largest, have occurred in October. The average October decline for the DJIA has been 0.15% since 1980. However, if the 1987 October plunge is ignored, the DJIA actually gained an average of 1.21% for this period. For the 1950–1997 period, the DJIA lost 0.05% during October. However, if the 1987 decline is ignored, the DJIA shows an average gain of 1.21% for October.

Contrary to common wisdom, September has been the worst month for the DJIA's average performance since 1950, with an average decline of 0.56%. Since 1980, the average monthly decline in September has been 0.55%. Also, since 1980, the DJIA has been up only six times in September.

An explanation for the market's volatility during September and October is the decrease in expectations among investors. At the beginning of the year, investors are optimistic about earnings and performance. However, by September, these expectations get tempered as realization sets in that only a few months remain for earnings forecasts to be met. This causes analysts to accelerate reductions in earnings estimates in September, just before the companies start reporting their third quarter results. This causes share prices to start declining.

Quarter end fluctuations

At the end of each quarter, the market sees above average volatility due to "window dressing" by portfolio managers. This is the time when fund managers are required to file their quarterly reports, which have to list the stocks that the fund is holding. To look good, fund managers sell their poorly performing stocks and "dress up" their portfolio with stocks that have outperformed recently and have had good press coverage. The utility of this technique is questionable because publicity gain does not generate any profits for the fund.

Monthly performance

Since 1950, the best month for the DJIA has been January, with an average gain of 1.74%. December has been the second best month, with an average gain of 1.73%. For a shorter period, from 1980 through 1997, January is also the best month with an average gain of 2.78%. The second best month is November, when the DJIA gained an average of 2.12%. Since 1980, the DJIA has declined only six times during December and five times in September. The good performance in December and January is attributed to large money inflows into mutual funds as well as pension and profit sharing plans.

The average gain by the DJIA from June through October during the 1980–1997 period has been 0.44%. During the November to May period, the average monthly gain has been 1.64%. Looking at a longer period, from 1950–1997, the results are similar. From June through October, the average monthly gain was 0.18%, while for the November through May period, the gain was 1.11%.

For some investors, this has been a very compelling argument for moving in and out of the market. However, rather than focus on probabilities, investors should be driven more by individual stock picking and valuations, rather than the expected performance of market averages in the next 6 to 12 months.

Table 9: Average monthly gain/loss for the DJIA

	Jan	Feb	Mar	Apr	May	Jun	Jul	Aug	Sep	Oct	Nov	Dec
1980–97	+2.78	+1.17	+0.21	+1.78	+1.84	+0.69	+1.72	+0.48	-0.55	-0.15	+2.12	+1.57
1950–97	+1.74	+0.24	+0.85	+1.70	+0.07	-0.01	+1.34	+0.18	-0.56	-0.05	+1.48	+1.73

Other seasonal factors

Market gains or losses in any given year are to some extent dependent on the market's performance in the previous year. Usually, a very good year will be followed by a year in which gains are lower. Some coincidental factors have also been observed. For example, it has been observed that presidential election years have been winning years for stocks. Other observations include:

- in the past 25 presidential election years this century, 20 years ended with gains
- in the last 10 presidential elections since 1960, there was only one down year for the market
- since 1832, stocks have fallen in the first year of every reelected president's 2nd term with one exception (Reagan)

How to play the seasonal observations

While an investor should be aware of seasonal factors, buy or sell decisions should not be based primarily or solely on seasonal factors. While it would be a mistake to ignore seasonal factors, they should not be given undue importance. Investors should be knowledgeable about the seasonal effects on stocks in order to better understand price movements caused by this phenomenon. However, to make informed investing decisions, other criteria for evaluating, selecting and selling stocks should be used. In general, to take advantage of seasonal effects, the following two guidelines can be used:

- planned stock purchases should be done near the beginning of the favorable seasonal period
- planned sales should be deferred till the end of the favorable period

MARKET VOLATILITY AND DROPS

Market volatility

Volatility is measured as the spread between the highest highs and the lowest lows on the S&P500. According to the Investment Research Institute, the average volatility has been 33% during the 28-year period starting in 1970.[18] The long-term volatility chart is shown in Figure 35, while the volatility numbers since 1990 are shown below:

Year	S&P500 volatility
1990	35%
1991	29%
1992	24%
1993	17%

[18] *Investor's Business Daily,* January 29, 1998.

Year	S&P500 volatility (cont'd.)
1994	20%
1995	17%
1996	26%
1997	33%

For the DJIA, the average annual volatility has been approximately 28% in the past two decades. In 1992, it was only 7.5%, the lowest in a century.

After-effects of a low volatility period

Investors should be aware that lack of volatility, characterized by flat behavior, indicates the potential for an explosive price movement. A drop in volatility usually follows an explosive year for the market. A low volatility year is typically, about 85% of the time, followed by a high volatility year. The movement can either be upward or downward. However, the initial move out of the trading range can often be misleading. When the market roars out of a narrow trading range, it can be a short-term move prior to a longer-term move in the opposite direction. For example, on October 5, 1992, the market initially dropped 100 points, recovered 82 points before finally closing 22 points down. This move was followed by a significant S&P gain of 9% in the next two months.

Guidelines for analyzing volatility

- the market may be flat and hide high volatility among individual issues; big down moves can cancel big up moves
- some groups may be canceling the effect of other groups (technology sector rising with real estate declining)
- NASDAQ volatility can be twice that of the S&P500 in a typical year.
- low volatility may reflect the use of derivative products, options and futures, for hedging

Daily volatility

The market periodically experiences extremely volatile days (Figure 36). For example, October 28, 1997, has been the market's worst session when it dropped 554 points, equivalent to a 7.2% drop. A day later, it recovered 337 points, a gain of 4.7%, on a volume of 1.2 billion shares. The NASDAQ gained 4.4% on a volume of 1.38 billion shares.

Figure 35

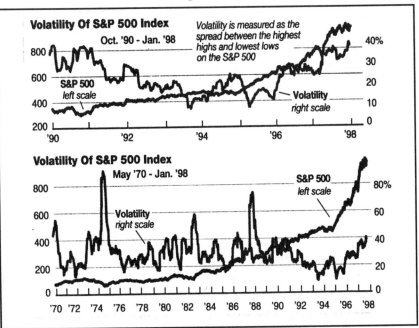

Source: Investment Research Institute and *IBD* (January 29, 1998)
Reproduced with permission of *Investor's Business Daily*

Daily gyrations, when the market moves up and down rather than in just one direction, are routine. For example, on March 8, 1996, the DJIA dropped 171 points. It started off dropping 120 points in the first 20 minutes of trading. After the initial selling, the DJIA rallied to cut the loss to 64 points within 90 minutes of trading. It then traded sideways for three hours when it collapsed further. At its worst point, it was down 217 points. In terms of the size of price drop, the largest declines of the DJIA are shown in Table 10.

In the past couple of years, 100+ point gains/declines have become quite frequent. Sometimes volatility can extend for many days in a row. For example, at the end of August 1997, the DJIA rose or fell at least 1% on seven of ten consecutive trading days.[19]

---

[19] *Time*, September 22, 1997.

Figure 36

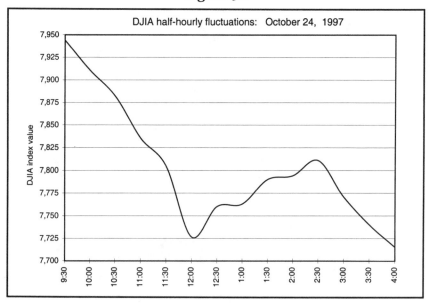

DJIA half-hourly fluctuations: October 24, 1997

Table 10: Largest declines for the DJIA

Largest point drops			Largest percentage drops		
October 27, 1997	554 points	7.18%	October 19, 1987	508 points	22.61%
October 19, 1987	508	22.61%	October 28, 1929	38	12.82%
August 15, 1997	247	3.11%	October 29, 1929	30	11.73%
June 23, 1997	192	2.47%	November 6, 1929	25	9.92%
October 13, 1989	190	6.91%	December 18, 1899	5	8.72%
October 23, 1997	186	2.32%	August 12, 1932	5	8.40%
March 8, 1996	171	3.04%	March 14, 1907	6	8.29%
July 15, 1996	161	2.90%	October 26, 1987	156	8.04%
March 13, 1997	160	2.28%	July 21, 1933	7	7.84%
March 31, 1997	157	2.33%	October 18, 1937	10	7.75%
November 12, 1997	157	2.07%	February 1, 1917	6	7.24%
October 26, 1987	156	8.04%	October 27, 1997	554	7.18%

The largest declines for the NASDAQ have been as follows:

- 11.35% on October 19, 1987
- 9% on October 20, 1987
- 9% on October 26, 1987
- 7.02% on October 27, 1997

The largest point gain ever for the NASDAQ was on October 28, 1997, when it rose 67.93 points, equivalent to a 4.4% gain.

CONCLUDING REMARKS

A number of stock market indexes and averages are available to investors for monitoring the health of the market. While some give a very broad view of the market performance, others focus on specific market sectors. An investor should monitor the broader averages as well as an appropriate index or average against which the performance of his stock or portfolio can be compared.

The stock market moves alternately in bull (rising price) and bear (declining price) cycles. While buying winning stocks is the key to reaping profits, the ability to understand market extremes, as represented by bull market tops and bear market bottoms, can enhance these profits significantly. These market extremes do not occur suddenly. They give investors ample signs that every investor should learn to recognize.

Investors should not view bear markets as disasters. Instead, they should be viewed as opportunities when stocks can be picked up at bargains. It is recommended that investors remain invested at all times. However, when market extremes are recognized, investors can either lighten up or increase their exposure to stocks. Also, they can use these cycles to invest in the sectors/groups most likely to benefit from the cycle in the next year or so. Investors should also be aware of seasonal patterns.

CHAPTER 7

UNDERSTANDING STOCK BEHAVIOR

MONITORING A BASING STOCK

Recognizing forces at work

No stock moves straight up in price. Even the strongest stock will pause at times in its relentless runup to digest and consolidate gains before continuing its upward move. These pauses can last several weeks or months. During this consolidation or "basing" period, also known as backing and filling, the following forces are at work:

- profit taking by short-term traders
- continued accumulation by long-term investors
- some selling by nervous long-term investors aimed at locking in profits already made

When a stock is correcting or consolidating recent gains, investors try to determine the direction in which it will make its next big move—up or down. An investor able to correctly recognize a bullish or bearish basing pattern can reap handsome profits or avoid losses. Such an investor can remain invested when the indicated pattern is bullish and reduce exposure if the pattern is bearish.

Signs of a stabilized basing pattern

After heavy selling, even a strong stock may break its long-term trendline and decrease in relative strength. Before such a stock can begin a sustained move back to the upside, it typically needs to go through a basing period. The following are some positive signs of a stock having stabilized in a basing pattern:

- stock that has been falling stops making lower lows

- the 50-day moving average line flattens out
- stock's price begins to go sideways
- accumulation starts taking place (volume increases on up days and decreases on down days)

Overhead supply

This refers to the higher price level at which a stock traded for some time before it declined. When a stock rises to a level where overhead supply exists, investors who previously bought at that level tend to sell. This happens because these investors attempt to break even and dump a stock in which they had losses. Usually, this occurs when a stock recovers from a correction or a sharp pullback.

If a stock has traded at an overhead supply level for a long period prior to its decline, its overhead supply will be large. Therefore, it becomes harder to push through such a level due to stiff resistance.

Monitoring guidelines and tips

A stock will ultimately move out of its basing pattern either to the upside or downside. Therefore, an investor needs to be alert to any potential moves out of the basing pattern. This requires regular monitoring of the stock's basing pattern and behavior. Factors that should be monitored to determine whether a basing pattern is bearish or bullish include:

- volume to price relationship
- trend of the prior advance
- basing pattern
- market and industry group behavior

While each basing pattern is different, in that price fluctuations are unique, there are some common characteristics for basing stocks. The following are some useful tips that can be used to monitor a basing stock:

- stocks tend to be supported at the top of previous bases
- stocks often retrace about 50% of their prior gain
- if a stock tries to advance off a base after soaring over 100% and not correcting much, be careful
- if a stock's price holds above its 200-day moving average line, it is a positive sign

- a declining stock does not always find support at support levels; if it does, it is a positive sign
- the strongest stocks usually hold during a correction, rally, retest their lows, and then turn higher
- tremendous profits can be realized if a leading stock is held, for a year or two, while it goes through several basing patterns

RECOGNIZING A WEAKENING STOCK

Signs of a weakening stock

Even if a stock has performed admirably in the past and has high EPS rank and RS rank, an investor should always be alert to its behavior because past performance is no guarantee of future performance. Any stock, including a winner, can weaken at any time for a number of reasons. The following are typical warning signs for a weakening stock:

- volume is heavy on down days and light on up days (sign of distribution)
- stock that declined recently rallies back on below average volume
- stock does not move in tandem with the market

Breakout failure

A sign of a weakening stock is when it tries to move higher after a consolidation period and then fails to do so a few times. Such action can signal a breakdown, or price failure, even though there may be no fundamental reasons for this behavior. A common explanation is that a stock that has reaped substantial profits by rising sharply higher presents an opportunity to a large number of shareholders to bail out. This happens even as momentum players are still piling up without being able to make the stock breakout. When momentum players start realizing that the stock is unable to make any upward progress, they also start bailing out, sending the stock into a tailspin. If the stock cuts the lower end of it price base or an important trendline, it initiates even more heavy selling from investors who previously placed stop sell orders.

Unexpected breakdown

Even if a stock has performed well and its behavior is normal, it can be hit by massive selling for a number of reasons. Typically, massive selloffs are precipitated by negative announcements. Usually, these concern earnings or some development with the potential to impact business prospects. Sometimes, even a good earnings report can trigger a selloff. This can often be attributed to an earnings report containing some negative item, such as slowing revenue growth, even though the overall report may look good.

Another common reason for a stock to be hit by massive selling is an unexpected change in the competitive environment, such as the introduction of a killer product by a competitor, entry of a formidable competitor into the industry or niche, loss of market share, etc.

How to avoid getting trapped

To avoid being trapped, investors should closely monitor their stock and note if any distribution is taking place. Distribution occurs when a stock trades on heavy volume but fails to make any upward price movement. When a stock closes lower or remains unchanged in price despite a heavy increase in volume, it is a good indication that distribution is taking place. After a major decline, if a stock rises on lower volume on the following day, it is a bearish sign.

Investors should monitor the stock's industry group leaders. Their behavior can be leading indicator of what is in store for the stock. If a group leader starts being distributed, it may not be long before the other stocks follow. Therefore, an astute investor will monitor his own stocks as well as their group leaders.

Finally, one should be an informed investor and constantly monitor the company's fundamentals. Usually, surprises are rare for those who keep on top and stay informed. Signs of deterioration in fundamentals are visible to most investors who keep a close eye on their investments.

HANDLING SIZZLING STOCKS

Periodically, the attention of investors becomes riveted on a stock that only seems to go higher and higher, defying all predictions for its fall. A question many investors ask when they see such a hot and sizzling stock is, "Should I buy this stock?" The answer to this question from seasoned investors will be quite obvious: "Look before you leap."

A sizzling stock has far greater risk and reward potential. Therefore, prior to buying it, it should be analyzed far more thoroughly than a normal stock. Unfortunately, many investors get carried away by their emotions and do not perform any meaningful investigation before buying such a stock.

Understand the reasons

A number of reasons can cause a stock to exhibit sizzling behavior. For example, a potential winner could just have been "discovered" and achieved legitimacy because an important institution started buying its stock or an influential analyst recommended it. Other common factors include the introduction of a new product, new technology, control of a niche market (with a unique product), a very small float or a short squeeze that forces short sellers to cover their positions.

A potential winning stock typically shows great strength. It is not unusual for such a stock to rise while others in the same group may be stumbling. In many cases, rather than rise steadily, such a stock shoots straight up. Prior to investing in such a company, an investor should determine whether the stock's price move is sustainable or is just a passing stage with the potential to burn investors.

What needs to be investigated

Before investing in a sizzling stock, it should be thoroughly analyzed and subjected to fundamental analysis. Factors that need to be investigated include:

- reason for the price behavior
- projected earnings
- business conditions: can they permit earnings to be sustained (or achieved)?
- P/E ratios
- competing products and companies
- barriers to the entry of competition
- management strength and quality
- strengths and weaknesses of company

Blowoff move

Signs of a blowoff move

The phenomenon of an advancing stock suddenly shooting straight up in price, as shown in Figure 37, is called a blowoff move. When the stock market makes a very powerful move, like the one which started in December 1994, it can put many stocks in positions that can make them go off into a blowoff stage. For those able to recognize such stocks, the profit potential is tremendous.

Among the signs of a potential blowoff move are:

• needle-like price formation with heavy volume; if this pattern shows up on a weekly price chart, it is an even stronger indicator
• stock price will move 80% or more above its 200-day moving average

Among the warning signs that investors should be aware of when monitoring a blowoff situation are:

• climatic top: this can occur if a stock that has been advancing rapidly gaps up at the start of the trading day
• reliable sign of a top: after trading with a wide spread, the stock price closes near its low for the day
• ultimate top: this may take place on the heaviest volume day since the move began
• if a price gain does not occur despite heavy volume, this indicates that the move is near its end
• new price highs on significantly lower volume is a bearish sign

Dealing with a blowoff situation

Traders have some choices available for dealing with stocks after recognizing a blowoff pattern or after the blowoff move actually takes place. These include:

• selling a portion of the holding; selling too early misses additional gains, while a delay in selling results in lost profits
• using trailing stop orders based on the stock's chart pattern

Investors, while scaling back, can continue to maintain positions because such a stock may still be in an uptrend and, therefore, can continue its upward move after a consolidation period. An example is

Figure 37

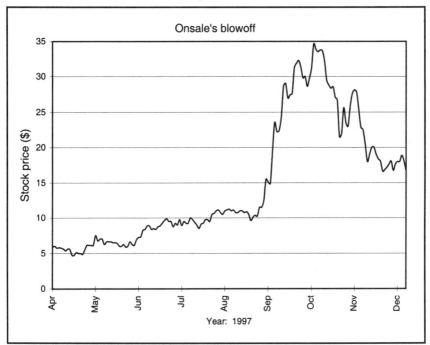

Micron Technology, which was trading at 22 in January 1995. It then experienced a blowoff move which caused it to rise 8 ½ dollars, from 34 ⅛, in just over a week. It consolidated for 6 weeks and then continued rising to a high of 94 by September 1995. It then reversed direction and declined to 29 by January 1996. Micron ultimately declined to a 1996 low of 16 ⅝ (refer to Figure 8). This decline occurred while the DJIA was making major gains.

Investing in a superhot stock

<u>Irrational behavior</u>

At times, a stock suddenly takes off like a rocket, defies all logic, and continues to move higher for a while. For example, Comparator Systems leapt 32 fold in only 5 trading days in May 1996. On just a single day, May 6, its price rose 400%. When momentum players see such a streaking stock, they jump on it no matter what its price or valuation. They expect such a stock's momentum to realize quick profits for them. However, serious investors should maintain a different attitude and never buy a stock based only on its price momentum.

Ultimately, superhot stocks run out of gas. When this happens, rather than base like ordinary stocks, they fall very rapidly and with devastating effect. For example, Presstek, a developer of digital-imaging technology soared 74% in a month to a high of 200 on May 21, 1996. It then dropped to a low of 60 by June 1996, triggered in part by news that the SEC had started an investigation of Presstek.

Netscape Communications Corp., which develops Internet products including the web browser, has been another recent superhot stock. It went public in August 9, 1995. It was priced at $28 a share, opened at $71 and closed that day at 58 $1/4$. It continued to rise to 174 before ending 1995 at 139. By the summer of 1996, it had traded as low as 69 (split adjusted). While this company had an excellent product, its lofty stock price had no relationship with its current or projected earnings for years to come. As was to be expected, after the initial euphoria died down, the stock declined precipitously.

Dealing with a superhot stock

An investor cannot easily determine a superhot stock's future direction. However, it is quite obvious that high risk is associated with such a stock; therefore, it needs to be handled with caution. Using some guidelines, the risk from such a stock can be minimized. For example, an investor can determine:

- the cause of the move; this should be fundamental rather than speculative; do not buy a stock rising on speculation
- if the story make sense
- whether the effect of the news or rumor propelling the stock (new products, turnaround, etc.) has already been discounted (through a price increase) and to what extent
- what the company's competitors are doing
- if a short squeeze (when short sellers are forced to cover their positions) is driving up the price; once short sellers have covered, the stock can be expected to quickly run out of gas

- if the fast rising stock is extended; it should not be purchased when it is trading:
  - 10% above its 50-day moving average
  - 10% beyond the breakout point from its base, which is the trading range where the stock traded for at least 7 weeks on relatively low volume
- available float: a company with a small float can be very volatile and difficult to sell during a decline

FACTORS BOOSTING SHARE PRICE

Share buybacks

There are a number of ways in which companies try to boost the share price of their stocks. A common way is to buy back their own company shares in the open market. This reduces the total number of outstanding shares. Since EPS is calculated by dividing net income by the total number of shares, any decrease in the total number of outstanding shares boosts the EPS. Often, a company announcement that it will buy back its shares causes an upward push in its stock price.

Manipulation

Investors should realize that stock prices can be manipulated in a number of ways. Self-serving changes in brokerage analyst recommendations do occur, though not frequently. Sometimes, an analyst will issue a negative rating on a stock, in order to make its price drop intentionally. The usual reason, in such a case, is to give the analyst's brokerage company the opportunity to buy the stock for its own clients at a lower price.

A few years ago, a well-known analyst issued a buy rating on a biotechnology company, which had no products in production or in the pipeline. Since the company had just started its R&D effort, it had no expectations for having a product in production for at least 5 to 7 years, the time typically required to bring a drug to the market. The analyst's buy recommendation made the stock rise from 12 to 18 within a few weeks. When the stock reached 18, the analyst downgraded the stock to a "hold" because of "high valuation." The stock dropped to 14 within a few days. At 14, the analyst again issued a buy recommendation based on its "current reasonable valuation"! Obviously, no one can value such a company, with no products except hype, so precisely and accurately within a $14 to $18 range. This was a classic case of manipulation.

Sometimes, a company will issue press releases to shore up its stock price—to counter negative news on the company. At times, short sellers start rumors in order to put pressure on the stock. In short, investors should realize that stock prices are subject to some degree of manipulation. However, in the long run, what ultimately matters is the company's earnings. What investors should do is be careful, focus on the fundamentals, and remain informed about developments that have the potential to affect the company's fundamentals.

Stock splits

Stock splits are primarily carried out to reduce the price of each share in order to make it more attractive to individual investors who prefer to buy lower priced shares. Suppose an investor has 500 shares of a $50 stock. After a 2 for 1 split, the price of each share will decrease to $25, while the number of shares will double to 1,000. Therefore, the stock split will result in no change in the total value of the shares held by the investor.

Advantages

An advantage of a split is that it increases the float, which makes the company's shares more liquid. If a company has a total of 50 million outstanding shares, a 2 for 1 split will increase the total number of outstanding shares to 100 million shares. As a consequence of the split, the stock's daily trading volume will increase. Sometimes, an increase in a stock's daily trading volume makes it eligible for investment by some institutions. The reason for this is that many institutions are restricted from investing in stocks whose daily trading volume is below a certain limit.

Long-term effect

The effect of a stock split on a stock's price is debatable. In many cases, a split increases the stock price prior to the actual split due to increased interest. After the split, usually, a sell-off occurs due to profit taking. In the long term, the effect of a split is negligible because, ultimately, a stock's price is dependent on the company's fundamentals. A disadvantage of a stock split is that trading commissions increase because, usually, they are based on the number of shares traded, which increase when a stock split occurs.

INFLUENCE OF A STOCK'S INDUSTRY GROUP/SECTOR

To understand the behavior of any stock, an investor needs to study more than just the company. Also to be understood and monitored is the behavior of other stocks in the same industry group.

What is an industry group

To monitor, compare and analyze groups of stocks, usually with similar characteristics, many sector and industry groups have been created. The reason for creating such groups is that stocks within a group act together. Hence, if a stock's group is underperforming, the stock cannot be expected to outperform. Usually, stocks in the same group, with exceptions, follow the same trend. Therefore, knowledgeable investors monitor and compare the performance of their stocks to other stocks in the same industry sector or group.

It is important that an investor determine which groups/sectors his stocks belong to. Then, as part of his monitoring activities, he should regularly compare the behavior and performance of his stocks to that of the relevant group.

Obtaining fundamental information on specific industries

A useful source for conducting industry research are the S&P Industry surveys, which examine the prospects for the industry in question. The S&P surveys analyze trends and problems. These are examined with reference to historical data and behavior. Also, within an industry, important sectors are highlighted in these surveys.

Monitoring industry specific indicators

A number of indicators are used by investors to monitor the health of various industries. For example, the retail industry uses the same store sales figures to compares sales, while the semiconductor industry has been using the book-to-bill ratio.

Understanding an industry-specific indicator

The book-to-bill ratio is obtained by dividing the month's bookings number by the billings number. Suppose the booking number is 105 while the billings number is 100. In this case, the book-to-bill ratio will be 105/100 = 1.05. This indicates that for every $100 of products shipped, new orders for $105 were placed. The ratio is calculated on a three-month moving average to smooth out fluctuations and is adjusted seasonally.

Some analysts consider a book-to-bill ratio of 0.8-0.85 as a buy signal, while a ratio of 1.15 to 1.2 is considered to be a sell signal. In 1995, when this ratio remained consistently high, the semiconductor group had a huge price runup. When it started declining, the semiconductor group collapsed.

What investors should do

An investor should become familiar with the relevant industry specific indicators, if they exist, for his stocks and should understand their importance and implications for his investments.

Monitoring an industry group rank

Investors should note the group that a stock belongs to and its rank. *IBD* provides the relative rank of 197 industry groups, which is based on the price performance of all stocks in the industry in the last six months. Also indicated are the positions held a week ago, as well as three months ago, for comparison purpose. Comparison of industry group ranks can provide useful information. For example, if a group has a high rank or it is rising, it is a positive sign. On the other hand, if its rank is low or decreasing, it is a warning sign. When the signs based on an industry rank are negative, an investor can lighten up by selling part of the position.

Picking the leaders

The action in a group can be a tipoff to the movement of institutions into that group. When institutions move into a group, P/E ratios and prices of stocks in the group invariably start to rise. An astute investor can jump on the bandwagon and be rewarded, provided the fundamentals of the company are sound. Therefore, to take advantage using the performance of industry groups, an investor should:

- note the industry groups showing an increase in stocks making new highs
- focus on stocks with an EPS rank above 90 in such a group (potential leaders will typically be found here)
- predict industry groups having the best growth prospects in the next 2 to 3 years (because institutions pick the best companies in such groups)

Failing to monitor industry groups

For those who fail to monitor their stock's group, the consequences can be disastrous. Consider the case of investors who owned semiconductor stocks in 1995. The technology sector, including the semiconductor group, had a banner year until September when the semiconductor group started falling apart. Those who did not monitor the semiconductor group failed to see it deteriorate in the last quarter. They got badly burned because the technology sector, and the semiconductor group in particular, had a massive downturn. Remember that the stock market is a very dynamic place and no one can afford to be complacent.

Monitoring other groups and sectors

Tool for forecasting market direction

Even if an investor owns stocks in only one industry or sector, he needs to monitor other sectors also because they can provide clues to the future direction of the market. For example, cyclical stocks (automobile manufacturers, home builders, paper products and basic chemicals) tend to advance when a recession appears to be ending because the profits of such companies tend to rise and fall with the state of the economy. If an investor waits for a recession to end and an economic upturn to become fully apparent in order to jump in, he will miss most of the profits that can be generated by anticipating such a move. Typically, by the time the economy is growing at a healthy pace, cyclical stocks have already made their most significant move.

On the other hand, defensive stocks (such as P&G and ADM, the largest food processor) and utilities grow steadily. Therefore, the earnings of such companies are fairly predictable. These companies find favor when the economic growth starts slowing at the end of an economic cycle. Since these companies are slightly affected by a slowing economy and any downturn is relatively mild, investors flock to them for parking their money. If this sector starts improving during a bull market, it is a sign that the market may have trouble ahead because investors usually start moving their money defensively to this sector in anticipation.

Limitations of using sector behavior as a forecasting tool

Sector behavior does not always correctly forecast future market moves because assumptions of investors and market participants can be wrong and the market has a way of its own. For example, when it appeared that the economy was slowing fast during mid-1995, investors flocked to defensive companies after getting rid of cyclical companies. However, the economy grew much stronger than these investors expected.

Riding with winning groups and market leaders

Recognizing leadership signs

A very successful way to recognize a winning stock is to identify an industry, or a group, that is poised to take over market leadership. A group in an uptrend will typically have many stocks making new highs. This is a sign of current leadership. Such a group can be expected to continue its leadership role in the near future. An example is the technology sector, which led the market during its powerful rise during most of 1995. Within the technology sector, the semiconductor group was the leader. An analysis of this group, for that period, reveals many winners including Intel, C-Cube Microsystems, Applied Materials and Motorola.

Avoiding suspect leadership

Do not invest in a sector or group even if it is in an uptrend with many new highs if its fundamentals are suspect or the future is cloudy. A group with healthy and rapidly improving earnings with potential to beat estimates handily should be the ideal one for investment. An example is the technology sector and its semiconductor component whose exploding earnings rocketed the sector in 1995.

Be wary of investing in a group that has been a leader for some time because the best move may already be behind it. A safer approach involves taking the following three steps:

- pick the industry group moving up or showing a big percentage of new highs
- observe which stocks in the group are making new highs
- pick the stock(s) with the best fundamentals

Sources to scan for group leadership

Industry leaders can be identified from the data for various sectors, groups and industries that is provided in various publications. The most comprehensive data is provided by *IBD*, which tracks 197 industry groups. It provides the following important data:

- *IBD* industry prices showing top industry groups
- groups with the greatest percentage of stocks making new highs (Table 1)
- performance of market sector indexes (Table 6)

The performance of various sectors and groups can be easily obtained these days. While some newspapers and magazines publish this information, *IBD* is the best source for comprehensive and timely data. On a daily basis, it provides charts for some market sectors, including high tech, junior growth and consumer indexes. Weekly data is provided for some sectors such as banks, health care and defense sectors.

CONCLUDING REMARKS

The price movement pattern of every stock is unique. However, there are some common characteristics among individual stocks, such as basing (after a rise or fall from its prior level), weakening and breakdown. Developing the ability to recognize signs of danger, and opportunity, for a stock can aid an investor in making an informed and profitable decision—avoiding a stock when it is about to collapse or riding a winner as it takes off.

In general, stocks in a group rise and fall together. Therefore, the performance of a stock is also influenced by the state of health and performance of its industry group. Hence, it is important that a stock's industry/group be monitored as part of an investor's monitoring activities. A serious investor should also monitor the performance of other industries/groups because their performance can often provide early indication of trend changes.

It should be realized that stock prices can be boosted or manipulated in a number of ways. However, keep in mind that the effect of any such attempt is temporary because the ultimate level of a stock's price is dependent on its earnings.

CHAPTER 8

INVESTMENT PRINCIPLES AND STRATEGIES

INVESTING REQUIREMENTS

Investors use a number of investment strategies and techniques because a prerequisite for success in the stock market is the use of a strategy. Investing without a strategy is an invitation to disaster. Therefore, an investor must chose a strategy, fine tune it according to his own needs and experience, and then stick with it. A strategy need not be sophisticated. What is important is the need to follow a strategy—no matter how simple it is.

Some strategies work in specific investment environments but will fail under certain unfavorably changed circumstances or a paradigm shift. Even very successful Wall Street investors, such as Benjamin Graham, have had to modify their strategies with changing times. Therefore, periodic strategy and techniques review should be made and, depending on the results achieved to date, appropriate changes should be made.

In general, there are five basic requirements for achieving success in the stock market, which are described in the following sections.

A method

Before investing in the stock market, an investor should establish objectives, assess his risk tolerance, determine the length of time for investing, and decide on the investment plan and strategy to be followed. What should never be done is to randomly buy a stock based on the hope that it will go higher. Instead, expectations for success in the stock market should be based on a method or system.

A method should clearly spell out the decision-making process for buying and selling stocks, which can be based on simple rules. For example, an investor can have the following basic rules that will be followed strictly:

- for buying:
  - company's earnings growth rate must be at least 25%, and
  - P/E ratio must be less than 15
- for selling:
  - stock does not meet earnings expectations
  - stock price appreciates 30% or declines 12%
  - earnings growth rate declines
  - the reason(s) for buying no longer exist

A method should be followed consistently. While a method can be changed or improved, based on experience gained, it must not be changed frequently.

Discipline to follow your method

An investor should not follow a method from year to year, season to season, or from trade to trade. For success, the discipline to follow a method consistently is required. A decision to use or discard a method should never be based on a unique experience.

Experience

Before starting to trade in the stock market, a potential investor can gain some experience by simulating trades. Such trading is useful for testing a methodology, but it has practically no value in the real world because it cannot simulate emotions involving real gains and losses. For an inexperienced investor, it is advisable to start with a strategy that has been proven over the years. Some well-known strategies are described later on in this chapter.

Attitude

To be successful in the stock market, an investor requires patience and the discipline to hold on to, or add to, investments through both declining and rising markets. Making a fast buck should not be an investment goal. An investor must have the mental fortitude to accept the fact that losses are a part of the investing game. Instead of blaming professional traders, program trading, insiders and others for losses, an investor should try his best to improve and outperform most of the competition.

Having a long-term horizon

Investment in the stock market should be made for the long-term. One should not be a trader and try to time entry into and exit from the stock market. Timing is a far less important factor for those with a long-term horizon than it is for short-term traders. Timing is something that only very knowledgeable and experienced investors should attempt. Average investors should remain invested in the best-performing stocks and let their profits run.

INVESTMENT PRINCIPLES AND STRATEGIES OF SOME PROS

There are many investment principles and strategies espoused by stock market professionals. Some confine their strategy to a few basic principles while others follow a fairly extensive list. This section lists the principles and rules followed by a highly successful individual investor, some well known and successful investment professionals, as well as rules followed by the authors.

Anne Scheiber's rules

Anne Scheiber has been one of the most successful stock market investors in recent times. Her $5,000 investment, made in 1944, grew astronomically into a $22 million portfolio by 1995. This works out to a 22.1% annual return,[20] which compares very favorably against the 12.4% per year gain of the S&P500. It even bettered Benjamin Graham's 17.4% return. However, it was just shy of the returns generated by the best investors the stock market has known: Warren Buffet (22.7%) and Peter Lynch (29.2%). The following were Scheiber's basic investing tips:

- favor firms with growing earnings
- capitalize on your interests (convert what you like into investment themes)

[20] *Money,* January, 1996, pg. 64.

- invest in leading brands
- invest in small bites (dollar cost averaging)
- reinvest your dividends
- never sell
- keep informed

Warren Buffet's principles
- buy a business—not a stock; focus on four tenets:
  - business tenets
  - management tenets
  - financial tenets
  - market tenets
- don't worry about the economy
- turn off the stock market (don't pay attention to the overall market fluctuations and movements)
- manage a portfolio of businesses

A money manager's basic investment philosophy
- don't be an extremist (on the upside or downside)
- let your profits run
- be humble and admit your mistakes (and learn from them)
- combine technical analysis with fundamentals
- rely on industry group movements

John Templeton's investment factors
- P/E ratio
- present and anticipated growth rate in earnings/share
- "perfect blend" consisting of the highest possible growth rate for the lowest possible P/E
- rising pretax profit margins
- consistency of earning rates (consistent earnings growth is a plus; however, too high growth rates often signal trouble ahead)
- validity of a company's long-range planning
- level of effectiveness of the company's competitors
- major company challenges other than competition
- maintaining a degree of flexibility
- everyone makes investment mistakes; know when to acknowledge them and cut your losses (sell)
- keeping a diversified portfolio

Cyber-Investing process (Brown and Bentley)
- find a list of stocks that most closely match your major investment goals

- narrow the list to a few top stocks
- maximize your profit potential with technical buy signals
- implement good portfolio management procedures
- reduce risk and enhance profits by a continual assessment of a stock's risk/reward relationship

The authors' rules

- invest for the long term; don't be a trader (don't try to time the market) unless you are a professional
- use a simple investing approach (use a minimum number of indicators)
- use the growth investing approach (focus on companies whose earnings are growing at an above average rate); favor small/mid cap stocks
- thoroughly research a stock prior to buying it
- ride your winners (do not sell early)
- analyze your past trades and mistakes
- do not follow the crowd
- stay informed (note anything that might materially affect your stocks)

THREE BASIC APPROACHES TO STOCK INVESTING

There are many approaches that are being followed for stock investing. However, over the years, only three have proved to be consistently successful. They are:

- growth investing
- value investing
- momentum investing

Growth investing

Objective and approach

This is the most widely used investing approach. The basic objective is to buy fast growing companies based on the expectation that large capital gains will be realized over time. Such companies have above average sales and EPS growth compared to the market as a whole. Investors expect a successful growth company's earnings to continue growing steadily at a good pace. Consequently, their expectation is that its higher earnings will be followed by a higher stock price.

Growth criteria

The primary criteria for those using this approach is the company's growth rate. The rate of growth acceptable to growth investors varies, depending on:

- type of growth company: aggressive or established
- investor's profile: conservative, moderate or high risk

Aggressive growth companies: These are new and fast growing companies, which are usually low priced. They have a shorter performance track record and are quite volatile. The risk and reward associated with these companies is much higher compared to the more well-established growth companies. It is not unusual for such companies to be growing at a 25 to 50% annual rate.

Established growth companies: These are relatively large companies that have been in business for a number of years. These companies, while still growing at a healthy pace, have lower growth rates compared to aggressive growth companies. Their share prices are less volatile. The risk and reward associated with such companies is lower compared to aggressive companies. Typically, such companies grow at a 15 to 20% annual rate.

Characteristics of promising growth companies

With the primary objective being to pick a growth stock, investors should learn how to recognize the characteristics of growth stocks. This will increase the probability that a winning stock with the potential for good price appreciation will be selected for procurement. In general, the following are the characteristics of good growth stocks:

- growing at an above average rate (revenues and earnings)
- profitability is based on revenue growth (not through cost controls, restructuring, disposal of assets, etc.)
- earnings growth rate higher than its P/E ratio
- belongs to a growing industry, which will permit the company's growth rate to be maintained or increased
- has some unique advantage(s) over its competitors (product/service, technology, market niche, etc.)
- able to grow without requiring heavy debt financing
- minimum or no debt

- adequate cash reserves and lines of credit (provides flexibility)
- high return on equity (usually over 15%)
- early in a theme; is a leader

Potential reward and expectations

The growth investing approach has the potential to achieve high returns for investors prepared to take higher risks. For growth stocks, the market has high expectations. Any positive surprise, over expectations, results in a stock getting handsomely rewarded through exceptional price appreciation. However, stocks failing to meet growth and earnings expectations get severely punished.

Value investing

A stock's true worth is derived from its earnings and the value of its assets. Therefore, these criteria are used by value investors to determine if a stock is overvalued or undervalued. An undervalued stock currently trades at a price substantially below the company's true (or liquidating) value. To a value investor, such a stock is a bargain that can be bought at a substantial discount. Such an investor sees little risk in buying something for 70 cents, or even substantially lower, when its true value is $1.

Objective and approach

The primary objective of investors following the value investing approach is to buy undervalued stocks. Value investors seek above average returns by acquiring a stock that is underpriced relative to the underlying "value" of its earnings and yield potential. In other words, the aim is to acquire a stock at considerably less than its real worth. The logic is that if a stock is bought at a price less than its true worth, risk is minimized while the potential for gain is maximized.

The value investing approach is based on a two-step process:
1. determining the intrinsic value of a stock in terms of its earnings, dividend and yield
2. comparing the value, determined in the first step, to the current share price

If the stock price is lower than its intrinsic value, it is considered to be undervalued and, therefore, attractive for investment and vice versa.

Value criteria

To determine if a stock is trading below its intrinsic value, a number of criteria such as P/E and price-to-sales ratios are used. Typically, value investors focus on buying stocks with low P/E ratios. The belief is that such a stock protects them from a steep decline because the P/E, due to its already low value, can fall only a limited distance. However, it should be realized that a very low P/E is a reflection of the market's concern about the company's business in addition to expectations of reduced earnings. Therefore, such a company clearly indicates weak prospects for growth. Hence, there always exists the danger that such a stock can languish, for years, and tie up valuable capital for a long period.

Potential reward and expectations

Stocks with relatively low P/E ratios that are expected to increase can be very rewarding to investors. Typically, these companies are those that have been out of favor for some time but are expected to turnaround. Indications of a potential turnaround and, consequently rising P/E, include buying by insiders, improving margins, earnings estimates being raised and expanding volume.

For an undervalued stock, the market expects very little or nothing. Therefore, any positive surprise results in the stock being rewarded with exceptional gains. However, before investing, an investor should determine the reasons for a company being undervalued. Typically, reasons include economy slowdown, business cycle, product cycle, management change, unappreciated assets, fundamental problems, etc. An undervalued stock with fundamental problems, and a deteriorating business outlook, should not be bought.

Momentum investing

Objective and approach

The term momentum refers to the rapid price movement of a stock or a market index. Momentum investing has been described as "buying because others are buying." Momentum investors are those who primarily base their buy and sell decisions on a stock's pattern and price momentum. Typically, momentum stocks are characterized by rapidly growing earnings and/or price appreciation momentum. However, if either one of these start slowing, momentum players sell the stock immediately.

Momentum criteria

Momentum players do not pay much attention to high P/E ratios, insider trading or other fundamental indicators. Instead, they only try to identify stocks with the greatest price, earnings and industry group momentum. Once a stock with these characteristics is recognized, they jump on it. They continue riding it until its momentum slows down or they find a faster moving stock.

Momentum investors do not agree with the logic "buy low and sell high." Their argument is that no one knows precisely when the market or a stock is at its low point. They point out that too often a high flying stock comes crashing down, loses 50% or more of its value, looks "cheap" and "close to the bottom," only to fall another 50% shortly. An example is Borland, which went down from $87 to $8 in less than one year. In this case, cheap became cheaper every few days.

In contrast to the "buy low and sell high" principle, momentum investing is based on the principle "buy high and sell higher." Momentum investors believe that if a stock starts rising rapidly, the probability is very high that it will continue to rise for some time to come. They do not believe in buying value stocks. Their investment approach does not allow them to hold a problem stock and wait for it to turnaround. Instead, they prefer to board a rising stock with upward earnings and/or price momentum. This approach involves waiting until after a stock hits bottom, forms a base, and then breaks out as it starts a major new advance. Buying is done only after a breakout. Before boarding a stock, momentum players like to see the stock having earnings and/or price momentum. They also prefer to see high relative strength rank over 80, which indicates that the stock has been outperforming in price.

Risk of momentum investing

Momentum investing can expose an investor to big risks. At the first sign of trouble for a stock, momentum players bail out en masse, magnifying any normal decline. In 1991, momentum players hitched onto biotechnology stocks causing them to rise to very lofty levels. When they started to exit, the biotech stock suffered tremendous price declines, from which they took years to recover. The declines were magnified because many stocks in this group had risen to stratospheric levels, without the support of any tangible earnings. Again, in late 1995, momentum players bailed out of semiconductor stocks when the group started to lose momentum. For those who failed to jump ship in time, the losses were tremendous.

The most dangerous period for momentum investing is at market tops in a bull market. This is the period when trend following reaches a climax. However, if an investment has been made in a fundamentally strong growth company, which is part of a strong group, the damage during a declining market will be limited.

CONCLUDING REMARKS

There are a few basic points that every investor should understand. First, stock market investing should be done for the long-term. Second, it is imperative that an investment strategy be used, which need not be sophisticated. Even successful professional investors use only a few simple rules to their advantage. Once selected, it is important that investors follow a method with consistency and discipline.

There are three basic approaches to investing in the stock market: growth, momentum and value. Growth investing, which is the most widely used approach, aims to invest in companies that are growing at an above average rate. Value investing is based on investing in stocks that are undervalued. Such stocks currently trade at a price substantially below the company's true (or liquidating) value. Momentum investing is not based on fundamentals and, therefore, exposes an investor to relatively higher risk.

Growth investing is the most viable approach for the vast majority of investors who do not have the patience to sit and watch a stock for years before it makes a profitable upward move. While growth-investing rewards are not inferior to momentum investing, it is inherently safe because it is based on sound fundamentals.

Investors should learn to recognize change, with the basic objective being to profit from change. The art of investing is based on an investor's ability to recognize change and adjust investment goals accordingly.

CHAPTER 9

SCREENING AND SELECTING STOCKS: AN OVERVIEW

BASIC REQUIREMENTS

Understanding the investing environment and challenge

The stock market has always been characterized by a dynamic environment. However, in recent years, it has become even more dynamic and challenging due to:

- massive corporate structural changes forced by an increasing competitive environment (global and domestic)
- availability of instant information to investors

Due to the changing nature of business, rapidly changing conditions and ever shortening cycles, very few companies find their business environment stable for any length of time. This impacts the profits that can be earned, which in turn affects stock prices. Consequently, a serious challenge is created for investors who have to deal with the shifting fortunes of a company.

In the current environment, an investor cannot afford to invest in a good stock and then take it easy. No one can afford to stop monitoring a company in the belief that its price will appreciate in the years to come, just because it is a good company. Gone are the days when an investor could buy a stock and just hold it forever. However, this also presents an opportunity. If an investor researches diligently and picks stocks that are going to perform well, excellent profits can be reaped in a shorter time span.

Objective

The basic objective for achieving long-term success in the stock market is to buy the shares of a company in which financial success is expected. Such a company will be characterized by revenues and profit margins that are currently increasing at a healthy pace or expected to do so in the near future. Typically, a winner will have some positive fundamentals such as new products (or services), is riding a recently established trend in the economy, has an improved business outlook for its industry or has new management.

Prerequisites

Investing in the stock market and picking winning stocks requires discipline and diligence. Any investor can have a hot year or so. However, to get consistently high returns, especially in a market which changes quite rapidly, investors need to:

- have a methodology for selecting stocks that meets their investment goals
- use selected indicators for monitoring the health of individual stocks and the market
- have a selling strategy

Every investor should be prepared to conduct self-analysis periodically. If the results are consistently below expectations, the investment objectives and strategy need to be reviewed to determine if they require to be changed or modified. However, this should not be done frequently. Finally, it should be realized that no investment yardstick remains successful forever. Over time, investment selection formulas become obsolete and need to be replaced by more successful ones.

Selecting the investment strategy

Most investors follow one of three commonly used investment strategies: growth, momentum and value. Before starting to invest, an investor should determine which strategy and risk level is appropriate based on his own investment objectives. Once a strategy has been selected, it should be adhered to. All successful investors, even though they may have different strategies and techniques, use a disciplined and methodical approach to investing that they follow rigorously. Those who are not disciplined enough to develop or follow a strategy and lack dedication are the ones who frequently lose in the stock market.

An investor need not pick stocks based on only one strategy. For example, a stock investor who picks all stocks based on the growth strategy can make an exception by picking one or two stocks based on the momentum strategy. Another investor may plan to invest 80% of his money in growth stocks and use the value-based strategy for the remaining 20%. However, the rules defining any such deviations should be specific.

Recognizing and picking winning indicators

Widely used indicators

There are many indicators that an investor can use. Therefore, one needs to be selective and choose only a few, but powerful, indicators. These should be based on the investment approach that has been selected. While indicators used by the various approaches are usually different, a few indicators are used by all three approaches. However, the acceptable value for each indicator, for the three investing approaches, may be quite different. The most widely used indicators are:

- Projected long-term earnings growth rate
- Annual and quarterly earnings increase
- Revision in earnings estimates
- P/E ratio
- P/E-to-growth ratio
- Relative P/E ratio
- Insider buying
- Number of analysts following company
- Stock price
- Market capitalization
- Institutional ownership
- EPS rank
- Relative strength rank (RS)
- 200-day moving average
- Accumulation and distribution
- Return on equity (ROE)
- Debt/equity ratio
- Cash flow growth rate
- Company management

Assigning weights to picked indicators

Winning indicators are not equal in terms of their ability to help select a stock or to forecast its future price level. Also, the relative importance given to each indicator by investors following the different investment approaches can vary significantly. Therefore, to reflect the relative importance of each indicator, for ranking stocks in the screening and selection process, a weighting system can be used. This means assigning a "weight" to each indicator based on its relative importance. The higher the weight, the more important the indicator. Weights are assigned arbitrarily, based on the investor's experience and preference. For example, an investor can assign weights as follows:

- indicator #1 = 100%
- indicator #2 = 75%
- indicator #3 = 50%

In this example, indicator #3 has only half the "weight" or importance as indicator #1. Indicator #2 too is less important than indicator #1. These weights can be assigned using different scaling methods. For example, another method assigns weights on a scale ranging from 1 (lowest) to 10 (highest). This method, using a scale from 1 to 10, is explained in Chapter 10 (Tables 14 and 17).

The advantage of using weights is that an indicator assigned the highest weight will become the most important indicator and, therefore, will bias the selection process in favor of stocks scoring high on this indicator. However, it should be noted that while assigning weights has its advantages, it is not a requirement for stock selection.

Recognizing characteristics of winning stocks and leaders

Investors should realize that the leaders of one bull market are not necessarily the stars of the next. Latching on to a former high flyer just because its re-entered the atmosphere is not a winning technique that should be followed by serious investors. The danger exists that even after a drastic price drop a stock may still be overvalued and its best gains may already be history.

A better way to succeed is to find potential new winners. To do this, investors need to recognize the characteristics of winning stocks and leaders. Once they are able to do this, they can independently pick stocks with the best attributes.

Common characteristics of winners

Table 2 showed some important characteristics of some very successful stocks of recent years. In general, the following are the common characteristics of winning stocks and leaders:

- accelerating earnings (quarterly and annual)
- growth better than its industry, sector and the S&P
- excellent sales and EPS growth over the last 3 to 5 years
- small capitalized company
- low, but increasing, institutional ownership
- insider buying with no insider selling
- high relative strength
- new price highs
- positive technical indicators such as relative price, moving averages, etc.
- financial ratios better than its industry or sector: key ratios include margins, ROE, debt level and inventory turns
- high R&D expenditure

Characteristics of winning small cap stocks

An analysis of successful small stocks shows many common characteristics, which include the following attributes:

- good steady growth
- controls a niche area
- product(s) that large numbers of people will buy
- new product or service that represents a breakthrough
- low labor costs and minimum government regulation
- benefit from high industry entry barriers
- diversified customer base
- the company is following the trend of the industry into new technology
- is a user of technology
- institutions either do not own the stock or have only a small presence in the stock
- few, or no, analysts follow the company
- insiders have a heavy stake in the company or are buying the stock
- is a spin-off
- company is buying back shares

Characteristics of leaders emerging from corrections

It can be very profitable to pick a leader as it emerges from a correction and is poised to make a significant move up. The important factors that indicate emerging new leadership include new highs, high relative strength and improving fundamentals. Generally, in a bull market correction, growth stocks decline 1½ to 2 times the market averages. Those that do not correct much, or even rise, are the potential leaders when the rebound occurs. A stock maintaining a high relative strength (RS) rank stands out as a potential winner because the RS of leading stocks usually tend to drop sharply during a falling market. When the market rebounds, such a stock has a greater probability of rising significantly higher.

STOCK SELECTION PROCESS

After the basic requirements have been met, an investor can proceed to screen and select stocks in a five-step process that includes:

1. Identifying stocks for investing
2. Screening
3. Ranking
4. Fundamental analysis
5. Timing the purchase—technical analysis

Figures 38, 39 and 40 show the processes for screening stocks using manual and computerized methods. Each process and the individual steps indicated in the diagrams are described in the following sections.

Step (1) Identifying stocks for investing
Common sources

In this step, a number of stocks are initially identified for potential investment. Usually, these investments can be identified through one of the following conventional methods:

- Investment sources such as Zacks, Value Line, S&P, investment newsletters, newspapers, magazines, Internet, Online services, etc.
- Personal network (colleagues, friends, business partners and others)
- "hot" tips from colleagues, friends, neighbors, unsolicited investment literature, etc.

- *IBD:* companies featured in the "New America" section and mutual fund lists (small cap and growth)
- *Individual Investor:* America's fastest growing companies (those showing at least a 100% gain in quarterly earnings) and the Magic 25 list

Stocks identified in this step need to be handled in two different ways:

- subject the stock to the full screening and analysis process: this means starting the process from step (2a)
- subject the stock to fundamental analysis without going through the screening process: this means starting the process from step (4)

Computerized databases

These are huge databases that contain historical and current investment data on all publicly traded stocks. These databases can only be tapped using a computer and investment software. Investors using this source, for identifying stocks for potential investment, will directly proceed to step (2b).

Best sources

The authors' experience shows that for the average investor, the best sources for initial identification of stocks for investment are:

- *S&P Outlook*
- *Zacks Analyst Watch*
- *Value Line Investment Survey*
- *Investor's Business Daily*
- *OTC Insight*
- *Individual Investor*
- *Investor's Digest*
- *California Technology Stock Letter*

These sources contain recommended lists, company profiles, performance tables, screening lists and more. It should be noted that this list is not based on any recommended order. It should only be used by investors as a starting point for their research and analysis. Using such a list can help investors who do not use computerized tools save considerable time and effort in their research efforts.

Step (2) Screening

<u>a) Manual screening without computerized tools</u>

Stocks identified in step (1) are put through a manual screening test using indicators such as earnings, growth rate, P/E, moving averages, etc. The limitation of this manual method is that only a few stocks can be screened due to the time and effort involved. However, this is not a problem for most individual investors because, typically, they will be screening only a few stocks for potential investment at this stage.

Screening process for a single stock

This process is shown in Figure 38. Screening for a single stock can be done in one or two passes. In the first pass, only a few indicators are used. If the stock passes this screening, it is subjected to the second pass screening, which is performed using more stringent criteria and additional indicators. Stocks surviving the second pass can be directly subjected to fundamental analysis, as shown in step (4), because no ranking will be required for a single stock.

Screening process for multiple stocks

This process is shown in Figure 39. Screening for multiple stocks can be performed in one or two passes. If too many stocks survive the first pass, a second pass is made in order to reduce the number of passing stocks. This elimination is required for limiting the number of stocks to be processed in subsequent steps, especially for the time consuming fundamental analysis process described in step (4). The second pass is performed either by:

• using more stringent criteria (for the indicators used in the first pass)
• using additional indicators

If only a few stocks pass the screening step, the ranking process (step 3) can be skipped and they can be directly subjected to fundamental analysis (step 4).

<u>b) Screening with computerized tools</u>

If a brand new search needs to be performed, with all stocks in the major exchanges to be considered for potential investment, then a

Figure 38

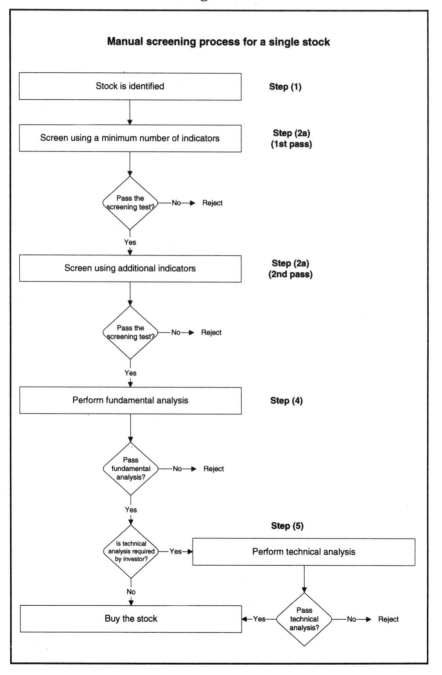

Manual screening process for a single stock

Figure 39

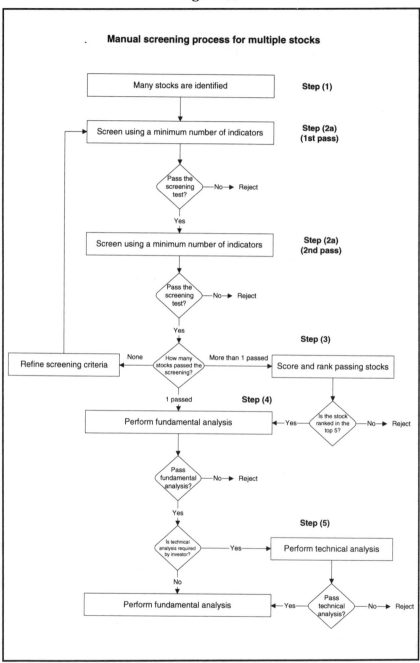

Manual screening process for multiple stocks

rigorous method for identifying, screening and selecting stocks is needed, which is shown in Figure 40. For all practical purposes, this cannot be done manually. However, a computerized tool running against an Online database, containing data on thousands of stocks, can efficiently narrow down the number of stocks using specific screening criteria.

To tap these gigantic databases, software programs are required. Using specific search/screening criteria, they can eliminate undesirable stocks and narrow down prospects to a manageable number. Typically, the screening criteria are based on one of the three main investment approaches: growth, momentum and value investing. The actual combination of indicators used for specifying the screening criteria reflect the investment philosophy and risk tolerance of the investor.

Some indicators, like market capitalization and stock price range, can appear in all three investment approaches (growth, value and momentum). For example, the P/E ratio can be used in both growth and value strategies. However, the values selected for this indicator will be quite different for each strategy. For example, a value investor will make sure that a stock with a P/E greater than 15 is screened out, while a growth investor might use a screening value of 30 for the same indicator.

Depending on the search criteria specified, a search can return a few or even hundreds of stocks. If too many stocks pass the screening test in this step, the screening process can be repeated after specifying more stringent search criteria. Depending on the number of stocks surviving the screening process, the next step in the process can either be:

- ranking (step 3)
- fundamental analysis (step 4)

c) Screening on the Internet

This is basically a variation of step (2b), which also requires the use of databases and computerized tools. The main difference is that

Figure 40

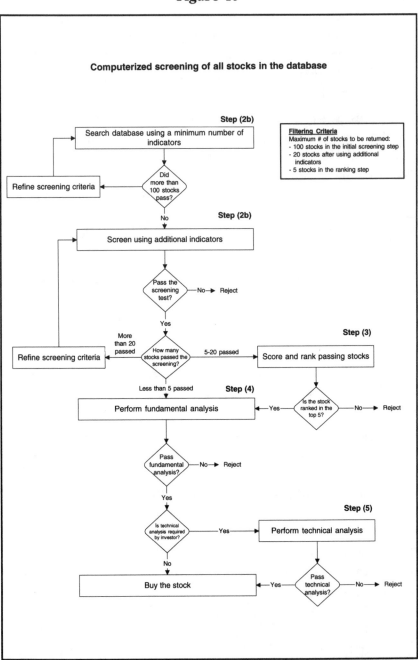

access to the database is provided through the Internet. The up-to-date screening/selection software and data is provided by various service providers. The advantages are that the user does not need to connect to the database through a modem or periodically update the database manually, as required in step (2b). However, the principle and process are exactly the same as step (2b).

Step (3) Ranking

The ranking process is used to eliminate stocks with the lowest rank. It is usually required when more than the required number of stocks survive the screening test (step 2). Ranking may be required if more than 5 to 6 stocks pass the screening test in steps (2a), (2b) or (2c). This step is optional and some investors do not use this step. For the ranking exercise, stocks can be scored and ranked based on:

- indicators used in step (2)
- all indicators used in step (2) supplemented by additional indicators
- some indicators used in step (2) supplemented by additional indicators
- a completely different set of indicators compared to those used in step (2)

The scoring and ranking methodology is shown in a step-by-step process in Chapter 10 (Tables 12–18).

Step (4) Fundamental analysis

In this step, every company that passes the screening and, where applicable, ranking process is analyzed thoroughly. This analysis includes in-depth research on the company. As part of this effort, an investor studies company research and earnings reports that can be obtained from S&P, Zacks, First Call and other sources. These reports include review of the company's earnings history and estimates, financial statements, news articles and other fundamental data.

It is possible that further ranking may be required after fundamental analysis, if more than the desired number of stocks survive in-depth fundamental analysis. The new ranking process will be similar to the procedure in step (3) with the difference being that more stringent, and possibly different, screening and elimination criteria may be used.

Step (5) Timing the purchase - technical analysis

If a company passes the fundamental analysis evaluation, an investor can buy its stock confidently. However, technical analysis may be used in conjunction with other factors to determine a more beneficial entry point. This can increase the long-term profitability of the investment. Such a step will require technical analysis of both the company and the overall market. For a long-term investor, with a 3 to 5 year horizon, this step has less significance than a trader who has an investment horizon of one year or less. Many long-term investors, including very successful ones, ignore technical analysis completely.

CONCLUDING REMARKS

An investor's ability to pick winning stocks depends on his skills in selecting winning indicators and recognizing the characteristics of winning stocks. If these skills are mastered, such an investor's stock screening and selection process will ensure that only superior stocks, which can be expected to outperform significantly, get picked.

The first step in the stock selection process is screening. It enables the filtering of stocks that fail to meet a specified screening criteria. The indicators used for the screening criteria, as well as their values, are specified by the investor based on his investment approach, experience and risk tolerance. This screening can be performed either manually or through computerized tools.

In the next step, stocks passing the screening test are ranked in order to narrow down the list of stocks passing the screening test. However, if only a few stocks survive the screening process, they can be directly subjected to fundamental analysis, which involves in-depth company research and analysis. Companies passing the fundamental analysis test can be subjected to technical analysis, which can help determine a more appropriate time for buying the stock.

CHAPTER 10

SCREENING AND RANKING STOCKS: THE DETAILS

SCREENING PROCESS

Basic objective

The objective of the stock screening and selection process is to find promising growth stocks, especially those in their fastest growth period. The reason why investors desire to select such stocks is because they are aware that the top 1% of growth stocks will consistently beat the market averages by 50 to 100%.

The process

The basic process for screening stocks involves the following steps:

A) Eliminate stocks using preliminary screening criteria matching the investor's objective and investment philosophy in order to narrow the search universe. Initially, only a limited number of indicators are used. If required, more stringent criteria or additional indicators can be used to further narrow the search.

B) Stocks passing the screening test, in step A, are scored and ranked using a number of indicators. Usually, step A indicators are used for this purpose. If required, scoring and ranking can be done using step A indicators supplemented with additional indicators. The purpose of these additional indicators is to enhance the screening criteria, and if needed, to bias the selection process to stocks with specific characteristics. The result is that stocks with preferred characteristics get pushed to the top of the list.

SCREENING

Screening without computerized tools

Potential investors who are limited by their ability to use computers need not worry that they will be unable to screen and select stocks without using software tools. This limitation is a real handicap for professional investors and traders because they need to select stocks from the gigantic databases on a continuous basis. An individual investor, on the other hand, typically analyzes only a very limited number of stocks, and can do this without a computer, even though the manual process is slower and requires additional effort.

Ordinary investors, especially those who cannot use computers, can quickly screen and analyze an individual stock using the "Express Method" which was introduced in Volume I. This is an easy, fast, hands-on method for screening individual stocks. To complete the "Express" table, which even unsophisticated investors can use, only a calculator and 5 to 15 minutes of simple data entry and calculations are required.

It is strongly recommended that every investor, including those who are not computer savvy, review the following section, "Screening with Computerized Tools," because it contains fundamental concepts and basic screening/selection criteria that every investor should be familiar with.

Screening with computerized tools

A number of computerized search tools can be used for screening stocks' databases. Their cost ranges from a few hundred to thousands of dollars. These tools have very sophisticated features. They can access Online databases that contain a wealth of investment data, current and historical, about every exchange-listed stock.

Screening process

The screening process is fairly simple. To start with, an investor specifies the screening criteria on easy-to-use screens. In the next step, the search tool extracts and lists all stocks meeting the specified criteria, after eliminating all companies failing to pass the screening test. If too many stocks are returned, the search criteria is modified using more stringent criteria and/or additional indicators, so that fewer stocks pass the screening test in the next pass. Most investors prefer to end up with 10 to 20 stocks in this step.

Screening criteria

Computerized search tools contain scores, some even hundreds, of indicators that can be combined in various permutations to create different search strategies. The combination used should reflect the investment philosophy being followed: growth, value or momentum. The following is an example of a search based on four screening criteria:

- P/E ratio should be lower than 45 and greater than 5
- highest historical earnings
- highest estimated earnings over next 3 years
- stock price above $5 and below $75

A single indicator is very rarely used for screening. However, neither should too many indicators be used because they will eliminate too many good stocks. Typically, 3 to 5 indicators are used.

Backtesting

The most important test of a search is to see how it performs over time—during different business cycles as well as in up, down and sideways markets. Such an exercise can help refine an investor's search technique. Therefore, users of computerized screening tools should perform backtesting. This means conducting a search, using historical data, and seeing how a search criteria performed over time. Such a test evaluates stocks on the basis of their values at the time of the search rather than their current values.

Screening on the Internet

Investors can use easy-to-use software available on the Internet, as well as the Online services, to perform custom screening of stocks. The process is exactly the same as used for "Screening with computerized tools."

An Internet site that individual investors can use is Zacks' "Analyst Watch on the Internet" (http://aw.zacks.com or http://www.reswizard.com). Its

"Custom Equity Screening" function allows an investor to interactively screen Zacks' 5,000 plus equity database using any combination of 81 investment criteria. For example, it can search for companies that have experienced significant changes, such as:

- earnings surprises
- price movements
- changes in analysts' buy/hold/sell recommendations
- changes in analysts' earnings/share estimates

Some of the specific criteria that can be used for screening, using "Analyst Watch on the Internet," include the following:

- best EPS surprise
- best change in:
  - current quarter consensus EPS estimate
  - next quarter consensus EPS estimate
  - current fiscal year consensus EPS estimate
  - next fiscal year consensus EPS estimate
  - long-term growth estimate
- best average recommendation
- largest increase in average recommendation
- best industry recommendation rank
- best change in industry recommendation
- highest dividend yield

Zacks' system is flexible enough for an investor to design, build, backtest and operate virtually any fundamental or technically based stock selection system. More information on "Analyst Watch on the Internet" can be obtained from (800) 399-6659.

An Online source that can be used for screening and selecting stocks is the "Strategic Investor." It is a versatile tool, which can use stock selection models such as CANSLIM and the Graham/Dodd model. This service can be accessed through Prodigy.

SCREENING CRITERIA FOR THE 3 APPROACHES

The indicators to be specified for screening stocks depend on an investor's investment approach and risk tolerance. In the following sections, search indicators and screening criteria based on four approaches, three well known and one uncommon, are described. The four approaches are:

- growth
- momentum
- value
- combination (based on criteria picked from the other approaches)

Growth investing search indicators

Objective

The objective of this search is to pick companies with superior growth prospects. In general, the following requirements are desired for selecting winning growth stocks:

- strong earnings growth and momentum
- insider buying with no insider selling
- belongs to a strongly performing industry group
- small capitalization company
- low level of institutional ownership

Indicators commonly used

There are many indicators used to search for growth companies with winning characteristics. The most important and widely used screening criteria used by growth investors are:

- earnings growth rate (higher the better)
- earnings that are rising (higher than a specified rate)
- upward changes in earnings estimates by analysts (the higher the upward revision, the better)
- positive annual earnings history for the prior five years
- absolute P/E (should be in line with its industry/group range)
- relative P/E (preferred below 50%, must not be near the high end of its range)
- insider buying (the greater, the better)
- stock price range (between $5 and $75)
- market capitalization (preference for small cap)
- bullish technical situation:
  - prefer to be above 200-day moving average line
  - should not be more than 5 to 10% below its 200-day moving average line

Screening criteria: an example

A specific screening criteria for growth stocks could be based on the following three indicators:

a) earnings growth rate greater than 20%
b) one-month change in analysts' earnings estimates—upward revision
c) stock price in the $5 to 50 range

Secondary screening

After the first step elimination has been performed with the three indicators (a), (b) and (c) in the previous section, additional indicators can be used to screen the surviving stocks. For example, the following secondary indicators can be used:

d) relative P/E ratio less than 60%
e) stock trading over its 200-day moving average line

Scoring and ranking

The following is a typical grouping of indicators used to score and rank stocks passing the screening test in the previous step:

• earnings growth rate (the higher, the better)
• insider buying (the higher, the better)
• one-month change in analysts' earnings estimates—upward revision (the higher, the better)
• relative P/E (the lower, the better)
• market cap (bias towards small caps)

Indicator weighting

To reflect the investor's bias and/or experience, each indicator can be assigned a different weight. This will cause some indicators to be favored at the expense of others. The advantage is that it permits the tailoring of a search to a particular goal or objective. For example, a screening criteria favoring insider trading can be weighted as follows:

• insider buying: 100%
• earnings growth rate: 90%
• one-month change in earnings estimate: 75%
• relative P/E ratio: 10%

Similarly, if an investor wanted to favor projected earnings, the following weights could be used:

- projected earnings: 100%
- historical earnings: 80%
- P/E ratio: 40%

Momentum investing search indicators

<u>Objective</u>

The objective of this search is to pick companies with good price and earnings momentum. This search is not concerned with indicators like insider selling, high P/E ratios and other fundamental yardsticks. The overriding criteria is momentum, with everything else being secondary.

<u>Indicators commonly used</u>

The main objective of momentum investors is to find stocks with the greatest:

- price momentum (RS rank)
- earnings momentum (EPS rank)
- industry group momentum (Group rank)
- accumulation/distribution

<u>Screening criteria: an example</u>

There are many indicators momentum investors can use for their screening criteria. The following is an example of a primary screening criteria that a momentum investor might use to eliminate unwanted stocks:

- RS rank (at least 70%, preferably over 80%)
- EPS rank >80%
- accumulation/distribution indicator (A or B)

<u>Scoring and ranking</u>

The scoring and ranking done by a momentum investor on stocks passing the screening test can be based on the indicators used in the screening step or on a different set of indicators. For example, the following indicators can be used to score and rank stocks passing the screening test in the previous step:

- RS rank change in recent 1-week, 4-week and 8-week periods
- EPS rank change in recent 3-month, 6-month and 9-month periods
- Accumulation/distribution status

Value investing search indicators

Objective

The objective of a search for undervalued growth companies is to pick stocks that:

- are trading below their true value
- have had high historical growth
- have good projected growth

Indicators commonly used

Value investors use a number of indicators for determining valuation and screening stocks. The following are some important criteria used by these investors for picking value stocks:

- lowest P/E ratio
- very low price-to-book ratio (stock price currently trading below book value)
- yield is above an absolute value or yield is high compared to its historical yield
- meets a minimum 10-year growth rate (the higher, the better)
- low price compared to its long-term price trend (the lower, the better)
- high long-term price trend (the higher, the better)
- high projected EPS growth rate for the next five years (higher the better)
- projected earnings comparable to the historical growth rate

An interesting value-based selection method is the "Dow 10 yield" criteria. This concept is based on investing in the 10 stocks with the highest yield among the 30 DJIA stocks. It involves listing the DJIA stocks in the order of their current dividend return and then selecting the ten highest yield stocks. This strategy has been quite consistent in its returns. Almost every year, these stocks return more than the DJIA itself. Between 1973 and 1995, this method yielded a 17.7% annual compounded return. An even better result is achieved by buying the 5 lowest priced stocks from among the 10 highest yielders. The low-priced yield system beat the DJIA in 18 out of 23 years, usually by a substantial margin.[21]

Screening criteria: an example

The following is an example of a screening criteria that value investors might use to search for value stocks:

- P/E ratio below 10
- rising earnings in the past five years
- stock price below book value

Scoring and ranking

The scoring and ranking done by a value investor, on stocks passing the screening test, could be based on a different set of indicators such as:

- relative P/E ratio
- lowest price/sales ratio
- dividend yield

Combination searches

It is possible to combine elements from the different investment approaches to create a combined search criteria. However, this must be done with extreme care. Suppose that an investor wants to combine the undervalued and momentum search criteria. The preliminary search can usually be conducted without a major problem. However, tricky problems arise when the indicator results need to be scored and ranked. Due to their bias, the different investment approaches may require a particular indicator to be scored differently. For example, the value investing approach will tend to assign a high score to indicators such as dividend yield and P/E ratio, while the momentum investing approach will tend to assign them a low score.

To get around this problem, two independent searches based on the two investment approaches can be run initially. This will create two lists: one each for momentum and value criteria. If the same stock appears on both lists, though it is going to be rare, it is reasonably certain that a winner has been identified.

---

[21] *Individual Investor,* March, 1996, pg. 10.

SCREENING/SELECTION CRITERIA USED BY SOME PROFESSIONALS

Range of indicators used for screening

Successful stock pickers are able to generate above average returns because their stock selection methods are superior. The portfolios of such pros consist of unique stocks, which have distinct characteristics pertaining to earnings growth rate, historical earnings, P/E ratios and other indicators. Investors can learn from these market pros by analyzing their screening and selection criteria.

When the selection criteria used by professional and successful investors is compiled, a vast array of indicators get listed. However, while some indicators appear frequently in the selection criteria used by these professionals, the combination of indicators used by each of these investors is somewhat unique.

Table 11 lists the basic screening criteria of some investment professionals and money managers. A review of this table shows the range of selection criteria being used in the stock market. As expected, some indicators appear in most lists. However, no two identical set of indicators are used by these professionals. Guidelines for using screening indicators, based on Table 11 and the authors' experience, are shown in Table 12.

Indicator combinations used for screening

Table 11 shows that investment professionals use different combinations and a varying number of indicators for their screening process. Even when the same indicator is used by different professionals, a different screening value for the indicator may be used due to two reasons. First, they may have a different investment approach (growth, momentum or value). Second, their acceptable risk levels may be different despite having the same investment approach. For example, one could be an aggressive growth investor while the other could be a conservative growth investor.

If Table 11 is analyzed, it will be observed that both #6 and #7 use the growth investing approach. However, they use the following criteria, which are quite different, for the same indicator:

- #6: P/E ratio no more than half the growth rate
- #7: P/E ratio less than the growth rate

Unusual combinations used for screening

The range, variety and combination of indicators that can be used are only limited by an investor's imagination. However, it is better for investors, especially inexperienced ones, to only use well-known and proven indicators.

An interesting combination is shown in Table 11, item #11, which searches for stocks with an EPS rank higher than 90 and an RS rank less than 20. Such a search will find companies that have had excellent earnings. However, while such companies obviously have performed well on the earnings front, they have failed to appreciate in price. The reasons for a depressed share price could be many, including litigation, actual/perceived competition, unsubstantiated rumors, poor marketing (not getting the story out) and others.

Using the screening criteria in item #11, hundreds of small stocks can be picked up at any time. However, any stock passing this screening criteria would need to be subjected to thorough investigation. This would require confirmation that the stock has good fundamentals, with solid product(s) and good future potential. If nothing fundamentally wrong turns up in an investigation, a company picked up in this search might turn out to be a good investment.

Table 11: Screening/selection criteria used by stock market professionals

#	Indicators
1.	• earnings outperform the S&P500 by 10% • volatility within 20% of the S&P500 • RS greater than 80 • EPS greater than 80
2.	• P/E ratio less than the 5 year earnings growth rate • P/E ratio below the latest ROE

#	Indicators
	• five straight years of profitability • price greater than $5 but less than $25 • price at least 20% below the stock's 52 week high
3.	• price above $5 • market capitalization greater than $150 million • three years annual earnings growth exceeding 12% • three years revenue growth over 8% • ROE greater than 11% • long-term debt to capitalization ratio less than 55%
4.	• market cap between $100 and $500 million • profits growing at least 15% per year • P/E ratio less than the growth rate
5.	• growth rate (sales and earnings) at least 20 to 40% • growth rate at least twice that of the S&P500 • high ROE (3 to 10 times the money market rates) • low debt (below industry average) • good cash flow • price momentum especially in the past few quarters (high RS)
6.	• revenues growing at least 30% a year • earnings growth keeping up with sales (>30%) • P/E no more than half the growth rate • earnings acceleration • high sales/price ratio • RS of 75 or higher (preferably 90 to 95)
7.	• earnings growth at least 30% • P/E ratio (based on current year's estimated earnings) less than the growth rate
8.	• earnings growth greater than 25% • earnings growing at a faster rate than the P/E ratio • sales growth greater than 25% • historical growth is greater than 10% • low debt • high ROE (16% or higher) • management ownership over 20%

#	Indicators
9.	• institutional ownership • accelerating quarterly revenue growth • earnings estimates being raised • earnings growth rate (for the next year) to be greater than the P/E ratio
10.	• sales: $200 million or less • daily trading volume dollar volume: $3 million or less (ideally between $50,000 and $3 million) • price between $5 and 20 • net profit margin: 10% or more • RS 90 or higher • earnings and sales growth: 25% or greater • insider holdings: at least 15% • cash flow from operations: a positive number
11.	• EPS rank 90+ • RS rank less than 20
12.	• sales growth greater than 15% • pretax margin greater than 15% • ROE greater than 15% • R&D expenditure greater than 7% of sales

Additional factors that were listed as being important by some of these professional investors:
• growth should be sustainable
• growth should be from existing operations, not any acquisitions
• among top two companies in a niche market
• high industry ranking (#1 to 3 ranking)
• barriers preventing new competition
• superior product line—no dependence on a single product
• strong upcoming product cycle
• excellent management team
• conservative accounting, with a minimum of deferred expenses

More rigorous screening: an example

Table 11 showed examples of preliminary screening, using some basic criteria, which are used as a springboard for launching in-depth analysis. The following example is based on a professional money manager's rigorous analysis, based on a number of indicators and criteria that evaluate both the stock and the market. His overall selection process involves a three-step approach:

In the first step, basic screening is done, using the following criteria:
- projected revenue growth in the next 5 years: greater than 25%
- projected earnings growth in the next 5 years: greater than 25%
- market capitalization less than 1 billion
- total debt less than 40% of market cap
- ROE approximately 20%

In the next step, the absolute value of the stock is determined. This requires discounting projected earnings with reference to the long-term interest rates. Additionally, the P/E-to-projected growth ratio is analyzed. For this pro, a stock is considered attractive if this ratio is less than 0.75 and overpriced when it is greater than 1.25.

In the last step, relative value is established. This is done by comparing the P/E of a well-known diversified growth fund to that of the S&P500. The comparison helps determine whether growth stocks are currently overvalued, or undervalued, compared to the S&P500. This helps the investor avoid growth stocks during their period of underperformance, relative to large caps, which occurs in cycles lasting a few years. As a final supplement, other indicators (market, sentiment and economic) are analyzed in order to determine the overall market health and investment climate.

CANSLIM method for selecting winners

William O'Neil, author of the best-selling book "How to make money in stocks", and founder of *Investor's Business Daily,* has developed the CANSLIM method for picking stocks. Mr. O'Neil conducted a comprehensive study of the top performing equities just before they began their major price moves. He analyzed virtually every big winner during seven or eight market cycles dating back to 1953.

The analysis covered most fundamental and technical variables, for each company, including sales, earnings, products, profit margins, P/E ratios, relative strength etc. It was observed that there were seven common variables in almost all the top-performing companies. He assigned a letter to each of these seven characteristics and created the acronym CANSLIM. These seven characteristics are:

C - current quarterly earnings per share
A - annual earnings per share increase
N - new products, new management, new highs
S - shares outstanding
L - leader or laggard
I - institutional sponsorship
M - market direction

According to this stock picking methodology, the following are the basic requirements that a stock should meet before it can be selected for investment:

"C" Current quarterly earnings/share for the most recent quarter should be higher by a significant percentage compared to the same quarter of the previous year. This desired increase is at least 18 to 20%.

"A" The annual EPS should have increased at a meaningful rate compared to the previous year's earnings for each of the prior five years.

"N" This refers to the company having either a significant new product (or service), new management or a change in industry conditions. It also means that one should buy a stock when it is close to, or has made, a new high in price after having had a correction and spent time in a base building phase.

"S" Evaluate the supply and demand for a stock. A stock should have a small number of outstanding shares. A stock with small capitalization and with fewer shares available for trading is believed to have a better chance of moving significantly higher than a large cap stock, if all other factors are equal.

"L" This is the price performance of a stock. This method recommends buying a leader, with high RS, rather than a laggard (even though it looks very cheap). The stock's relative price strength should be very high. Only stocks having an RS rank of 80 or higher are considered for investment.

"I" Do institutions own the stock? The presence of 3 to 10 institutions is considered reasonable. Ownership by too many institutions is not desired.

"M" Determine the state of the general market. An investor should understand market behavior and be able to interpret general market indexes. This will enable an investor to determine the overall market direction—up or down. This requirement is based on the fact that during declining markets, even good stocks lose value.

Summarizing the screening criteria

A wide array and combination of indicators are used by professional investors; the value used for each of these indicators can be quite different, depending on the investor's approach and risk tolerance. This can be very confusing for most ordinary investors, who do not have easy access to indicator guidelines available in an easy-to-use format. Therefore, it is very difficult for individual investors to choose the right indicators and their acceptable values.

To help the ordinary investor select values for the most commonly used indicators, Table 12—"Guidelines for screening indicators," has been compiled. These guidelines are based on data compiled in Table 11 and the authors' own experience.

Table 12: Guidelines for screening indicators

#	Indicator	Preferred value
1.	Projected long-term earnings growth rate	more than 20%
2.	Annual and quarterly earnings increase	more than 25%
3.	Revision in earnings estimates (1 month change)	positive
4.	P/E ratio	less than growth rate

Table 12: Guidelines for screening indicators (cont'd.)

#	Indicator	Preferred value
5.	Relative P/E ratio (ignore for young companies)	less than 70% for established companies
6.	P/E-to-projected annual earnings growth rate (PEG ratio)	less than 0.75; not more than 1.0
7.	Insider buying	at least one buyer
8.	Number of analysts following company	three or more
9.	Stock price	between $5 and $75
10.	Market capitalization	small cap
11.	Institutional ownership	more than 20% and less than 50%
12.	EPS rank	greater than 80%
13.	RS rank	greater than 80%
14.	200-day moving average	within +/- 10% of stock price; trending up
15.	Accumulation/distribution	A or B
16.	Return on equity (ROE)	15% (minimum); prefer more than 20%
17.	Debt/equity ratio	below industry average
18.	Cash flow growth rate (historical)	more than earnings growth rate
19.	Profitability	three or more years

RANKING PROCESS

The concept of scoring and ranking stocks will be shown through examples in this section. The objective of these exercises is to score and rank two stocks, "A" and "B," using a number of indicators. The assumption is that only two stocks "A" and "B" have survived the screening process. The exercise will be conducted in two parts:

• Case 1: using indicators based on the growth investing strategy
• Case 2: using indicators based on the momentum investing strategy

The results, not surprisingly, are different for the two cases. Stock "B" is favored using the growth strategy indicators, while stock "A" is favored when the momentum strategy indicators are used. The reasons are obvious: different indicators and weighting factors were used in the two cases.

Case 1: Growth investing strategy

Table 13 lists the five indicators that will be used to score and rank stocks "A" and "B." These indicators are based on the growth investing philosophy. Table 14 lists the scores to be used for different values of each indicator. For example, if the projected long-term growth rate of the company is 24%, its score will be 7 because it falls in the indicator value range of 20 to 24%. In the real world, the actual scores used will be provided by the investor based on his own experience. For the inexperienced investor, the values shown in Table 14 can be used in the beginning.

The data

For the ranking exercise for stocks "A" and "B", the following three tables will be required:

- Table 13: Contains the actual values of five indicators for both stocks ("A" and "B").
- Table 14: Contains the score for each possible indicator value based on the growth investing approach.
- Table 15: Worksheet for calculating the total scores required to rank stocks "A" and "B." The indicator values and corresponding scores required to be plugged into this table are extracted from Tables 13 and 14 respectively.

Table 13: Actual values of indicators (growth)

# Indicator	Stock A	Stock B
1. Projected long-term growth rate	30%	24%
2. P/E-to-projected growth rate	1.0	0.7
3. # of analysts following the company	3	7
4. Insider buying	0	2
5. EPS rank	90%	80%

Table 14: Growth investing indicators and scores

#	Indicator	Indicator value	Score to be used
1.	Projected long-term growth rate	35% or higher	10
		30–34%	9
		25–29%	8
		20–24%	7
		15–19%	6
		less than 15%	5
2.	P/E-to-projected growth rate	less than 0.5	10
		0.5–0.59	9
		0.6–0.69	8
		0.7–0.79	7
		0.8–0.89	6
		0.9–0.99	5
		1.0–1.09	4
		1.1–1.19	3
		greater than 1.19	2
3.	Number of analysts	greater than 10	10
		7–10	9
		3–6	8
		1–2	7
		None	0
4.	Insider buying	3 or more buyers	10
		2	9
		1	8
		one	0
5.	EPS rank	90% or higher	10
		80–89%	9
		70–79%	8
		less than 70%	5

The calculations

Table 15 can be completed as follows:

- Assign a weight for each of the five indicators in the "weight" column (W) to reflect the indicator's relative importance.

- For Stock "A":
  - Enter the "Value" column data (X1) for each of the five indicators. This data is extracted from Table 13.
  - Enter the "Score" column data (Y1), corresponding to the (X1) column value, for each of the five indicators. This data is extracted from Table 14.
  - Calculate "Total Score" (Z1), for each of the five indicators, by multiplying columns W and Y1.
  - Obtain the "Grand Total" by adding the five calculated values in the "Total Score" column (Z1).
- For Stock "B":
  - Enter the "Value" column data (X2) for each of the five indicators. This data is extracted from Table 13.
  - Enter the "Score" column data (Y2), corresponding to the (X2) column value, for each of the five indicators. This data is extracted from Table 14.
  - Calculate "Total Score" (Z2), for each of the five indicators, by multiplying columns W and Y2.
  - Obtain the "Grand Total" by adding the five calculated values in the "Total Score" column (Z2).

Table 15: Ranking based on growth investing approach

# Indicator	Weight (W)	Stock A Value* (X1)	Stock A Score** (Y1)	Stock A Total Score (Z1=W*Y1)	Stock B Value* (X2)	Stock B Score** (Y2)	Stock B Total Score (Z2=W*Y2)
1. Projected long-term growth rate	10	30%	9	90	24%	7	70
2. P/E-to- projected growth rate	10	1.0	4	40	0.7	7	70
3. No of analysts	7	3	8	56	7	9	63
4. Insider buying	6	0	0	0	2	9	54
5. EPS rank	5	90%	10	50	80%	9	45
Grand Total:				236			302

* Values obtained from Table 13
** Scores obtained from Table 14

The result

The result of the ranking exercise, as shown in Table 15, is:
- Stock A = 236 points
- Stock B = 302 points

Hence, based on this analysis, it is indicated that stock "B" should be favored over stock "A" due to its higher overall score.

Case 2: Momentum investing strategy

Table 16 lists the four indicators that will be used to score and rank stocks "A" and "B." These indicators are based on the momentum investing philosophy. Table 17 lists the scores to be used for different values of each indicator. For example, if the EPS rank of the company is 85%, its score will be 9 because it falls in the indicator value range 80 to 89%. Again, the scores used in the real world will be provided by the investor based on his own experience. For the inexperienced investor, the values shown in Table 17 can be used in the beginning.

The data

For the ranking exercise for stocks "A" and "B", the following three tables will be required:
- Table 16: Contains the actual values of four indicators for both stocks ("A" and "B").
- Table 17: Contains the score for each possible indicator value based on the momentum investing approach.
- Table 18: Worksheet for calculating the total scores required to rank stocks "A" & "B." The indicator values, and corresponding scores, required to be plugged into this table are extracted from Tables 16 and 17 respectively.

Table 16: Actual values of indicators (momentum)

#	Indicator	Stock A	Stock B
1.	EPS rank	90%	80%
2.	RS rank	85%	90%
3.	Accumulation/distribution	B	A
4.	200-day moving average: % extended	+1%	+6%

Table 17: Momentum investing indicators and scores

#	Indicator	Indicator value	Score to be used
1.	EPS rank	90% or higher	10
		80–89%	9
		70–79%	8
		less than70%	5
2.	R/S rank	90% or higher	10
		80–89%	9
		70–79%	8
		less than 70%	5
3.	Accumulation/distribution	A	10
		B	9
		C	6
		D	4
		E	2
4.	200-day moving average: % extended	1–1.9%	10
		2–3.9%	8
		4–5.9%	6
		6–7.9%	4
		8–9.9%	2
		greater than 9.9%	0

The calculations

Table 18 can be completed as follows:

- Assign a weight for each of the four indicators in the "weight" column (W), to reflect the indicator's relative importance.
- For Stock "A":
  - Enter the "Value" column data (X1) for each of the four indicators. This data is extracted from Table 16.
  - Enter the "Score" column data (Y1), corresponding to the (X1) column value, for each of the four indicators. This data is extracted from Table 17.
  - Calculate "Total Score" (Z1), for each of the four indicators, by multiplying columns W and Y1.
  - Obtain the "Grand Total" by adding the four calculated values in the "Total Score" column (Z1).

- For Stock "B":
  - Enter the "Value" column data (X2) for each of the four indicators. This data is extracted from Table 16.
  - Enter the "Score" column data (Y2) corresponding to the (X2) column value, for each of the four indicators. This data is extracted from Table 17.
  - Calculate "Total Score" (Z2), for each of the four indicators, by multiplying columns W and Y2.
  - Obtain the "Grand Total" by adding the four calculated values in the "Total Score" column (Z2).

Table 18: Ranking based on momentum investing approach

#	Indicator	Weight (W)	Stock A Value* (X1)	Score** (Y1)	Total Score (Z1=W*Y1)	Stock B Value* (X2)	Score** (Y2)	Total Score (Z2=W*Y2)
1.	EPS rank	10	90%	10	100	80%	9	90
2.	RS rank	10	85%	9	90	90%	10	100
3.	Accumulation distribution	7	B	9	63	A	10	70
4.	200-day moving avg: % extended	7	+1%	10	70	+6%	4	28
	Grand Total:				323			288

* Values obtained from Table 16
** Scores obtained from Table 17

The result

The result of the ranking exercise, as shown in Table 18, is:

- Stock A = 323 points
- Stock B = 288 points

Hence, based on this analysis, it is indicated that stock "A" should be favored over stock "B" due to its higher overall score.

CONCLUDING REMARKS

Stock screening is performed by specifying screening criteria using a combination of indicators. The selection of these indicators depends on the investment approach being used: growth, momentum and value. The number of indicators used by investors for screening and selecting stocks is very large—spanning the broad spectrum of variables available to stock market investors. However, only some indicators appear in the selection criteria of most professionals and successful individual investors. Also, while some indicators appear frequently in their selection criteria, the combination of indicators used by each of these investors is somewhat unique.

Successful stock pickers are able to achieve above average returns because their stock selection methods, based on winning indicators, are superior. Their portfolios consist of unique stocks with distinct characteristics pertaining to earnings growth rate, historical earnings, P/E ratios and other indicators. Investors can learn from these market pros by analyzing their screening and selection criteria, which have been summarized in this chapter.

Screening can be done in a couple of passes. In the first pass, a few indicators are typically used to conduct preliminary screening. This is followed by secondary screening done with the same indicators (but with different values) or using the original indicators supplemented with additional indicators. Screening is followed by scoring and ranking, which allows the selection of the top stocks with the best characteristics, if winning indicators are used. In this step, weighting factors can be used to give more importance, based on the investor's bias and experience, to specific indicators.

CHAPTER 11

ANALYZING STOCKS: THE DETAILS

FUNDAMENTAL ANALYSIS

Basic requirements

Every stock identified as a potential investment during the initial screening and selection process must be thoroughly analyzed prior to buying using fundamental analysis. In this step, a company's current health and business prospects are evaluated. This complete process involves quantitative as well as qualitative analysis.

Choosing the right indicators and criteria

Many criteria and indicators can be used to subject a company to fundamental analysis. However, an investor must not use too many indicators for evaluating stocks. Besides requiring too much effort, it has the potential to cause confusion and lead to the wrong conclusions due to conflicting signals. Therefore, only a few indicators should be chosen that conform to the investor's investment strategy, goals and risk tolerance. Where possible, indicators should be prioritized and ranked in the order of importance. This can typically be done by using weighting factors.

Indicators should be analyzed with care. When working with many indicators, flexibility is also needed. For example, if a few relatively unimportant indicators get a low score during analysis, they can be ignored safely. However, if a single important indicator is negative, it must never be ignored.

Basic indicators for evaluating a company's fundamentals

In fundamental analysis, a number of indicators are used to analyze the health and future business prospects of a company. In this section, only the most important indicators used in fundamental analysis, described in-depth in earlier chapters, are presented in a summarized form. These indicators, it may be noted, are also used for preliminary stock screening and selection as shown in the previous chapter.

Earnings per share (EPS)

Investors analyze two types of EPS numbers: quarterly EPS and annual EPS. More than the dollar/share number (EPS), investors focus on the percentage change in quarterly EPS compared to the previous year's comparable quarter. Investors want the current quarterly EPS growth rate to be higher by a significant percentage compared to the same quarter of the previous year. A company with accelerating earnings growth, such as growing from 20% to 25% to 30%, is highly favored by investors. Also, the annual EPS should have been increasing consistently for a number of years.

Projected earnings per share (quarterly and annual)

This is the consensus annual earnings estimate from analysts monitoring the company for the following year. Quarterly earnings estimates for the next quarter, and in some cases for each quarter of the next fiscal year, are also provided by these analysts. The higher the projected earnings, relative to a company's current earnings, the better it is.

Projected five-year earnings growth rate

This is a very important indicator. Successful growth stocks should have a historical earnings growth rate of over 20%. Generally, a company with a forecasted 3 to 5 year growth rate of 20 to 30% is a very good investment. Unless there are exceptional circumstances, avoid companies with historical annual earnings growth rates below 15%.

Earnings estimate revisions

Periodically, analysts revise their earnings estimates for a company. Usually, this is triggered by an earnings release, news item or an improving/deteriorating business outlook for the company. An upward revision is considered positive and pushes the stock price up. A downward revision on the other hand tends to make the stock price decline. The number of changes in projected EPS are reported for 1-week, 1-month and 2-month periods. However, the most closely watched number is the one-month change in projected EPS.

Revenue (sales) growth

Revenues are reported by companies every quarter and annually. These should be growing at a healthy pace. Without revenue growth, the earnings growth of a company is going to be limited. A useful number to track is "quarter sales percent change." This is the percentage change in quarterly sales compared to the same quarter of the previous year.

P/E ratio

This valuation tool, obtained by dividing the current stock price ($) with the earnings/share ($/sh), is used very widely. For this indicator, extreme values are undesirable. Typically, very low (P/E under 5) or very high (P/E over 35) ratios are undesirable. A high P/E ratio needs to be justified by the company's revenue and earnings growth rate. In general, fast growing growth stocks may have a P/E ratio ranging from 20–40 without being considered overvalued by growth investors.

Relative P/E ratio

This indicates the current value of a company's P/E ratio when compared to its own historical P/E range, with 100 being the highest historical value. Value and growth investors want this number to be low, or within accepted norms, depending on the growth rate of the company. Momentum investors do not place any emphasis on this number.

P/E-to-projected growth rate

This ratio is obtained by dividing the P/E ratio by the expected annual earnings growth rate. If the P/E ratio is 30 and the annual earnings growth rate is 40%, the P/E-to-projected-growth ratio is equal to 0.75 (30/40). Generally, a stock is considered attractive if this ratio is less than 0.75 and overpriced when it is over 1.25.

Insider trading

Investors view it as a very positive sign if insider buying is taking place in a company. The greater the number of insider buyers, the more positive is the sign. Insider selling should be noted even though it does not have the same significance as insider buying.

Number of analysts following the company

This is not a direct indicator of a company's health. However, it is an important number because it indicates the degree of importance that can be given to earnings projections. More the number of analysts that follow a company, the higher is the confidence generated in the accuracy of the forecasts. The greater the number of analysts, the lower the chance that a single wrong estimate will distort the average estimate figure being reported.

Cash flow

This is the net cash generated during the reporting period. Good cash flow is vital for growth companies. Poor cash flow can force borrowing (which affects overall earnings) or the issuance of more stock (which affects earnings/share). Both of these are a negative for the stock price. Cash flow/share is used for analyzing a company's cash flow. It is equal to the cash provided by operations divided by the total number of outstanding common shares.

Five-year cash flow growth rate

The more cash generated by a company, the better it is. Positive cash flow helps a company to finance its growth and weather business downturns. It is a positive sign if the company's cash flow growth rate is significantly higher than its earnings growth rate.

Debt-to-equity ratio

A company's debt burden is analyzed by investors because it can affect profitability. Obviously, the lower the debt/equity ratio, the lower is the risk, and consequently, the safer it is for the company and the investment. Therefore, avoid buying a company with a high debt/equity ratio. If the debt/equity ratio has been decreasing in the past 2 to 3 years, or even in recent quarters, it can be viewed positively. A company's debt/equity ratio should be compared to other companies in its industry. It should be in line with or less than the industry average.

Return on equity

Return on equity is a measure of how effectively a shareholder's investment is being used. It is calculated by dividing net income (after taxes) by the common stockholders' equity. The higher a company's ROE, the better it is as a prospective investment.

Return on sales

This is a measure indicating the percentage of sales that a company converts into profits. The higher the return on sales, the more efficiently the company is converting sales into net income and managing its business.

Performance indicators

A number of indicators are used to gauge the performance of a stock. The most popular of these performance indicators, which are particularly favored by momentum investors, are:

Relative strength (RS) rank

This measures and compares a stock's price performance over the past year, with the last quarter being given greater weightage, against all other stocks. In general, a company having an RS rank greater than 80 is preferred. Such a stock has the potential to be a leader or a winner, rather than a laggard.

Earnings per share (EPS) rank

This is a measure of a company's EPS growth over the past five years and the stability of that growth. It measures, and compares, a stock's earnings momentum against all other stocks. Since the best stocks, the leaders, have the highest EPS rank, stocks with an EPS rank over 80 are preferred.

Accumulation/Distribution

Accumulation indicates professional buying by institutions, while distribution indicates selling. Stocks with an "A" or "B" rating indicate accumulation and positive momentum. "D" and "E" ratings indicate distribution while "C" indicates a neutral rating.

UNDERSTANDING THE COMPANY

The stock market heavily favors informed investors. For such investors, consistent success is quite common. While success is also achieved by casual investors who invest without conducting any meaningful research, it comes their way only occasionally. In the long run, the odds do not favor those who venture into the stock market depending on hunches and hopes. It should be realized that for success to be achieved, the stock market requires investors to:

- conduct adequate research prior to investing in any company
- remain informed by constantly monitoring their stock investments

Research requirements

For initial research prior to procurement and for subsequent monitoring, investors need to review the quantitative and qualitative aspects of an investment. The quantitative aspect includes review of earnings projections and trend, dividends, financial statements and operating performance. The qualitative aspects include company profile, competition, business prospects and management quality. For analysis, neither the quantitative or qualitative aspects should be ignored because both provide important perspectives and information.

Investment information sources

Company research report

Investment information can be obtained from many sources. The best source of investment data and news on a particular company is a "company research report," which is typically issued by a brokerage company or an investment firm. Such a report, which is readily available to ordinary investors, typically includes financial and performance data as well as important news affecting the company in the prior 12 to 18 months. Important sources of company research reports include S&P, Zacks and Value Line as well as the Internet. Sample company reports have been included in the Appendixes (B and C).

All company research reports contain earnings data. However, only some reports contain comprehensive historical, current and projected earnings data. To supplement information contained in the company research reports, investors can use the more focused earnings reports from First Call Corporation or Zacks Investment Research.

The company being researched

A very good source of information is the company itself. Upon request, companies will provide their own investment literature free of charge. Besides the annual and quarterly reports, they typically provide other reports (10K and 10Q), copies of news articles concerning the company and press releases. Some companies also provide free of charge company research reports issued by analysts following the company. To obtain any report or other pertinent information, contact the company's "Investor Relations" department, which every publicly traded company is expected to have.

Other sources

There is no dearth of sources for an investor prepared to spend the time and effort required to conduct investment research. The most useful sources are described in Chapter 6 of Volume I. (See page 275)

Where to get company research reports

Brokers provide a complete company research report package for their clients. This package, generically called a "company research report" or a "stock report." is usually a collection of reports and data from multiple sources. Such reports include data sheets from multiple sources such as S&P, Zacks, First Call and other research information providers. Instead of collecting this information from multiple sources, it is better for an investor to obtain it from a broker, which will save considerable time and effort. The Internet is also an excellent source for getting company research reports.

Company research reports: what they contain

A company research report is extremely valuable in that it can reveal material information, which can be positive or negative, such as:

- company related news
- press releases and announcements by the company
- consensus earnings estimates (from analysts)
- comments on earnings estimates
- changes in competition and environment
- product cycle and any delays
- fundamental and performance data

Typically, a detailed company research report will include the following general, performance and financial data pertaining to a particular company:

General information

- company business summary, comments on performance and earnings trend, important developments and news items referencing the company
- industry outlook
- ratings:
  - S&P issues 5 stars to a company recommended as a buy; 1 star is issued to a company with a sell recommendation
  - Zacks rates companies from 1 (best) to 5 (worst)
  - Value Line from 1 (highest) to 5 (lowest) for both "Timeliness" and "Safety"
- risk associated with the stock (beta)
- price chart and average daily volume
- shareholder's data (outstanding shares, insider ownership, percentage of institutional ownership)
- market capitalization
- the number of analysts following the company
- breakdown of analysts' buy/hold/sell recommendations and the mean value of recommendations

Performance indicators

- EPS (quarterly and annual): current and historical

- EPS projection: for the next 2 quarters as well as the next 2 years
- EPS projected growth rate: for the next 2 years; the average for the next 3 to 5 years
- EPS growth rate comparison (versus the industry and the S&P500)
- earnings revisions: average revision in each estimate, upward or downward, over the past 7, 30 and 60 days
- earnings surprises: comparison of actual earnings to the analysts' earnings estimates
- P/E ratio (current and 5-year average)
- relative P/E
- comparison of current vs. projected P/E ratio
- sales (revenues): quarterly and annual (current and historical)

Financial data and information

- summarized financial data
- income statement
- balance sheet and other financial data
- net margin (current and 5-year average)
- return on equity (current and 5-year average)
- debt levels and ratios
- analysis of key financial data

Historical and comparison data

- 5 to 10 year historical per share data including:
  - book value, cash flow, earnings, dividends
  - stock price: high and low
  - P/E ratio: high and low
- comparison with the industry average (and the S&P500) of various indicators including current P/E, estimated 5-year EPS growth, price/book ratio, price/sales ratio, dividend yield, net margin, ROE and debt/capitalization ratio

Examples of news items in company research reports

A company research report lists major news items relating to that company, which were reported in the prior 12 to 18 months. This information can be very useful for relating the company's performance and price gyrations to specific news items. The following are examples of news items from two such reports:

April 25, 1997: "Qualcomm shares up 8% today on news that Motorola's motion for preliminary injunction and restraining order against

Qualcomm has been denied...Motorola claims that Qualcomm's 'Q' phone infringes Motorola's patents related to its StarTAC phone."

April 2, 1997: "Informix down $7/8 to $9...Robertson Stephens & Gruntal, Inc., reportedly downgraded stock...Yesterday, company forecast substantial 1st quarter operating loss, net loss due to weakness in all regions."

Tips for analyzing a company

General tips

There are many factors that need to be evaluated when analyzing a company. Besides the guidelines listed in Table 12, which can be used for analyzing a company, investors can use the following tips:

- 10 to 20% institutional ownership is a sign that they have started buying; indicates that plenty of institutional buying remains to be done
- company must have solid products or services (no fad products)
- status of product cycle and upgrades
- study quarterly and annual sales results; check for seasonality
- breakdown sales categories, which can be helpful in pinpointing strong and weak areas
- international sales as a percentage of revenues
- determine market share
- market control: is the company a leading player or established in a niche market?
- compare to competition: identifying a better competitor might indicate a superior investment prospect

Performance tips

- sales growth is insufficient by itself; it must be accompanied by expanding profit margins
- simultaneously expanding sales and margins can fuel exceptional growth
- sales growth combined with margin expansion and P/E expansion will rocket a stock price
- profit margins are useful in comparing profitability of companies within the same industry
- analyze net profit margins (measures a company's margins after taxes)
- realize that margins will eventually level off

- rapidly contracting margins can be disastrous
- determine positive trends

Analyzing company management

The ability of a company to perform successfully or continue doing so is dependent to a large extent on its management. A company's management should have the ability to lead and execute its strategic plans. Therefore, an investor should try to determine the quality, experience and aggressiveness of the management team. Any changes that might improve or diminish the team's effectiveness should be noted. If management makes excuses for poor results, it should serve as a warning sign. However, if management has a large stake in the company, but not large salaries, it is a positive sign.

The impact of quality management on the performance of a company cannot be minimized. This is understood by Wall Street, which places high value on company management. For example, the president of Project Software & Development left the company in late July 1996. He had been most closely associated with Maximo—the software product that accounted for most of the company's revenues. Following his departure, the stock slid from 49 $^3/_4$ in early July to a low of 27 $^1/_2$ in the second week of August. The reason was investors' concern that a visionary had left the company and that his leadership would be missed.

Investors can obtain the name of a company's Chairman, Chief Executive Officer (CEO), and Chief Financial Officer (CFO) from its annual report. This can be a starting point to work backwards, to determine how successfully the executive(s) performed at the last company he worked for. Usually, the performance of that company is a good indication of the executive's prior performance.

Analyzing the industry group/sector

A company should never be analyzed, purchased or monitored in isolation. Instead, its environment should be studied and analyzed at every stage. An investor should never forget to look at the bigger picture because picking winners involves more than just selecting good companies. In simplified terms, this means observing the behavior of the market as well as the industry group/sector to which the company belongs.

Why analyze the industry group/sector

It is well known that the long-term performance of a company rests on its ability to earn profits and grow at a healthy rate. However, the short-term performance quite frequently depends on two important external factors:
- outlook for the industry or group the company is a part of
- the state of the economy

Therefore, it becomes imperative for an investor to understand which industry group/sector his stocks belong to—such as technology, financial services, etc. This will enable him to understand and compare the behavior and performance of his stocks to similar stocks.

Industry analysis should be an integral part of a solid investment strategy. Being able to understand the future prospects for the industry, and where the stock being analyzed fits in the bigger picture, can be crucial for enhancing the profits to be made.

What to do

An investor should determine the group/sector to which his stock belongs. Sometimes this is not very obvious. For example, technology stocks are considered by some to be cyclical stocks even though they are growth companies. Their cycles are quite different than those of conventional cyclical companies.

After a company's industry group/sector has been determined, an investor should understand, monitor and forecast, if possible, its expected performance relative to other groups and the market. This will enable him to forecast, to a reasonable degree, the expected performance of his own stocks. When it appears that the group/industry performance is going to deteriorate, he can lighten up. When the future performance of the group is forecast to be positive, he can increase his exposure to the group by adding to existing holdings or by taking up new positions.

TECHNICAL ANALYSIS

After a company has passed the fundamental analysis exercise, an investor can confidently buy its stock. However, it can be worthwhile to subject the stock to technical analysis, at least a limited one, in order to determine a more profitable entry point.

Entry point determination

A basic technical analysis test is to determine if a stock is trading over its 200-day moving average. A stock trading over this line is considered to be in a long-term uptrend and, consequently, this is considered bullish. If a stock pushes above its 200-day moving average line, many investors consider this to be a buy signal. On the other hand, if a stock slides below its 200-day moving average, these investors consider this to be a bearish signal and, therefore, they sell the stock. Similarly, if a stock trades over its 50-day moving average line, it is considered to be a bullish sign by short-term traders. These players use the 50-day moving average line both as an entry and exit point.

A profitable time to buy a stock occurs after it has had a price correction and undergone consolidation, i.e., experienced a 2 to 15-month basing period. According to technicians, a stock should be bought after it has emerged from a base building period and when it is close to or actually making a new high in price. Horizontal support and resistance lines are also used by some investors as entry/exit points. A support line is used as an entry point if the stock has reversed direction and other indicators are also positive.

Limitation

Technical analysis is no substitute for fundamental analysis. It should be used only for a limited purpose. For example, by determining resistance and support levels, an investor can have a better understanding of a stock's price swings and behavior. In general, the following guidelines should be used when using technical analysis:

- use it to confirm fundamentals
- do not buy a stock even if technical analysis provides confirmation, if little or no research material is available

- if market analysis shows that the market is making a top, reduce overall stock holdings

ANALYZING A COMPANY IN-DEPTH: AN EXAMPLE

In this section, a company will be analyzed in-depth. The objective is to introduce the reader to fundamental analysis using a specific, real-world case. The basic procedure involves:

- extracting important statistical, performance and financial data from company research reports
- collecting business information, industry data and performance prospects from various sources including company annual reports, company research reports and trade publications
- evaluating the potential price appreciation from the collected data
- highlighting specific parameters in support of or against the case for buying the stock

The company

The company to be analyzed is Oracle Corporation, an enterprise software and information management services company. The company develops, markets and supports computer software products used for database management, network communications, applications development and end-user applications. The company's core product is the Oracle7 relational database management system (RDBMS). The company offers its products, along with consulting, education, support and systems integration throughout the world.

Statistical and shareholder data

An analysis of the shareholder data, presented in Table 19, indicates that most of the factors analyzed are positive. The company has a very large number of outstanding shares, which usually is a negative since it tends to make it difficult for a stock to make a major move, either up or down. However, this is balanced by the very high percentage of insider holdings, considered to be a very positive factor.

Table 19: Analysis of Oracle's basic statistical and shareholder data

	Miscellaneous data and values	Observations and analysis	Investment perspective
Industry	data processing	high forecasted growth	+ve
Group	computer–software	above average growth	+ve
Shares outstanding	654 million	very large float	-ve
Average daily volume	3.89 million	high	neutral
Insider holdings	40%	very high	very +ve
Institutional holdings	54%	high	-ve
Beta	0.83	near S&P average	+ve
Risk	average		+ve
Current stock price ($)	$37\,^1/_2$	10% below recent high	+ve
52 week range ($)	$23\,^3/_8$–$42\,^1/_8$		
Insider activity	neutral		neutral
12-month P/E	41.7	5-year average = 41.2	+ve
P/E on 1997 estimate	29.3	below 35% estimated growth rate	+ve

Data sources being used for analysis

The primary sources of data used in the analysis are 1996 earnings and company research reports on Oracle Corporation. Data from 1996 has been used because it will permit comparison of Oracle's forecasted performance, based on its fundamental analysis using these reports, with its actual performance in 1997 and 1998. The reports used in this analysis are:

- Appendix A: First Call "Earnings estimate report"
- Appendix B: S&P stock report
- Appendix C: Zacks' company report
- Appendix D: Zacks' "Analyst Watch" report

It may be noted that it is not necessary to use all four sources for analysis. These reports contain a considerable amount of duplicate data. For most practical purposes, one or two reports are adequate. It should also be noted that reports from different sources can contain minor data discrepancies, which can usually be ignored. The reason is that occasionally the data included in these reports is preliminary and subject to minor changes.

For example, the S&P report shows Oracle's 1996 earnings equal to $0.90/share (Appendix B), while the number reported by Zacks' report is $0.95/share (Appendix C). The $0.05 difference is attributed to the $0.05/share charge that Oracle took in the first quarter of 1996 to reflect costs associated with an acquisition. So depending on when the data is updated, reports issued by different sources may contain slightly different numbers. If the difference is material, the data should not be used prior to making an investigation.

Table 20: Oracle's revenues (million $)

Fiscal year ending May	1996	1995	1994	1993	1992	1991
1st quarter	771.8	556.5	398.0	307.0	245.0	215.0
2nd quarter	967.2	670.3	452.2	353.0	284.0	257.0
3rd quarter	1,020	722.3	482.8	370.0	290.0	269.0
4th quarter	1,464	1,018	668.1	472.6	235.0	287.0
Year	4,223	2,967	2,001	1,503	1,178	1,028

Source: Appendix B (S&P stock report)

Table 21: Oracle's earnings ($/share)

Fiscal year ending May	1996	1995	1994	1993	1992	1991
1st quarter	0.08	0.09	0.06	0.02	0.00	-0.05
2nd quarter	0.21	0.14	0.09	0.05	0.02	0.00
3rd quarter	0.22	0.16	0.11	0.04	0.03	0.02
4th quarter	0.40	0.27	0.17	0.10	0.04	0.01
Year	0.90	0.66	0.43	0.21	0.10	-0.02

Source: Appendix B (S&P stock report)

Performance and financial data

- Revenues: 4.22 billion for fiscal year ending May 1996
- Total revenues in the 4th quarter of fiscal year 1996, ending May, grew 44% year-to-year
- Growth in business areas:
  - core database licenses: +49%
  - applications: +73%
  - tools: +13%
  - services: +44%

- current ROE = 41%; compares favorably with:
  - 12% for industry average
  - 20% for the S&P500
  - 33.9% for Oracles 5-year average
- net margin: 14.3% vs. average 10% for the last 5 years
- net margin: 14.3% vs. average 3.3% for the industry
- long-term debt/capitalization:
  - current = 0%
  - 5-year average = 11%
- EPS growth rate for last 12 months: 42%
- price/book ratio: 13.1 vs. 3.5 for the industry average
- price/sales: 5.8
- price/CF 29.8 versus 19.9 for the industry average

Source: Zacks' Company Report (Appendix C)

Broker recommendations

- from Zacks (Appendix C):
  - strong buy: 12
  - moderate buy: 10
  - hold: 4
  - sell and strong sell: nil
- from First Call (Appendix A):
  - mean of recommendations based on 20 brokers (analysts): 1.4 where 1 = buy, 2 = buy/hold, 3 = hold, 4 = sell/hold, 5 = sell

STOCK PRICE FORECAST

Earnings assumptions and estimates

For the purpose of this analysis, earnings data and estimates from First Call's "Earnings Estimate Report" have been used as the primary source. Where required, data from Zacks' company report, Zacks' "Analyst Watch," and S&P's stock report have been used to supplement the primary data from First Call.

Table 22: Oracle's earnings estimate ($/share)

Fiscal year end in May	1996 (actual)	1997 (estimated)	1998 (estimated)
Mean estimate (EPS)	$0.90	$1.28	$1.69
No. of analysts making estimate		25	20
Estimate range		$1.22-$1.34	$1.55-$1.79

Source: Appendix A (First Call "Earnings estimate report")

Forecast calculations for fiscal year 1997

- EPS growth in the last fiscal year (1996): 35%
- Estimated EPS: $1.28
- Earnings growth estimates (short-term: 1 year):
  - S&P report estimates that earnings will grow over 35% during fiscal year 1997
  - Zacks' "Analyst Watch" report also estimates a 35% EPS growth for fiscal year 1997
- Report date: September 7, 1996
- Months remaining till the end of the current fiscal year (May 1997): 9

Forecast price at the end of the current fiscal year (May 1997):

= annual earnings growth rate x estimated EPS

= 35% x $1.28

= $44.8

Forecast price rise:

= $44.8 - $37.5 = $7.3

% price increase:

= ($7.3/$37.5) = 19.47%

This means that the stock is forecast to rise 19.47% in the next 9 months (ending current fiscal year, May 1997). On an annualized basis, this equals:

19.47% x (12/9) = 25.96%

Forecast calculations for fiscal year 1998
- Estimated EPS: $1.69
- Earnings growth estimate (long-term):
  - First Call estimate from analysts: 29.6% (average annual long-term growth rate)
  - Zacks estimate: 33%/year (fiscal year 1998)
  - for this analysis, we will be conservative and use the lower EPS annual growth rate (29.6%) for fiscal year 1998
- Report date: September 7, 1996
- Months remaining until the end of fiscal year (May 1998): 21

Forecast price at the end of the next fiscal year (May 1998):

= annual earnings growth rate x estimated EPS

= 29.6% x $1.69

= $50

Forecast price rise:

= $50 - $37.5 = $12.50

% price increase:

= ($12.5/$37.5) = 33.33%

This means that the stock is forecast to rise 33.33% in the next 21 months (ending fiscal year, May 1998). On an annualized basis, this equals:

33.33% x (12/21) = 19%

OVERALL ANALYSIS

The big picture

Corporate America is competing in a very competitive global market. Efficiency (lean and mean) and increased productivity are some of the traits of successful companies competing in this environment. To either become or remain competitive, companies need many tools including robust enterprise software. Companies providing these tools will benefit from the efficiency and productivity improvement trend, which is expected to continue for many years. Oracle is a leader in this group and stands to benefit tremendously from this continued push for efficiency.

Positive business factors

- Oracle is a well-established company growing at a very rapid pace: such growth is usually associated with smaller companies
- Software industry growing : database sector also growing very fast; Oracle expected to grow in tandem
- Overall business growth is excellent: revenues grew 44% in the last quarter (ending fiscal year May 1996)
- Core database business is strong: secondary businesses are also good with the exception of tools
- Market share: 37.9% of the relational database software market
- Diversified product line: core product is supplemented by tools, education and consulting
- Difficult for new companies to enter their business
- Strong balance sheet
- International presence
- Very high percentage of management ownership
- Excellent management team

Positive technology factors

- Technical leader: its products dominate the market
- Software is available on all hardware platforms: enables customers to easily migrate from other platforms
- Well positioned to take advantage of two of the hottest trends in the computing world: Internet and Data Warehousing
- Internet and Data Warehousing products being introduced rapidly

Negative factors

- Potential of price war, with severe impact on earnings, if Microsoft enters the enterprise database market
- A company as large as Oracle may be unable to maintain its current high growth rate for too long

Price appreciation potential

Oracle's current price (year: 1996) is $37.5. As calculated earlier, Oracle's stock has very good price appreciation potential in the next two years as tabulated in Table 23:

Table 23: Oracle's forecasted price appreciation potential

Current price $37 ½	Forecasted price	Rise over current price	Annualized return
ending fiscal year, May 1997	$44.8	19.47%	25.96%
ending fiscal year, May 1998	$50	33.33%	19%

Financial data analysis

An analysis of Oracle's financial tables, shown in Appendix B, shows that it is in a very strong financial position, with most ratios and debt status improving year after year. Its balance sheet is very strong. The following is a summary of the financial data analysis:

- cash balance increasing consistently since 1990
- cash flow increasing every year since 1991
- long-term debt decreasing every year since 1991
- debt ratios decreasing every year since 1992
- return on assets increased in 4 out of the last 5 years
- return on equity increased in 4 out of the last 5 years

Performance data analysis

The performance indicators, shown in Table 24, are very positive with the exception of the price/book ratio which is high compared to its industry.

Table 24: Analysis of Oracle's performance data

	Value	Comparison	Investment perspective
ROE — current	41%	12% for industry average 20% for S&P	very +ve
ROE — 5-year average	33.9%		very +ve
Net margin	14.3%	10% for last 5 years 3.3% for the industry	very +ve
LT debt/ capitalization	0	11% average last 5 years	very +ve

Table 24: Analysis of Oracle's performance data (cont'd.)

	Value	Comparison	Investment perspective
EPS growth rate last 12 months	42%		very +ve
price/book ratio	13.1	3.5 for the industry	-ve
P/E (current)	41.7	41.2 average last 5 years	+ve

Technical indicator analysis

Most of the technical indicators shown in Table 25 are positive. Both the short-term and long-term trend indicators are positive. The accumulation/distribution indicator is neutral because Oracle, along with other members of the technology sector, suffered a correction during the summer that decreased the value of this indicator to "C."

Table 25: Analysis of Oracle's technical indicators

Indicator	Value	Investment perspective
Accumulation/distribution	C	neutral
RS rank	79	neutral/+ve
EPS rank	98	very positive
% above 10-week moving average line	12%	+ve
Trading above 200-day moving average line	Yes	+ve

Source: *Investor's Business Daily*

Confirmation signals

The fundamental analysis of Oracle Corporation reached a positive conclusion. As a final check, we can compare our conclusion to the recommendations being made by the professional analysts (Appendixes A and C). Not surprisingly, they are also very positive:

- no sells
- very high percentage of buy recommendations (22 out of 26)
- high mean of recommendations (1.4)

Recommendation and logic

It is quite clear that Oracle's fundamental health is good. Fundamental, technical, performance and financial analysis indicate a positive investment climate. The current fiscal year's estimated profit potential is excellent (25.96%). In the following year, the rate of return is expected to decrease to 19%. With such a positive forecast, it is recommended that the stock be bought.

As indicated earlier, an investor should continuously monitor a company, even if everything looks good. Oracle is no exception. It should be monitored regularly. At the first sign of slowdown in its earnings or revenue growth rate, the company should be thoroughly reevaluated to determine if it should continue to remain in the portfolio.

If Oracle continues to maintain its growth rate, analysts will periodically increase its earnings estimates. In tandem with the revised earnings forecasts, reruns of the calculations (with the new earnings and growth figures) should be done. Such an exercise will enable an investor to determine if the forecasted ROI is acceptable and also help determine the new target price.

Actual performance in 1997 and 1998

The performance of Oracle Corporation was in line with expectations derived from its fundamental analysis. The company continued to grow at an excellent pace in fiscal year 1997. Not surprisingly, its stock price appreciated in tandem with the growth in its revenues and earnings. Compared to a forecasted price of $44.8, Oracle was trading at $46.62 at the end of the 1997 fiscal year (May 1997).

It had been forecast that the stock would appreciate to $50 by the end of the 1998 fiscal year (May 1998). This price level was reached in June 1997—much earlier than expected. The stock continued to appreciate—reaching a high of $63 before starting to decline. This decline came as no surprise because the stock had appreciated far more than its forecast earnings warranted. By January 1998, Oracle had declined to a low of $27.09 (after adjusting for a 3-for-2 stock split that took place on August 15, 1997). A strong rebound followed and the stock had recovered to $47.82 by April 1, 1998. This placed it within a shade of its May 1998 forecast price of $50.

CONCLUDING REMARKS

Every company passing the screening test must be subjected to fundamental analysis, which helps determine its health and future business prospects. For performing in-depth company analysis, investors use a number of indicators. The relative importance of these indicators depends on the investing approach, philosophy and risk tolerance of the investor.

The most important indicator is earnings, which is analyzed in many different ways including annual and quarterly earnings, EPS rank and earnings history. Other commonly used indicators include revenue (sales) growth, P/E ratio, cash flow and debt level. A number of performance indicators, such as relative strength rank, are also used. As part of fundamental analysis, a company's management and its industry/group/sector are also analyzed.

Finally, after passing the fundamental analysis test, a company can be subjected to technical analysis. This can help determine a more appropriate time for buying the stock. However, most investors do not use technical analysis for timing their procurement.

CHAPTER 12

SELLING STRATEGIES

COMMON PROBLEMS

Poor selling performance

Any investor, despite thorough research and analysis, can make a mistake and pick a loser that will need to be sold. In fact, not even the best and most savvy investors are immune to making mistakes. Also, even though it is recommended that profits run, every winner needs to be sold ultimately. Therefore, every investor has to deal with selling issues at some time or the other. However, it has been observed that while many investors are good stock pickers, their performance in selling stocks leaves much to be desired. The disinclination to sell, in many cases, can be attributed to:

- belief that a sound, long-term investment has been made that precludes selling
- refusal to acknowledge that a mistake has been made

Lack of selling strategy

Generally, investors focus their attention only on buying stocks and, in many cases, do not have any selling strategy. However, to be a successful player, an investor must have both buying and selling strategies. Therefore, it is imperative that every investor pick a selling strategy—no matter how simple. Otherwise, selling will be based on emotional factors, hunches and reaction to events.

PLAN YOUR SELLING

Avoid forced selling

Deciding when to sell a stock is as important as making a buy decision. Every investor must have a strategy, or a rules list, for determining when to sell a stock. An investor must not let circumstances, such as needing money for immediate needs, force a sell decision. Letting such needs influence a selling decision is a sure recipe for losing money. Funds invested in the stock market should be those that will not be needed in the near future. If the investment horizon is short, or the possibility exists that such funds may be required soon, other financial instruments more appropriate for holding short-term funds should be used.

Select a selling strategy

An investor must have a selling plan, for cutting losses, profit taking (short term) and for disposing long-term winners. Without a specific strategy, for individual stocks and the market, an investor will not be able to effectively react to changes. However, an investor with a pre-determined strategy is always better prepared. For example, such an investor will be better prepared, than one with no strategy, when deciding whether to sell or buy more shares if there is an unexpected price decline.

No strategy will work forever. Even good strategies need to be modified and fine-tuned occasionally. Also, it is natural for investors to make mistakes. Therefore, periodic self-analysis should be conducted in order to pinpoint mistakes and subsequently refine or change the strategy.

Set price targets

When buying any stock, price targets should be set for loss selling, short-term profit taking and long-term profit taking. A common tool for this purpose is the limit "sell order," which is an order that gets executed only if the stock reaches a specified price. Such an order can be placed with the "good until canceled" condition, which usually remains in effect for two months. If such an order expires, a new order can be placed. If needed, it is possible to increase the target sell price while such an order remains in effect.

COMMON REASONS FOR SELLING

Profit taking

This refers to selling a stock after it has appreciated in price. This can occur after a short price runup which leads traders to dispose of a stock for profit taking. However, the majority of selling involves investors disposing stocks, for capital gains, after an appreciable price increase. A fair amount of selling is also done by investors, after varying holding periods, even though they may have only a limited amount of capital gains.

Loss exceeds a percentage

Many market advisors recommend that an investor should sell, no matter what the reason, if a stock drops more than 7 to 10% below the buy price. This makes an assumption that the stock has been bought at the correct (exact) buy price. This may be an acceptable strategy for well-established blue chip companies and utilities, whose price movement in either direction is limited. However, for small growth companies, whose price fluctuations can routinely be 20% or more, such a strategy will not work satisfactorily. An investor in such companies can easily get whipsawed if this method is used. A more practical strategy may be to place a mental stop loss about 10 to 15% below the purchase price. Investors already having profits in a stock can be more flexible when determining the acceptable price fluctuation limits.

Laggard performance

Sometimes even the best research and analysis does not prevent an investor from picking a stock that fails to meet expectations. Such a stock, despite good earnings and favorable news, does not rise as can be expected of a company posting good results. Herein lies the difference between a good company and a good stock. A good company does not always translate into a good stock. Examples are Seagate Technology and AMD in the early 1990s. Both are good companies, which turned in hefty profits for a number of years. However, they did not excite investors and failed to rise to their potential. During the period that these two companies under-performed, other companies with far lower profits handsomely rewarded their shareholders.

Portfolio pruning

Investors buy both losers and winners. While ultimately all stocks need to be sold, some are required to be dumped very quickly, while others can be sold after a long holding period. Periodically, investors should evaluate their holdings and get rid of dead wood, which improves the portfolio performance in the long run. This pruning should be an ongoing process. When evaluating stocks for pruning, favor selling the losers first. These should be followed by those with small profits and those which failed to meet expectations.

Tax reasons

Capital gains can be offset by capital losses. Therefore, investors sell their losers in order to compensate for the capital gains tax liability generated by selling their winners. Typically, this is done at the end of the year, when the tax situation is more clear than at the beginning of the year. If a decision to sell a winner is reached at year-end, it is advisable to postpone selling until the new year starts. This permits an investor to defer the tax liability and, consequently, take advantage of the time value of money.

SELLING SIGNALS

Common sell signals

The most important reason to sell a stock is the deterioration of its fundamentals. In such a case, it should be sold without any hesitation or delay. Besides deteriorating fundamentals, a number of other factors can indicate trouble for a stock. These need to be analyzed as part of an overall analysis for holding on to a stock. In general, the following are signals which indicate that a stock might be a candidate for complete or partial selling:

General and market reasons

- stock does not appear to be meeting the investment goal
- earnings growth begins to slow or actually decline for two consecutive quarters
- reason/factors for buying the stock no longer exist
- stock has appreciated significantly:
  - profit taking appears in order
  - stock has become a larger than desired percentage of the portfolio and therefore needs to be partially sold
- stock continues to decline without any rally
- loss exceeds a predetermined percentage
- management actions seem irrational
- acquisition has had fundamental negative impact on the company
- market top is recognized

Technical reasons

- uptrending 200-day moving average turns into a downtrend
- stock price breaks below its 200-day or 50-day moving average line; break below 50-day moving average is a warning; break below the 200-day moving average is more serious
- stock is 70–100% above its 200-day moving average line
- price drop on heavy volume
- new highs on decreased or poor volume
- trading on heavy volume after an advance, without further price appreciation
- number of down days in price versus up days in price change after the stock starts declining
- stock is undergoing distribution
- decline appears more than a normal decline from a peak, i.e., a correction of 10–12% or so
- relative strength rank falls below 70, especially in a rising market
- group strength is weak and stock is acting alone
- support level fails
- trading band: failure swing at the top of the band or support failure at the 30-day moving average line
- trendline: occurrence of a trend break through a rising trendline, which signals the probable end of the trend

Additional sell signals for small growth, niche and one-product companies

- earnings growth rate decreases significantly, which does not justify its high P/E
- revenue growth does not meet expectations

- losing market share very fast
- poor financial health: high or increasing debt
- new company enters business, which changes the competitive picture materially
- competitor introduces killer product
- critical product is delayed or gets bad reviews after introduction
- pending litigation whose adverse judgment can materially affect the company
- adverse ruling in a major patent lawsuit or other litigation
- company starts wasting money on unnecessary nonproductive assets

Strong reasons to sell

While some sell signals can be ignored and usually need to be analyzed in conjunction with other indicators and signals, others are quite clear cut. These indicators are very strong sell signals and cannot be ignored without increasing the risk factor considerably. These include:

- company is in trouble: deteriorating financials or business prospects
- rate of quarterly earnings increase slows significantly or actually declines
- earnings actually decline for two consecutive quarters
- market share is lost for two consecutive years
- shares start declining due to fundamental weakness
- no new products are being developed
- spending in R&D has been curtailed
- company is resting on laurels and historical performance
- paid too much for an acquisition
- better opportunity: a stock with far more favorable prospects has been identified
- impending bear market has been recognized

Market as a sell signal

An investor should carefully check the overall market health and direction before leaping out of the market. One should not let some sharp selloffs, which can be isolated events, lead to the premature bailing out of the market. This can result in good stocks being sold too early. If that happens, the potential exists for missing a strong upward move following the selloff.

Warning signs from the market

The following are some signals emanating from the market that should raise warning flags:

- change in direction accompanied by increased volume
- leaders are among the casualties: this is an indication that the market will follow
- leaders decline on expanding volume
- if most declining stocks have low relative strength (RS below 80), it indicates that the weaker stocks are being hit
- if the mutual fund index shown in *IBD* falls significantly
- yields on long-term bonds exceed the S&P500 dividend yield by 6% or more: this is a very bearish sign

Riding out selloffs

Sharp selloffs are quite frequent and an investor needs to understand and profit from them. A very good example is the behavior of the market, on a very volatile day, when the NASDAQ dropped 1.3% and the DJIA fell slightly less. On the NYSE, losers beat gainers by a 5-3 margin. However, trading volume actually declined on all three major exchanges: NYSE, NASDAQ and the AMEX. The selloff subsided in just two days. On subsequent days, the market rebounded and the A/D line moved upwards, while volume declined.

Following a selloff, as in this case, low volume is viewed positively by analysts. Such a drop is more in line with an orderly correction than the start of a major market move in the opposite (downward) direction. Further analysis revealed that the leading stocks had suffered only minor pullbacks on decreasing volume. Investors who bailed out of the market missed the rebound. And as typically happens in such cases, bailed out investors continued to wait for the market to decline after the rebound in order to re-invest. However, the decline did not materialize.

MISTAKES TO AVOID

Common mistakes

Three of the biggest mistakes that investors make are:

- being extremely nervous, resulting in selling a stock prematurely

- continuing to hold a stock for too long even after its mediocre performance becomes apparent
- focusing too much on what was paid for the stock

A common mistake that many investors make, when deciding whether to sell, is to look at the current "loss" or "profit." Instead of basing a decision on the price paid basis, they should evaluate the stock's future price appreciation potential. They should not be driven by the "paper loss." If a stock's fundamentals are sound, a paper loss should not cause an investor to lose confidence. However, a sell decision should be taken immediately if the company's future looks cloudy.

Some long-term investors, who are paid a dividend, do not worry when their stock plunges. They do not evaluate selling such a stock because of the income it generates. The numbers in such a case do not add up: a 5% dividend yield minus a 30% loss equals a 25% loss! Such an attitude can be very costly if the company's fundamentals are not sound. First, the stock can fail to recover in price. Second, the risk increases that the company may ultimately be forced to cut its dividend.

When avoiding selling is not a mistake

Some signals appear to indicate selling. However, some stocks should not be sold despite these signals. The following are some guidelines for holding on to a stock, even though it is indicated that selling might be in order:

- pessimism is pervasive: do not be a crowd follower during pessimistic periods
- stock has appreciated significantly and appears "overvalued": ride a winner, do not sell early; do not sell just because of the price appreciation
- price target is reached: if fundamentals show an improvement, increase the price target
- stock has high P/E: do not use guideline P/E ratios for selling decisions; realize that winners can have 4 to 5 times the market's P/E ratio
- price drops: hold on if the reasons for buying remain valid
- leading stock gaps down in price: do not panic—may be due to a large block being sold by an institution

CONCLUDING REMARKS

Ultimately, every stock needs to be sold. The most common selling reasons are short- and long-term profit taking, profit target is reached, profit exceeds a percentage, laggard performance, portfolio pruning and tax reasons. However, despite this reality, too many investors confine their attention to buying stocks while ignoring selling, which is a very important aspect of investing.

A very common factor preventing selling is emotional involvement with a stock, which should never happen, and unrealistic hopes without any foundation. Every investor should have a selling strategy and an understanding of the factors that should trigger selling. This will prevent one from just reacting and making ad hoc decisions. Learn to recognize sell signals. Be aware of the common mistakes that investors make. Also, recognize the situations when avoiding selling a stock is not a mistake.

Typically, before a sell decision is made, other factors need to be studied in conjunction. However, there is one scenario which dictates that a stock be sold without any delay—deteriorating fundamentals. Also, once a sell decision has been taken, especially based on fundamentals, selling should not be delayed in anticipation of a minor rebound from current levels.

CHAPTER 13

RISK AND PORTFOLIO MANAGEMENT

LIMITING RISK

Common stocks are an excellent vehicle for making money but they are not suitable for everyone, especially for those who cannot tolerate price swings. While there are many opportunities in the stock market, it also has many risks associated with it. Stock market risks cannot be eliminated but they can be minimized. Some investors limit risk by staying away from the stock market altogether. However, for the vast majority, the stock market is the place to be. These investors need to strike a balance between risk and reward based on their individual risk tolerance and profit objective.

A very important way of reducing risk is by staying informed. An informed investor always stays on top, and instead of reacting to tips and events, makes calculated moves. Such an investor always comes out ahead. Besides remaining informed, an investor can use a number of methods, explained in the following sections, for limiting the risk faced by stock market investors.

Avoiding speculation

Every investor should understand the difference between investing and speculating. There is a great difference between picking a winner based on merits and speculating on hunches. The bottom line is that one should not speculate in the stock market. All stock selections should be made based on fundamental research and analysis.

Diversifying

A very common method for reducing risk is by spreading the investment among a number of stocks. This is based on the very old principle: Do not place all your eggs in one basket. By buying a number of stocks, an investor does not remain exposed to the fluctuations and performance of any one stock. While this strategy reduces the downside risk, it can also place a damper on any meaningful upside move by a winner.

The following are some diversification guidelines that can be used by investors:

- in general, 5 to 7 stocks are sufficient for an investment of $50,000
- overdiversification should not be done
- instead of owning a large number of mediocre performers, who can only drag down the overall portfolio, it is preferable to own a small number of top-performing stocks
- stocks with home run potential are inherently riskier than average stocks
- to reduce the risk for investors who want to invest in stocks with home run potential, diversification among several home run issues makes sense

Limiting risk from one-product companies

An important characteristic of a one-product company is that it is very focused. Another advantage is that it can control a niche that larger companies cannot enter profitably. Its stock also has the potential to rise appreciably. However, one-product companies have an above average risk associated with them. Depending on whether a company's single product succeeds or fails, its stock can soar or crash.

The key to evaluating potential investment in such a stock is to minimize risk while retaining the opportunity for reaping the big reward. A sensible strategy is to avoid having too many one-product companies in the portfolio. Once such a company enters a portfolio, it should be monitored with extra care. A key factor to monitor for such a company is its R&D expenditure. This is an absolute must because only a reasonable amount of R&D investment can ensure that the company maintains or extends its lead in the only product it sells.

Handling a "hot" tip with care

At some time or the other, every investor gets a "hot" tip. These tips from friends, neighbors and others should be thoroughly investigated before making any investment. The following is a useful action list for investors when dealing with a hot tip:

- separate the tip from the tipper
- if a story made the stock "hot," check it out; the story may already be discounted and the good news may already be reflected in the price
- study the company and its business
- analyze the company's fundamentals
- analyze analysts' earnings estimates and other indicators
- based on earnings estimates, estimate the potential price rise in the next year; compare this to the current price
- check out the industry's performance and determine its fundamentals
- investigate if any insider buying or selling has taken place
- invest only if everything investigated is positive and the ROE looks appealing

Using cash substitutes

Many investors prefer to remain invested even if there is uncertainty and worry about the economy (or the market) and the market is volatile. These investors can limit their risk by parking their money in the biggest companies, such as the DJIA components, whose price fluctuations are limited even during a volatile or declining market. These mega-stocks such as GE, which has a float of 3.23 billion shares, can become a cash substitute for such investors. Besides being relatively safe, such companies also pay dividends.

Using beta to limit risk

An investor's objective during the stock selection process is to identify stocks that will:

- rise faster than the average stock during a bull market
- decline less than the average stock during a bear market

Very few stocks can meet these desirable attributes. However, an investor can use beta to achieve one aspect of this goal. Beta can be used as a screening tool to eliminate stocks, even if they have had good price appreciation in the past, if they are too volatile. This can be done by buying a stock having a beta equal to 1 that, on average, will match the market's upside, as well as downside, swings at the same speed.

Each investor has to decide, based on one's personal risk assessment, the acceptable level of volatility. For someone prepared to experience more volatility, a stock with a beta greater than 1, which indicates higher than average volatility, may be acceptable.

Understanding the risk of leverage

Advantage of leverage

In its simplest form, leverage can be described as "more bang for the buck." Leverage is using borrowed money to buy stocks and can translate into doubling the gain or loss on an investment. Using margin, an investor can buy double the number of stocks that can be bought if only the cash in the account is used. Consequently, with double the number of shares, the potential loss or gain will be doubled. An alternative to playing margin is to buy stocks with above average volatility. The advantage of this technique is explained in the next section.

Alternative to margin investing

In a rising market, profits will be made by both techniques: margin investing and investing in high volatility stocks. During a rising market, a stock with above average volatility will rise higher. However, while a high volatility stock will appreciate more than a margined stock (which has lower volatility), the margin investor is compensated by having double the number of shares.

However, despite this advantage in a rising market, it is preferable to buy stocks with above-average volatility, even though they tend to be riskier, instead of playing margin. There are a number of reasons for this. With margin, an investor needs to buy double the number of shares (compared to a stock with double volatility). Therefore, a higher commission and margin interest will need to be paid. Also, during a declining market, the margin player's loss will be doubled. Another risk is that there always exists the danger of being forced to sell, due to a margin call, if the price declines too much. While a riskier, more volatile stock will fall more during a declining market, an investor's overall loss will typically be less with such a stock, than with a margined stock, because only half the number of shares will be owned.

Options

Calls and puts

There are two types of stock options: calls and puts. A call option conveys to the option buyer the right, but not an obligation, to buy the underlying stock from the call seller at a specified price called the strike price. This right expires on the expiration date of the contract. The option buyer pays a premium to the seller for giving him the right to exercise the option.

A put option conveys to the option seller the right, but not an obligation, to sell the underlying stock to the put buyer at a specified price called the strike price. This right expires on the expiration date of the contract. The option seller collects a premium from the buyer for giving him the right to exercise the option.

A call option buyer expects the stock price to rise, which will enable him to exercise the right to buy the stock at a price below the market value. If the stock fails to appreciate, the investor only loses the full amount of the option (premium), which is considerably less than the investment required for buying the stock itself. It should be realized that selling a call option does not protect against a price drop. However, buying a put option does protect against a price decline.

How an option works

Suppose that an investor owns 1,000 shares of ABC Company currently trading at $22. Let us assume that he sells a call option for 10 contracts, which is equivalent to 1,000 shares, at a strike price of $25 for expiry in March 1999. For getting this right, the call buyer will pay the investor a premium. If this premium is $2/share, the investor will collect $2000. In

March 1999, the call buyer can buy the stock from the call seller for $25/share. However, if the stock trades below $25/share on the expiration date, the option becomes worthless and the call buyer will lose his full investment ($2,000). However, if the stock trades at $30, he can still buy the stock for $25 from the investor. In this case, it means a net profit of $5,000 - $2,000 (profit - premium) for the call buyer.

Options are traded and quoted, just like stocks, with bid and ask prices. Their prices are reported in the newspapers such as the *WSJ* and *IBD*.

<u>Advantages and risks</u>

Stock options, when used correctly, can improve long-term returns and reduce risk. The advantage of using options is that during periods when a stock trades in a narrow range, when its price is not expected to rise appreciably, an investor can receive some income from the stock. However, the flip side is that if the stock makes a big move during the period that the option contract remains in force, the call writer (seller) will be unable to cash in on the major price move, which benefits the call buyer.

The shorter the expiration time limit, the greater is the risk of buying calls. On the other hand, the longer the term, the less the risk. To lessen the risk of buying options, options can be spread over several months. Risk can also be reduced by buying the options of solid companies. Writing naked calls, without owning the underlying stock, is very risky and should be avoided. Options should not be used by novice investors. When used, they should be used carefully and sparingly.

Hedging

A hedge is a strategy that offsets investment risk. This technique is used to cushion the risk of a major decline in the market. It involves balancing the "long" and "short" positions. A long position refers to investing in stocks, with the expectation that they will appreciate in price. A short position refers to shorting a stock, which is based on the expectation that the stock price will decrease. An investment in stocks is considered long while a position in an index, such as an S&P500 put or NASDAQ100 put, is considered short.

PORTFOLIO ANALYSIS

A very important aspect of investing in the stock market is portfolio management, which includes the following activities:

- asset allocation, which involves the distribution of assets among different investment types (stocks, bonds, money market funds, etc.)
- analysis of market conditions, which is used to determine the level of exposure to stocks in asset allocation
- managing diversification: determining which, and how much, of various sectors and industries are to be represented in the portfolio of stocks; for example, increasing exposure to interest sensitive stocks when the interest rate environment turns positive for such stocks
- periodic evaluation and review of the portfolio
- monitoring stocks in the portfolio
- sell decisions: determining whether to let profits run, cut losses, or switch stocks

CONCLUDING REMARKS

The stock market has many risks associated with it. However, while these risks cannot be eliminated, they can be managed and minimized. A number of tools are available to investors for reducing risk to manageable proportions. Two of the most important ways are by becoming an informed investor and diversifying investments—by spreading the stocks among different sectors and groups. While diversifying has its advantages, overdiversification should be avoided.

Investing for the long term in the stock market can reduce the risk caused by price fluctuations. Avoid speculation and select investments based on fundamentals. Be open to "hot" tips but analyze such companies thoroughly. When investing in one-product companies, be extra careful. They have extra risk and reward associated with them.

No portfolio should remain stagnant. The performance of every stock changes over time and, therefore, every stock in a portfolio should be periodically evaluated. This exercise will enable the pruning of underperformers and the infusion of new, faster growing, stocks in the portfolio.

APPENDIXES

▰FIRST CALL®

Earnings Estimate Report

Oracle Corp (ORCL)

Consensus Recommendation

	Buy	Buy/Hold	Hold	Sell/Hold	Sell
	1	2	3	4	5

▲

The mean recommendation of 20 brokers is 1.4 with a range of 3.0 to 1.0

Fiscal Year Earnings Estimates

Price as of 09/09/96 .... $37.50
Dividend Yield .... N/A
Beta 0.8

Fiscal Year End is May	Actual 1996	FY 1997	FY 1998
Mean Estimate	$0.95	$1.28	$1.69
Date of Last Revision		08/30/96	09/05/96
Date of Last Confirmation		09/09/96	09/09/96
Brokers Included In Consensus		25	20
Range of Broker Estimates		$1.22-$1.34	$1.55-$1.79
Median Estimate		$1.28	$1.70
Implied P/E ratio		29.3	22.2
Average long-term growth rate predicted by contributing brokers			29.6%
Five year historical growth trend in annual EPS			62.8%

Current Quarter Earnings Estimates

The next quarterly earnings announcement is expected September 12, 1996.

Quarter End is August	Actual Q1 96	Q1 97
Mean Estimate	$0.13	$0.17
Brokers Included In Consensus		25
Range of Broker Estimates		$0.16-$0.20
Median Estimate		$0.17
Implied Growth Rate Over Comparable Quarter		30.8%

Revision Momentum

The total number of upward and downward estimate revisions received from all contributing brokers during the last 90 days.

Brokers Revising Estimate Upwards	Q1 97	FY 97	FY 98	Q1 97	FY 97	FY 98	Q1 97	FY 97	FY 98	Q1 97	FY 97	FY 98
					1			2		3	19	2
Brokers Revising Estimate Downwards	1	1		1	1		2	1	1	4	2	2

Last 7 Days	Last 30 Days	Last 60 Days	Last 90 Days

To Order Additional Reports Call: 1-800-544-4699

Appendix B—S&P stock report for Oracle Corporation

STANDARD &POOR'S
STOCK REPORTS

07-SEP-96

Oracle Systems   **4876T**

Nasdaq Symbol **ORCL**

In S&P 500

Industry:
Data Processing

Summary: Oracle supplies computer software products used for database management, applications development and decision support, as well as end-user and other applications.

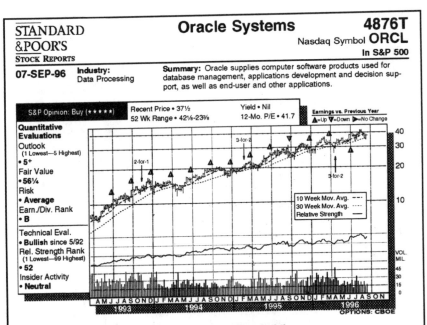

S&P Opinion: Buy (★★★★★)

Recent Price • 37½
52 Wk Range • 42⅛-23⅜

Yield • Nil
12-Mo. P/E • 41.7

Earnings vs. Previous Year
▲=Up ▼=Down ▶=No Change

Quantitative Evaluations

Outlook
(1 Lowest—5 Highest)
• **5+**

Fair Value
• **56¼**

Risk
• **Average**

Earn./Div. Rank
• **B**

Technical Eval.
• **Bullish** since 5/92

Rel. Strength Rank
(1 Lowest—99 Highest)
• **52**

Insider Activity
• **Neutral**

10 Week Mov. Avg. ----
30 Week Mov. Avg. ------
Relative Strength ———

OPTIONS: CBOE

Overview - 25-JUN-96

Revenues should increase at a 35% to 40% rate in FY 97 (May), reflecting strong demand for the company's relational database management system, aided by new releases of application products, accelerated growth in software develpment tools, driven by strength in the Windows market, continuing robust demand for services, and continued expansion of worldwide economies. Products for the UNIX and desktop environments (which account for about 90% of total revenues) should continue to grow rapidly, and proprietary systems growth is reaccelerating, led by strength in products tailored for Digital Equipment computers. Net profit margins are expected to be maintained, as volume efficiencies and cost controls are offset by a higher tax rate. Earnings should benefit from the greater revenues, steady margins and absence of the $0.05 a share non-recurring charge recorded in the FY 96 first quarter.

Valuation - 25-JUN-96

Earnings should rise over 35% in FY 97. The database software segment is growing rapidly, as organizations cope with managing and utilizing the massive data stored on their computer systems. ORCL's leadership position bodes well for future results; the core database server business is strong, applications software revenues should continue to grow rapidly, the database tools business should increase, and there is a continuing need for additional services. The shares, which reached new highs in June, were recently trading at a P/E of about 85% of the projected growth rate over the next several years, based on FY 97 projections. The strong earnings growth that we expect should help the stock outperform the market in coming months.

Key Stock Statistics

S&P EPS Est. 1997	1.25	Tang. Bk. Value/Share	1.87
P/E on S&P Est. 1997	30.0	Beta	0.83
Dividend Rate/Share	Nil	Shareholders	4,000
Shs. outstg. (M)	654.2	Market cap. (B)	$ 24.5
Avg. daily vol. (M)	3.896	Inst. holdings	54%

Value of $10,000 invested 5 years ago: $ 214,258

Fiscal Year Ending May 31

	1996	1995	1994	1993	1992	1991
Revenues (Million $)						
1Q	771.8	556.5	398.0	307.0	245.0	215.0
2Q	967.2	670.3	452.2	353.0	284.0	257.0
3Q	1,020	722.3	482.8	370.0	290.0	269.0
4Q	1,464	1,018	668.1	472.6	235.0	287.0
Yr.	4,223	2,967	2,001	1,503	1,178	1,028
Earnings Per Share ($)						
1Q	0.08	0.09	0.06	0.02	0.00	-0.05
2Q	0.21	0.14	0.09	0.05	0.02	0.00
3Q	0.22	0.16	0.11	0.04	0.03	0.02
4Q	0.40	0.27	0.17	0.10	0.04	0.01
Yr.	0.90	0.67	0.43	0.21	0.10	-0.02

Next earnings report expected: mid September

Dividend Data

Amt. of Div. $	Date Decl.	Ex-Div. Date	Stock of Record	Payment Date
3-for-2	Mar. 14	Apr. 17	Apr. 02	Apr. 16 '96

A Division of The McGraw-Hill Companies

Appendix B—S&P stock report for Oracle Corporation (cont'd.)

Oracle Systems Corporation

4876T

07-SEP-96

Business Summary - 03-JUL-96

Oracle Systems Corporation develops, markets and supports computer software products used for database management, network communications, applications development and end-user applications. Its principal product is the ORACLE relational database management system (DBMS). The company offers its products, along with consulting, education, support and systems integration services, worldwide.

Database management systems software permits multiple users and applications to access data concurrently while protecting the data against user and program errors and against computer and network failures.

Database management systems are used to support the data access and data management requirements of transaction processing and decision support systems. The ORACLE relational DBMS runs on a broad range of massively parallel, clustered, symmetrical multiprocessing, mainframes, minicomputers, workstations and personal computers using the industry standard SQL language.

A variety of applications development products, sold as add-ons to the ORACLE relational DBMS, increase programmer productivity and allow non-programmers to design, develop and maintain their own programs. Access tools enable end users and decision support analysts to perform rapid querying, reporting and analysis of stored data.

The company also offers an integrated family of end-user financial applications, including general ledger, purchasing, payables, assets, receivables and revenue accounting programs, as well as manufacturing and human resource applications. These application products use the ORACLE relational DBMS and related development and decision support tools.

ORCL offers consulting, education and systems integration services to assist customers in the design and development of applications based on company products.

Important Developments

Jun. '96—Total revenues in the fourth quarter of FY 96 (May) grew 44%, year to year; core database license revenues rose 49%, applications rose 73%, tools were up 13% and services advanced 44%.

Sep. '95—In the first quarter of FY 96, ORCL recorded a $51 million ($0.05 a share) charge to reflect costs associated with the acquisition of the online analytical processing business of Information Resources.

Capitalization

Long Term Debt: $897,000 (5/96).

Per Share Data ($)

(Year Ended May 31)	1996	1995	1994	1993	1992	1991	1990	1989	1988	1987
Tangible Bk. Val.	2.85	1.87	1.15	0.82	0.69	0.56	0.66	0.40	0.25	0.16
Cash Flow	1.23	0.89	0.52	0.30	0.18	0.07	0.25	0.17	0.09	0.04
Earnings	0.90	0.67	0.43	0.22	0.10	-0.02	0.19	0.14	0.07	0.03
Dividends	Nil	Nil	Nil	Nil	Nil	Nil	Nil	Nil	Nil	Nil
Payout Ratio	Nil	Nil	Nil	Nil	Nil	Nil	Nil	Nil	Nil	Nil
Cal. Yrs.	1995	1994	1993	1992	1991	1990	1989	1988	1987	1986
Prices - High	32½	20⅜	16¾	6⅝	3¾	6¼	5¾	2½	2⅛	1³⁄₁₆
- Low	17¾	11⅜	6	2⅜	1¼	1¹⁄₁₆	2¹⁄₁₆	1¼	⁹⁄₁₆	⅜
P/E Ratio - High	36	31	39	30	39	NM	30	18	29	29
- Low	20	17	14	12	13	NM	11	9	8	13

Income Statement Analysis (Million $)

Revs.	4,223	2,967	2,001	1,503	1,178	1,028	971	584	282	131
Oper. Inc.	1,124	797	485	297	165	81.0	226	143	75.0	33.0
Depr.	220	148	65.2	56.2	50.9	54.5	35.9	19.7	10.6	4.6
Int. Exp.	6.6	7.0	6.9	9.0	18.6	24.0	12.1	4.3	1.5	1.2
Pretax Inc.	920	659	423	218	96.0	-13.0	173	120	65.0	28.0
Eff. Tax Rate	34%	33%	33%	35%	36%	NM	32%	32%	34%	44%
Net Inc.	603	442	284	142	62.0	-12.0	117	82.0	43.0	16.0

Balance Sheet & Other Fin. Data (Million $)

Cash	841	586	465	358	177	101	50.0	49.0	49.0	38.0
Curr. Assets	2,284	1,617	1,076	842	641	586	569	337	192	109
Total Assets	3,357	2,425	1,595	1,184	956	858	787	460	250	144
Curr. Liab.	1,455	1,055	682	551	406	479	284	178	102	48.0
LT Debt	0.9	81.7	82.8	86.4	95.9	18.0	89.1	33.5	5.4	9.0
Common Eqty.	1,870	1,211	741	528	435	345	388	231	135	83.0
Total Cap.	1,880	1,321	862	623	541	369	499	276	147	95.0
Cap. Exp.	308	262	251	41.3	46.6	60.7	89.3	68.4	31.0	16.9
Cash Flow	823	589	349	198	112	42.0	153	101	54.0	20.0
Curr. Ratio	1.6	1.5	1.6	1.5	1.6	1.2	2.0	1.9	1.9	2.3
% LT Debt of Cap.	1.0	6.2	9.6	13.9	17.7	4.9	17.9	12.1	3.6	9.5
% Net Inc.of Revs.	14.3	14.9	14.2	9.4	5.2	NM	12.1	14.0	15.2	11.9
% Ret. on Assets	20.9	22.0	20.4	13.2	6.7	NM	18.6	22.6	21.5	15.1
% Ret. on Equity	39.1	45.2	44.6	29.2	15.6	NM	37.5	43.9	38.8	27.4

Data as orig. reptd.; bef. results of disc. opers. and/or spec. items. Per share data adj. for stk. divs. as of ex-div. date. E-Estimated. NA-Not Available. NM-Not Meaningful. NR-Not Ranked.

Office—500 Oracle Parkway, Redwood Shores, CA 94065. **Reincorporated**—in Delaware in 1987. **Tel**—(415) 506-7000. **E-mail**—investor@oracle.com **Website**—http://www.oracle.com **Chrmn**—J. A. Abrahamson. **Pres & CEO**—L. J. Ellison. **EVP & CFO**—J. O. Henley. **SVP & Secy**—R. L. Ocampo, Jr. **Investor Contact**—Catherine Buan. **Dirs**—J. A. Abrahamson, M. J. Boskin, J. Costello, L. J. Ellison, J. Kemp, D. L. Lucas, R. P. McKenna, D. W. Yocam. **Transfer Agent & Registrar**—Harris Trust & Savings Bank, Chicago. **Empl**— 14,830. **S&P Analyst:** Peter C. Wood, CFA

Appendix C—Zacks' company report for Oracle Corporation

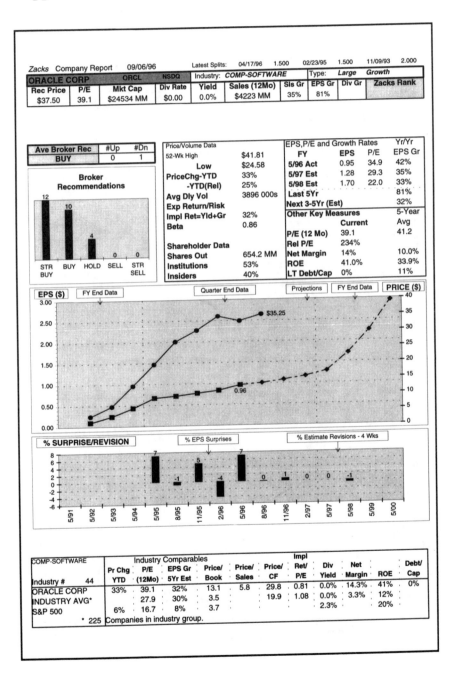

Appendix D—Zacks' "Analyst Watch" report

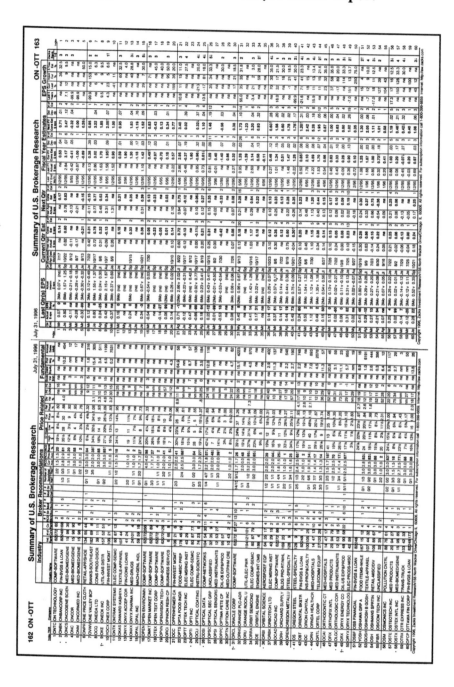

Appendix E

Volume I: *Stock Investing for Everyone:*
Select Stocks the Fast & Easy Way

What It Contains

This book aims to empower investors who in the past relied on others for their stock investment decisions and now desire to take a more active role in their investments. The objective is to provide them access to an inexpensive resource, which can arm them with the basic tools that a stock market investor needs.

To understand Volume I, which introduces the reader to the world of stock market investing, no prior knowledge of stocks is required. It is basic enough for beginners to use and yet has sufficient depth of information to make it very useful to somewhat experienced stock market investors.

Volume I starts off by laying the background and the case for investing in the stock market. It then describes the high level factors influencing stock prices and valuations. In the next step, investors are taught the basics of how to trade in stocks. This is followed by an introduction to stock market variables and behavior. Next, details are provided on where and how to conduct the investment research required for stock investing. This volume also contains an in-depth discussion of the commonly used methods for valuing stocks,

In Chapter 9, a fast and easy way for screening stocks and determining their price appreciation potential is introduced. This procedure, called the "Express©" method, is explained in a step-by-step manner. Specific real-world examples, with actual data, are provided for different scenarios illustrating when to buy or not to buy. While this procedure can be used by most investors, it is ideally suited for the majority of investors who either are unable to, or cannot, invest the time and effort required to analyze a company in-depth before buying its stock.

Next, the reader is introduced to theme investing. Also, a number of stocks with good investing potential are identified. Finally, a large number of comprehensive, easy-to-understand, stock market investing guidelines and tips are provided, in a summarized format, which readers will find very valuable.

Ordering Information

ISBN number for Volume I is: 0-9660863-0-9
Price: $14.95

Direct orders to the publisher can be placed at:
Stocks Advisory Group
P.O. Box 700003
San Jose, CA 95170

e-mail: StocksAG@aol.com

The book can also be ordered from:
BookWorld Services
1933 Whitfield Park Loop
Sarasota, FL 34243

Toll free order line: (800) 444-2524

International orders: (941) 758-8094

http://www.bookworld.com

Orders can also be placed through Ingram or the Internet:
http://www.amazon.com
http://www.borders.com
http://www.barnesandnoble.com

GLOSSARY

Acquisition: The procurement of all, or enough, shares of another company for taking control of its operations.

All-or-none order: An order that has to be executed completely or not at all.

Annual report: A comprehensive annual financial statement issued by every public company. Mandated by the SEC, this report indicates the financial health of the company.

Ask: The lowest price that a stock is being offered for sale. Also called the "offer" price. Ask price is higher than the bid price.

Asset: Items of value owned by a company such as cash, inventory, land, buildings and equipment.

Average down: Buying more shares of a company after its price declines. This results in the average cost of all the shares to decrease to a value somewhere between the purchase prices of the two transactions.

Balance sheet: A company's financial statement indicating what it owns (assets), what it owes (liabilities) and their difference known as stockholder's equity or net worth.

Bear: A pessimistic investor who expects stock prices to drop.

Bear market: A market which declines steadily for an extended period; usual decline is 20–30% and can last months or years.

Bearish: Price expected to decline.

Beta: A measure of a stock's price volatility compared to the market as represented by the S&P500 index. A beta equal to 1 is equivalent to the market's volatility. A beta higher than 1 means that the stock is more volatile than the market, while beta less than 1 means that the stock is less volatile than the market.

Bid price: Highest price at which a market maker is willing to buy a stock from a seller. Bid price is lower than the ask price.

Board of directors: A small but powerful group, elected by shareholders every year, who are empowered to take important decisions including acquisitions, appointing officers, issue shares, increase/decrease dividends, etc.

Bond: A debt instrument maturing in a period extending over a year from the date of issue.

Book value: The per share value of an outstanding share of stock. Calculated by subtracting a company's liabilities from its assets and then dividing the resulting number by the outstanding shares.

Broker: A brokerage company's registered (licensed) representative who handles customer accounts and executes orders.

Brokerage: A company licensed to execute investor orders for securities.

Bull: An optimistic investor who expects stock prices to rise.

Bull market: Stock market characterized by rising prices over a period of months or years.

Bullish: Price expected to rise.

Call option: An agreement which gives the buyer the right to buy a stock at a pre-determined price, known as the strike price, before the expiry date of the agreement. Agreements are made in terms of "contracts," where each contract is equivalent to 100 shares.

Capital gain: Net profit resulting from the sale or exchange of securities.

Capital loss: Net loss resulting from the sale or exchange of securities.

Capitalization: Capital that is invested in a company. Includes common stock and preferred stock, long-term debt (bonds) and retained earnings.

Cash flow: The amount of internally generated cash that can be used for paying dividends, financing growth or purchasing assets. Commonly defined as net income plus depreciation.

Channel: Area between the straight line connecting a stock's price lows and the parallel straight line drawn for its price highs.

Closing price: The last price at which a stock transaction takes place on any given day. This is the price quoted by the newspapers.

Commission: The fee that a brokerage company charges an investor for buying or selling a security.

Common stock: The unit of ownership in a corporation that is represented by a share.

Corporation: The most common entity through which business is conducted in a free market capitalistic economy.

Covering: Buying back the shares of a stock, that has been sold short, in order to close the position.

Current yield: For stocks, the percent paid out as a dividend calculated in terms of the current stock price. For a bond, payout is the interest payment in terms of its price.

Day order: A buy or sell order that is canceled automatically at the end of the trading day if it has not been executed as per instructions.

Depreciation: A decrease in the value of an asset over a period of time.

Discount: The amount below the list price or face value of a security. Such a security is referred to be "selling at a discount."

Discounted: Already taken into account; for example, a stock may not react to good earnings because the expectations may already have been factored into the stock price by investors.

Discount rate: Interest rate that the Federal Reserve Bank charges on loans to member banks.

Diversification: To spread out the investment in the stocks, or other securities, of different companies and/or sectors/industries.

Dividend: The payment a corporation makes, usually quarterly, to its stockholders. The company's Board of Directors decides the payout amount. It is usually related to the level of profits earned by the company. Payment is usually made in cash though it can also be distributed in the form of additional shares.

Dollar cost averaging: Investment technique that involves buying shares, at regular levels, in a fixed dollar amount irrespective of the price. This enables the purchase of more shares at a lower price than when prices are higher.

Dow Jones Industrial Average (DJIA): A measure of the market, which is based on the price of 30 stocks making up the Dow Jones Industrial Average.

Earnings: The net profit of a company after all costs, expenses and taxes have been paid. Typically, reported as earnings per share, which is calculated by dividing the earnings by the total number of outstanding shares. Reported for each quarter and annually.

Equity: This represents the ownership of the company which, for a publicly traded company, is synonymous with its common stock.

Expiration date: The date on which an option, put or call, expires. Stock options expire on the third Friday of the month. The next Saturday is designated as the expiration date.

Float: The number of shares of a company currently available for trading. Float is calculated after reducing, from the total number of outstanding shares, the shares held by the founding family, management and/or institutions.

Fundamental analysis: A comprehensive study of a company. This analysis covers its financial statements, management and the industry of which it is a part.

Growth stock: The stock of a company identified as growing at an above-average rate and, hence, is expected to appreciate in price at a faster rate.

Income statement: A document that reports a company's financial results for a specific period. Includes revenues, costs, expenses, taxes and earnings.

Index: A measure for representing the combined value of a group of stocks.

Inflation: The phenomenon of rising prices for goods and services.

Initial public offering (IPO): The initial offering of shares to the public, in the stock market, of a company that has been held privately so far.

Insider: An officer or director of a company who has access to confidential information that is not available to ordinary investors.

Insider trading: Illegal stock trading by an individual (such as a company's officer or director) who has access to information, about the company, which is not available to the public.

Institutional investor: A large organization which invests in the stock market such as a mutual and pension funds, insurance companies, etc.

Leading economic indicators: A group of economic variables that help economists forecast the direction of the overall economy 6–9 months down the road.

Liabilities: Indicates what a company owes. Includes all debts and other claims against the company.

Limit order: An order that instructs that the order be executed at a specific "limit" price or better.

Liquidation: The selling of shares for conversion into cash.

Liquidity: The ability of a stock to meet all buy and sell demands without causing the stock price to be moved appreciably. Lack of liquidity can cause the stock price to swing considerably or even prevent the shares being sold when required.

Long-term debt: Liabilities that need to be repaid after one year.

Margin: Money borrowed from a broker for buying stocks, which are kept as collateral by the broker.

Margin account: An account in which stock purchases can be made using credit. In this account, the shares bought on credit are held as collateral by the broker.

Margin requirement: The cash or equity requirements that must be on deposit with a broker in a margin account.

Market breadth: A measure of the extent to which stocks are participating in a market advance. Often indicated by the number of stocks that advance or decline during a specified period. Also measured by the number of stocks hitting new highs or new lows.

Market capitalization: Total shares outstanding at the end of the most recent quarter multiplied by the stock's closing price.

Market order: An order to buy or sell a stock, as soon as possible, at the best available price.

Market maker: Maintains bid and ask prices on the NASDAQ; buys from sellers at the bid price and sells to buyers at the ask price.

Merger: Friendly takeover of a company by another.

Money-market funds: A fund whose investments are made only in short-term debt securities.

Mutual fund: An open-ended investment company through which investors can invest in the stock market. They are more safe and less volatile, due to diversification, than individual stocks.

Mutual fund cash: The cash held by mutual funds as a percentage of their assets.

NASDAQ: National Association of Securities Dealers Automated Quotations. This system is used for trading stocks in the over-the-counter market.

Net earnings: see "earnings."

Net income: see "earnings."

Net profit: see "earnings."

NYSE: New York Stock Exchange.

Open order: A buy or sell order that has not been executed as yet. Such an order remains in effect until it is either canceled or executed.

Option: An agreement which gives the buyer the right to buy, or sell, a stock at a pre-determined price, known as the strike price, before the agreement's expiry date. Options are written in terms of "contracts," where each contract is equivalent to 100 shares.

OTC: Over-the-counter: A network of brokers/dealers who mostly buy/sell stocks that are not listed on the major exchanges.

Par value: Stated value of a security.

P/E ratio: See "price-earnings ratio."

Penny stock: The shares of a company that sell for under a dollar per share. Some investors classify stocks selling under $3/share in this category.

Portfolio: The basket of stocks that an investor owns.

Premium: The amount above the list price or face value of a security. Such a security is referred to be "selling at a premium."

Price/earnings ratio (P/E): The ratio obtained by dividing a stock's price by its earnings/share for a specific period like a quarter or the year. A stock trading at $24 having an earnings/share equal to $2/share, has a P/E equal to 12.

Prime rate: The interest rate that commercial banks charge their most creditworthy customers.

Profit margin: A measure of the profitability of a company which relates profits to revenues. Commonly used profit margins are operating, pretax and net profit margins.

Profit taking: The selling of shares to lock in profits that have been realized in a stock.

Put option: An agreement which gives the buyer the right to sell a stock at a pre-determined price, known as the strike price, before the expiry date of the agreement. Agreements are in made terms of "contracts," where each contract is equivalent to 100 shares.

Quote: A stock's current highest bid and the lowest offer price for buying or selling.

Rally: The upward, significant, price movement of a stock or the overall market.

Retained earnings: A company's earnings that are not distributed to the shareholders as dividends. Instead, they are re-invested in the company.

Return on equity: Rate of investment return that is earned by a company on its stockholders' equity. Calculated by dividing net earnings by the average stockholders' equity.

Revenues: Income derived by a company though sales and other sources before the deduction of costs and expenses.

Sales: The value of goods/services sold by a company.

SEC: The Securities and Exchange Commission, which oversees and regulates the stock market.

Settlement: The day on which a stock purchase or sale is "settled" by the delivering the shares or making the payment for a transaction. Occurs three business days after the trade has been made.

Shares outstanding: The number of authorized shares that have been issued by a company.

Short selling: The technique of selling a stock, by borrowing it from a broker, before buying it. The expectation is that the stock price will decline and, consequently, the investor will be able to buy back the stock at a lower price. The re-purchased shares are then returned to the broker (or other lender). The difference between the sale and procurement price is the investor's profit.

Specialist: A member of the stock exchange assigned the responsibility of maintaining an orderly market for a particular stock by balancing its supply and demand.

Specialist short sales: Short sales made by an exchange specialist.

Speculator: Someone who takes on far higher risk with the expectation of far greater profit than an ordinary investor. Investment decisions made by speculators are often made on hopes and hunches instead of solid research.

Split: The division of a company's shares into a greater number of shares, with the most common being a 2-1 split. Its result is to double the number of shares, while halving the price per share.

Spread: The difference between the "bid" and "ask" prices of stock.

Stock dividend: A dividend that is paid out in shares rather than in cash.

Stock exchange: A market that facilitates the trading of stocks registered there.

Stockholders' equity: The stockholders' ownership in the company. Also known as "net worth," it is the difference between the total assets and total liabilities of a company.

Stop order: An order to buy at a price above, or sell below, the currently quoted price for a stock. An order becomes a "market order" when the stock sells at or below the stop price. A stop sell order is used to protect profits or limit a potential loss.

Strike price: A stock option's pre-determined exercise price.

Technical analysis: A technique for analyzing stocks. It is based on the study of the price fluctuations with the objective of predicting future price movements.

Volume: The total number of shares traded, of an individual stock or the entire market, in a specified period.

Yield: The annual return on an investment, from dividends or interest, expressed as a percentage of the current price.

Yield curve: The difference in the yield between short-term Treasury notes and long-term Treasury bonds.

STOCKS ADVISORY GROUP (SAG)

SAG is an investment advisory and publishing company. It is positioned to provide a number of services to individuals and small companies in the following areas:

- Investing:
  - consulting
  - managing stock portfolios for individuals
  - managing funds for small companies
- Publishing:
  - consulting services for publishing
  - book promotion and marketing (conventional & Internet)
  - book promotion for self-publishers and authors

SAG, headed by Arshad Khan, is based in the heart of Silicon Valley in Northern California. This is a technologically advanced area where exciting new companies are born, and innovative products introduced, every day. Therefore, SAG is uniquely positioned to recognize, and select, technology companies with winning products for its clients. However, while technology companies receive considerable attention, investments are also selected from non-technology sectors.

For further information, write to:

Stocks Advisory Group

P.O. Box 700003

San Jose, CA 95170

e-mail: StocksAG@aol.com

ABOUT THE AUTHORS

Vaqar Zuberi is an experienced stock market professional who works as a senior trader for Schonfeld Securities. He was ranked in the top 5% of proprietary traders from 1990-1997 in terms of trading profits. He trades over a billion dollars annually and has a stupendous investing record. In 1996, his annual returns were 47%. Since 1992, his annualized returns average 33.6%, which are higher than the 29% average returns credited to the legendary Peter Lynch.

Mr. Zuberi started his career as a financial analyst. He has an MBA, as well as an engineering degree, to his credit. He has also attended one of Europe's top business schools, Hautes Etudes Commerciales (HEC) in France, in their MBA Exchange program.

Arshad Khan is a versatile professional, an adjunct professor, and an established author. He is an experienced stock market player who heads SAG. He started his career with New Court Securities Corporation, a financial services and investment company. He has written books in diverse fields including stock market investing, performance improvement and engineering. His first book, published by Elsevier in 1986, was awarded a prize for the best engineering book.

Mr. Khan has worked in many diverse industries, for large and small companies, in a variety of roles. His broad experience, especially in management, has given him a unique ability to analyze the fundamentals of companies for stock market investing. Mr. Khan has taught at a number of Universities including the University of California (Berkeley and Santa Cruz Extensions), Golden Gate University and National University. He has a graduate degree in engineering as well as an MBA.

INDEX

H

hedging   156, 266

housing starts   115, 116, 117

I

IBD Mutual Fund index   71, 129, 130

income statement   3, 4, 42, 235

index of consumer sentiment   85, 88

indicator weighting   208

indicators, value of   220, 223

Individual Investor   195

industrial production   22, 101, 119

industry group   1, 6, 33, 152, 162, 164, 171, 172, 173, 175, 176, 180, 185, 207, 209, 237, 238

insider buying   92, 93, 94, 191, 193, 207, 208, 219, 220, 221, 230, 263

institutional buying   79, 236

institutional ownership   22, 78, 79, 82, 191, 193, 207, 215, 219, 234, 236

investment principles   iii, 177, 179

investment strategy   132, 186, 190, 227, 238

Investor's Business Daily (IBD) 6

Investor's Digest   195

Investors' Intelligence Survey   85

IRA   152

J

January effect   152

jobs growth   108, 109

L

leadership signs   174

Leading Economic Indicators (LEI)   101, 121

leading indicators   116

leverage   264

limiting risk   261, 262

long-term debt   6, 214, 247

M

manual screening   196

market bottom   52, 54, 66, 85, 88, 91, 97, 98, 99, 126, 134, 149, 159

market bottom signs   149

market breadth   iii, 21, 61

market capitalization   79, 129, 130, 191, 199, 207, 214, 216, 219, 234

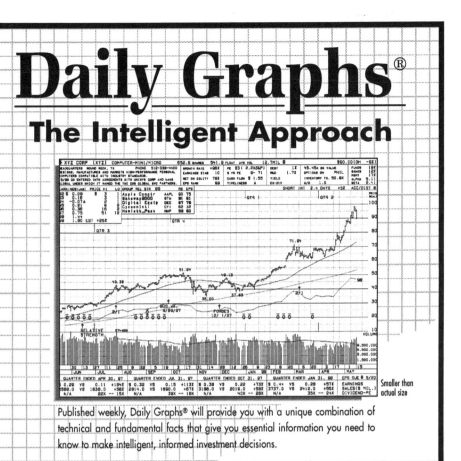